THE PRENTICE-HALL DIRECTORY OF EXECUTIVE SEARCH FIRMS

WILLIAM LEWIS
&
CAROL MILANO

Published by Prentice Hall Press
New York, New York 10023

Published by Prentice Hall Press
A Division of Simon & Schuster, Inc.
Gulf + Western Building
One Gulf + Western Plaza
New York, New York 10023

PRENTICE HALL PRESS is a trademark of Simon & Schuster, Inc.

Manufactured in the United States of America

1 2 3 4 5 6 7 8 9 10

Library of Congress Cataloging-in-Publication Data

Lewis, William, 1946-
    The Prentice-Hall directory of executive search firms.

    Bibliography: p.
    Includes index.
    1. Executives—United States—Recruiting.
2. Executives—United States—Recruiting—Directories.
I. Milano, Carol. II. Title.
HD38.25.U6L49 1986   658.4'07111'02573   85-30190
ISBN 0-671-55518-9

CONTENTS

INTRODUCTION

Often the best jobs are not advertised; they're obtained directly by approaching the decision maker who is empowered to hire. Because no one will ever have as deep an investment in your career as you do, it's essential that you control and direct your own job searches and vocational plans.

This doesn't mean, however, that you can't get excellent assistance and professional input as you advance up the proverbial ladder to success. We believe that experts in professional placement can provide valuable—at times, invaluable—information, encouragement, and access to jobs that would not be easily available to you on your own. *The Prentice-Hall Directory of Executive Search Firms* provides directions for locating appropriate firms or agencies to assist you and gives guidelines on approaching them and eliciting their cooperation and support in your own job search.

A bewildering assortment of placement entities exists today, and we will sort them out for you so that you know which types are best for your current situation. Interestingly, although the nomenclature can be confusing, a great deal of overlap exists among the services performed by supposedly different kinds of recruitment operations. A key fact to understand is that they all share two functions: finding a suitable person for an employer's current job opening and earning a fee for this service. By inference, then, any kind of placement or recruiting shop can profit by helping you find a suitable position—the better-paying, the better for all involved—so keep in mind that you're providing the personnel consultant with a situation that potentially benefits both of you.

It is never too early to take charge of your own professional direction. The executive search industry provides a service vital to both employer and employee. Let ethical, motivated experts in the personnel world bring you the best opportunities for your current circumstances—and never forget that they need *you:* your skills, talents, earning power, and over-all value in the job market.

PART I

HOW TO GET YOUR HEAD HUNTED

Chapter 1

DEFINING EXECUTIVE PLACEMENT

EXECUTIVE SEARCH FIRMS

Several thousand organizations in the United States consider themselves "executive search" companies. What does this vague term mean to you, the prospective job seeker? First, it signals that this firm, whether it be a massive international operation or a one-person shop, aims to find the right middle- to upper-level managers for job openings with its client companies. Most of the time, firms that choose this title don't place people at salaries below $30,000, and generally they work at levels well above this; some search firms won't deal with executives below the solid six-figure level.

Second, the choice of "executive search" as a title means the organization is not subject to the state licensing requirements that affect standard employment agencies. (Seven states have done away with this requirement, and seven others never introduced it.) Less regulation and supervision are provided for the consumer's benefit. Newspaper advertising is not strictly monitored for accuracy.

The third point is delicate. You've heard the colloquialism "headhunter" used to characterize executive searchers. How have they earned this mildly pejorative nickname? Executive searchers have to deliver the best-suited body to a client with a vacant spot; generally the best body is working elsewhere when targeted by the eagle-eyed executive recruiter. In almost every field today, competition is keen for the key positions at fine companies, and the top talent is widely coveted. Executive search organizations play an important role in seeking outstanding staff members from the corporations competing with their clients. The image of "body snatcher" was used even before the professional jungle was as densely populated as it has become in the mid-eighties, but it's unlikely to be replaced by a gentler expression in the immediate future.

Are these firms reputable? Many are; executive search firms regularly find CEOs, chairmen, and presidents for America's most prestigious companies. (In fact, Gerry Roche, chairman of Heidrick & Struggles, one of the "Big Six" search firms, virtually specializes in recruiting corporate chief executives, claiming to have placed more of them than anyone else in the business.) Executive search firms bill more than $1.5 billion in placement fees each year. If CBS, Pan Am, Marine Midland Bank, Monsanto, and thousands of others have all allowed search firms to fill their top positions, you can have confidence in the effectiveness and reliability of this resource.

The industry has been around for three decades now. Executive recruiting evolved after World War II, as American corporations began to move away from wartime activities toward new products requiring new technologies. Search services originated to restaff managerial ranks after the employment upheavals of the war. Sidney Boyden, who founded Boyden Associates, one of the Big Six, claims that the postwar period constituted virtually another industrial revolution for America because

> a large number of corporations laid plans for their participation in the production and marketing of these new sophisticated products, the know-how of which was limited to their established line of business. These included antibiotics, synthetic fibers, heavy chemicals, television, computers, space craft, communication equipment, automation, and dozens of other new products flowing from their research laboratories. Billions of dollars were invested in the construction of manufacturing plants to produce these products. Financial institutions provided the monetary resources for these new endeavors. Sources of raw material were exploited and developed. Manufacturing techniques were created, and consumer demand was stimulated.[1]

Capable management teams were needed, and few corporations had the skills or experience to identify the best employees, so a new field was born. "The executive search profession quickly grew into a worldwide professional service," Boyden continues. "This resulted from the need for international executives on the part of large American client companies who operate overseas, as well as foreign companies. The ever-increasing demand for international executives resulted in rapid growth on the part of executive search firms, many of whom have offices in foreign countries, staffed with associates familiar with local customs, languages, government controls, educational standards, compensation programs, and the know-how essential for appraising the qualifications of foreign nationals."

The industry has become so well established that the June 1984 issue of *Executive Recruiter News* featured this item: ***"New twist in resumes:*** Executive proudly names search firms responsible for putting him in last two jobs 'as an indication of my marketability and upward mobility' . . . says it's improved his response from recruiters."[2] As in every business, however, there are both ethical and unethical practitioners, and the burden is on you as a consumer or user of this service to shop around for a reliable provider.

Which responsibilities can you expect an executive search organization to perform for you, the candidate? First of all, never forget the recruiter is paid by the client company to fill a vacant position. You do not incur any expense in this process. The ad-

1. From *Handbook of Executive Search.* Copyright © 1974 by Consultants News, Fitzwilliam, NH 03447.
2. Copyright © 1984 by Kennedy & Kennedy, Inc., Fitzwilliam, NH 03447.

vantage, of course, is that you reap the benefits of the recruiter's expertise and job market information. The important caveat is that the executive search professional's primary concern is finding the best person for a client's vacancy rather than finding the perfect job for you.

You can expect the search professional to begin by comparing your background, experience, education, and talents with the requirements expressed by the client for a current opening. If a match seems possible, the recruiter will often make suggestions about revising your résumé to highlight your assets most effectively. At the same time the recruiter, who is also working with other candidates, keeps the client informed about the prospects. Usually the executive search firm will submit a list to the client company of the individuals it deems most suitable for the position. Interviews are then scheduled for each candidate.

When your job hunt reaches the point of scheduling interviews, a conscientious recruiter will help you prepare. He or she can give you solid information about the company and may also provide insights about the staff members you'll be seeing. Rehearsing and researching before an interview is always advisable, and with a well-informed recruiter assisting you, the advantages multiply. One executive recruiter told us he even accompanies his candidates on their interviews, introduces them to the executives who will conduct the session, and then stays for the entire interview! (He agrees this is an unusual degree of involvement with candidates but finds this work style effective with his clients.)

One of the main services firms perform for their corporate customers is research. They are paid to seek out, approach, and woo the best-qualified individuals. You can assume, therefore, that any reliable executive recruiter will check your credentials and references thoroughly.

You'll come across a wide array of terms as you explore the range of recruiting services available to you. We'd like to emphasize that you need not restrict yourself to organizations or individuals labeled "executive recruiting firm" or "executive search consultant." Here are some of the other categories that can help you locate the best position for your current professional level. Incidentally, you can utilize as many of these as seem potentially helpful, and there's no reason not to try one or two sources simultaneously.

EMPLOYMENT AGENCIES

All over the country, specialized employment agencies fill client openings by referring suitable candidates. The employer generally pays the fee, after hiring the new employee. Frequently the founder and many staff members of such agencies have experience in the firm's area of specialization, so they can direct you to companies with which your personality and temperament will be compatible. Again, remember that employment agency counselors are paid on commission, based on placements, so their first concern is filling the clients' openings. They'll supply a client with as many applicants as possible, placing the main responsibility for screening and evaluating on the employer. Agencies operate less covertly than the highest-level executive search firms, so they tend to advertise more, keep a higher profile, and welcome inquiries from job seekers with some experience in the specialty field. Many middle-management-level jobs are filled by specialized employment agencies.

How do they differ from executive search firms? "We have more volume," explains Eugene Pacifico, founder and president of the Staat Personnel Agency, a company specializing in insurance positions. "We can expose a casualty underwriter, for example, to many openings, while headhunters have fewer slots to fill at any one time. Staat clients come to us; headhunters are seeking and searching their clients out." A terse distinction is provided by David S. Ketchum, chairman of Ketchum, Inc., in describing his consulting firm's executive recruiting service: "Our goal is to find people for jobs, rather than jobs for people. We are not an employment agency."

Joyce Cooper, an executive recruiter with Advocate Search, was a personnel counselor at an employment agency for several years. She cites some differences between the two categories: "As a recruiter, I deal with candidates at a higher salary level. These candidates are more professional, offering greater experience and more education. The recruiter must be scrupulously honest, meeting and screening candidates more thoroughly. Executive search requires greater discretion and greater confidentiality. Because there are fewer candidates, I give them each more attention." Cooper has found over the years that "it's harder to persuade the higher-level professionals to make a significant job change."

William H. Clark, one of the founders of the Association of Executive Search Consultants, explains the legal background: "Perhaps the oldest legislation regarding employment practices was passed in the state of New York in 1904. Its purpose was to protect job seekers, many of them immigrants just arrived in America, from the abuses of so-called agents who for outrageous fees implied that they could find employment for these people. To correct these abuses, New York provided that employment agencies be licensed by the state, put up a bond, and adhere to agreed-upon fee schedules. No fee was due from job seekers unless they accepted a position. This New York legislation became the 'granddaddy' and prototype of similar employment agency laws in other states."[3]

MANAGEMENT CONSULTANTS

It's not widely known, but many management consulting firms perform executive search services for current clients or, in some cases, for any firm in the industry that wishes to draw upon their expertise. The fee is paid by the client company, and recruiters working at a management consulting firm operate just as recruiters in search firms do. If a respected management consulting group in your field maintains an executive search service, by all means take advantage of it.

In the mid-seventies, when pioneering recruiter Clark looked back at his field's development, he reported the difficulties faced by U.S. companies seeking the best talent in the years just after World War II. Growing demand for executives called for

3. From *Handbook of Executive Search*. Copyright © 1974 by Consultants News, Fitzwilliam, NH 03447.

innovation in recruitment methods. Traditional employment agencies no longer seemed the answer:

> While extremely useful for lower-level jobs, their primary function was to represent job seekers, not prospective employers. More significant was the fact that agencies were paid on a contingency basis and could not afford the time to learn in depth about the company's special problems, to carry out a search, and to investigate thoroughly the better prospects.
>
> Many companies turned for recruiting help to general management consulting firms, particularly those that had done other work for them and were already familiar with the company's problems. By 1950, the executive search work of a number of general management consulting firms had become a recognized specialty. Soon many of the consultants specializing in this field decided to start firms devoted exclusively to executive search. Today, for example, six of the largest search firms are headed by "alumni" of leading management consulting firms—four from Booz, Allen & Hamilton, and two from McKinsey & Company. . . .[4]

CAREER COUNSELORS

This specialty has been steadily expanding since the mid-seventies, as the nature of the American job market began to move from manufacturing to services, while a shift in work values simultaneously arose. The classic "work ethic" mentality had suggested staying with one's first employer until retirement and collecting the proverbial gold watch at one's testimonial dinner. As 45 million baby boomers, mostly college graduates, hit the professional work force, beginning in the late 1960s, it soon became clear that not everyone could scramble up the same pyramid. The surge of women clamoring for responsible jobs increased the crowding and necessitated a shift in the old system of unplanned career ladders.

Career counselors help people determine, refine, reassess, and redirect their vocational lives. Some corporations now provide in-house career planning departments; if your firm does, take advantage of the valuable professional input you may receive. If your employer does not offer this, seek out a trained professional who is experienced at working with groups or individuals in the process of evaluating their professional goals. Usually career counselors charge a fee for their services, often by the session. They can assist in preparing an effective résumé, too. The best way to find a competent career counselor is by personal referral. An alternative is to ask a local university's career services department to recommend a private practitioner in your geographical area. If a local college offers career counseling for employed adults, you may want to try its staff. A fourth source is a good national directory, such as the one published by Catalyst, the national nonprofit women's organization, which lists career counseling services all over the country.

Words of Warning: You'll probably find many advertisements for a category of

---

4. From *Handbook of Executive Search*. Copyright © 1974 by Consultants News, Fitzwilliam, NH 03447.

career services you don't want or need. These are high-priced marketing shops that charge you, the applicant, several thousand dollars to help you prepare a résumé and that give you "exclusive information" about the hidden job market. Several of these companies have been investigated by the offices of attorneys general in various states. These companies do not guarantee that they will get you a job, or even an interview. Some of the most notorious merely mass-mail a customer's résumé to hundreds of companies that may or may not have openings. Unsolicited résumés don't open doors, and mass mailings are an ineffective method of job hunting. In short, these expensive "executive planning" shops are dubious at best and not worth your time or money. Be wary of agencies that suggest executive placement in their titles but ask you to pay a fee for their services.

You should not bear the cost for any of the executive placement services we recommend. The only exception is *career counselors*, who do not do placement. They simply help an individual plan career goals, an advisory service for which they charge a relatively nominal fee that is stated in advance.

HEADHUNTERS

The most important element in your assisted search for an executive-level position will be the individual recruiter who helps you pursue your professional goals. Who are such recruiters, what can you realistically expect them to do for you, and, especially, how can you select the best recruiter for your job hunt?

The broad group we characterize as "executive search experts" includes many different titles on the practitioners' business cards. Staff members at reputable specialized employment agencies may call themselves *personnel consultant*, *employment counselor*, *account manager*, *specialist* in a particular industry, or any variation on these themes. At executive search firms, titles include *recruiter*, *executive search consultant*, *vice president* or *president*, and other officer designations. Many headhunters are sole practitioners, working independently for a small group of client companies; others may be part of large international firms with hundreds of employees. The best recruiters frequently have direct experience in the industry in which they now specialize. The placement field, in general, is receptive to career changers, so personnel professionals have a wide range of backgrounds.

Keep in mind that executive placement is at heart a sales and marketing business, and you're the product. Many recruiters have sales or marketing experience in some other field. No specific college or graduate training particularly prepares one to focus on executive search, since its skills derive from a happy combination of intuition and experience. Do recruiters enjoy the work? One executive search consultant was overheard exclaiming, at a professional association's cocktail hour, "It's great being paid to do something you love—gossip about people all day!"

Because no particular degree, such as accounting or law, exists in executive search, there's no national license or certification either. Two designations, however, are valuable for you to know. The National Association of Personnel Consultants, in Alexandria, Virginia, awards the Certified Personnel Consultant (C.P.C.) title to professionals who have been in the field for at least two years at a recognized firm, and have successfully passed a required examination. The Association of Executive Search Consultants (AESC), in Greenwich, Connecticut, has over fifty member firms who adhere to the AESC Code of Ethics, a model for the industry. We can assume that employees of any member firm are similarly bound by the association's code.

While these two designations can help you identify a recruiter who's trustworthy and reputable, don't assume their absence indicates a lack of integrity. On the contrary, the most successful and largest executive search firms don't belong to AESC, and this by no means suggests they don't merit your attention. As Windle B. Priem, a managing director of the world's largest retainer search firm, Korn/Ferry International, commented, "A large firm operating on a global basis doesn't share business issues with a two-person shop. The AESC is dominated by smaller firms."

Speaking of the Code of Ethics, we might as well address the question of the widely reported "sleaze factor" among headhunters. As in any business, some practitioners are more honest, sincere, and conscientious than others. Executive search has some distinctive features that can lend themselves neatly to duplicity.

The most abused practice is *rusing*, in which a recruiter attempts to collect confidential information about a successful, satisfied employee of a prestigious corporation. Naturally, corporations do not readily disclose private data about the earnings or responsibilities of their finest managers, so the resourceful recruiter may be tempted to employ a ruse. A common ploy is to give a fictitious name, claiming to be collecting information for a survey on executive preferences in automobiles, restaurants, or any suitable purchase category. This allows the alleged surveyor to ask a busy manager numerous questions, including all sorts of personal data to use in the demographic section of the fictional data bank. Clever recruiters will even offer the unsuspecting executive a copy of the completed survey, which involves getting the employee's name and home address. Other common ploys are for unidentified recruiters to call a firm stating they're collecting data for a new Who's Who or for a professional society's mailing. (In some cases, these bogus inquiries can be punishable by fines up to $1,000 or federal prison sentences as long as five years.)

Rusing, vehemently frowned upon by all reputable firms in the search industry, is one of the practices that has given headhunting its dubious image. Abuse of confidentiality is another. The head of one New York recruiting firm is notorious for letting the higher-ups in a company know when she is trying to place one of their most valued executives. This often results in the executive's being fired. The advantage to the recruiter is that she now has a new opening to fill with one of her other candidates—and she still has the opportunity to place the original job seeker, who is now desperate.

Recruiters are expected to do research; that's what they're paid for. Your concern is finding a thorough professional who performs the necessary research in respectable, overt, thorough, and effective ways, protecting the confidentiality of both the client company and all prospective candidates throughout the process. Reputable recruiters research by going through their detailed data banks to identify possible applicants for the position they're trying to fill. In addition, they'll ask their sources who are well established in the particular industry to recommend other individuals who may have the needed attributes for the immediate opening. The big executive search firms have full-time researchers who are hired to collect information for computerized storage so that the data are instantly available when a likely job order is received by the firm.

WHAT TO DO WHEN THE HEADHUNTER CALLS

The initial inquiry or screening call by an executive recruiter is an attempt to find out whether the employee would entertain the possibility of a new job at a competing company. A reputable recruiter begins such a conversation by saying, "This is John Smith, at ABC International, an executive recruiting firm. I'd like to talk to you about a position in which you may be interested." There is no ruse involved. The executive is free to express immediate lack of interest or listen to the specifics and then decline or arrange a face-to-face meeting with the caller. If the prospect declines, the recruiter will probably ask whether he or she can recommend a colleague who may be suitable. This is a perfectly legitimate, ethical practice in the search field. And yes, the prudent executive receiving such a phone call really ought to get up and close the door—and also should file the name and phone number of the caller for future reference, even if there's no immediate interest at all.

Some recruiters specialize in a particular field, such as the retail or computer industry. Others are more general, filling openings in a wide range of business activities. Our advice would be that you try to find a specialist rather than a generalist. Satisfied managers who were helped by executive recruiters cite familiarity with the industry, more frequently than any other factor, as the most important characteristic for the candidate. Seach firms that serve several industries will probably have individual staff members with expertise in specific fields. Try to find someone who's sensitive to the pulse of your industry, so you can get up-to-date information on opportunities, salary, the up-and-coming companies, and your own marketability in comparison with the competition.

The second critical factor is rapport. This recruiter is going to represent you to your prospective employer. It's vital that you and the recruiter communicate well (and often), share your best interests, and understand each other. This means you need to feel confident that the search consultant is clear about your goals; preferably, he has helped you to sharpen your professional focus. Art director Helen Lindberg declined to work with one recruiter she met because "I didn't trust her information or the agencies she suggested for me, and I didn't think she represented me well as an individual."

A native Californian, Lindberg comments that the West Coast style permits easier access to possible employers. In a more hectic, competitive work climate, such as New York, "a headhunter really does get you in the door." After working with several recruiters in her career, Lindberg wants her headhunter to be "quick, not to let my book collect dust. Recruiters can push you and be sensitive to your goals at the same time, rather than just send you off to any opening. They give pointers on improving your portfolio and on where to go to expand your credentials. The best recruiters are very familiar with the [advertising] industry, and who's doing what. They'll give insights or think of new possibilities; for example, a recruiter may know of a very creative group I'd never have heard about, at an otherwise unexciting agency." Lindberg's advice to future candidates is: "Tell the recruiter quite a bit about where you want to be. And try to find a person who loves your work, so he or she can push you hard."

Dan Gribbin, director of personnel at a "Big Eight" accounting firm, defines a good recruiter as "someone who knows my organization inside out and does enough homework on the company." He also collects recommendations from other personnel vice-presidents when seeking a recruiting firm.

Another trait for you to consider when scouting for your own recruiter is the per-, son's accessibility: does he or she return phone calls? You'll want to work with some-one who keeps you apprised of where your résumé or portfolio is headed; the profes-sional, considerate recruiter will check with you first about whether you'd like to be mentioned to a particular employer. Think, too, about a professional recruiter's relationship to your current employer. Another art director at a large international agency recommends, "If you're looking for a job, don't go back to the same headhunter who put you there! Increase your chance at confidentiality by dealing with a headhunter who doesn't have a relationship with your current boss or company."

Confidentiality is a critical issue in executive search. As a job hunter, you don't want your current employer, or executives at other firms you may be interviewing with, to know everything about where you're exploring. Similarly, corporate decision mak-ers don't want their competitors to know whom they're considering for open-ings—especially since most candidates probably work for one of the competitors. In fact, discretion is a major reason employers will turn to reputable executive search firms.

An experienced copywriter for America's fourth largest advertising agency pro-vides a succinct portrait: "The good recruiter *cares,* is personable and knowledgeable, makes recommendations, and has a 'hot line' to agencies with appeal. The recruiter I recommend seems to know something about people at the agencies she works with, and she acts as sort of an old-fashioned matchmaker. She'll say, 'Why go there when you're going to hate it?' I have confidence in her and feel comfortable with the open-ings she sends me to. She'll often tell me about jobs she doesn't feel I should apply for, so I know she's not just out for a quick buck. We've built a relationship, and I trust her."

Paula Jaye, an internal career consultant with a major international financial insti-tution, notes that a knowledgeable recruiter can provide an overview of your own in-dustry. "When you've been in one company for a while, your view narrows to focus on your firm; you lose sight of the industry as a whole."

Paul McCulley, an economist with E. F. Hutton, selected a recruiter carefully when he wanted to leave his previous employer. Preferring to work with a very specialized recruiter, he selected a New York-based search consultant with an outstanding repu-tation. "Because he'd been in the business for so long, he'd be marketing me to people he placed himself. I wanted to work with someone I knew could deliver." The recruiter he chose not only had "a stellar reputation" but was active in the National Association of Business Economists, "where he pressed the flesh actively." Involvement in profes-sional associations is another signal that a recruiter is well connected to your industry.

HOW EXECUTIVE RECRUITING WORKS

Personnel consultants are compensated in several ways, and you need to understand the nuances before you present yourself as an applicant.

Steven Ast, an experienced Connecticut-based recruiter, recommends that a candidate ask, "Who pays your fee? How are you compensated?" He admits some recruiters will resent the question, "but if they're clean, they'll tell you. Contingency search firms don't do the kind of meticulous search and research that get the best fit. Contingency firms send numbers of people" rather than only the very likeliest candidates. Ast is undoubtedly biased toward his own *modus operandi,* but let's look at the terminology more closely.

Executive search firms are paid on either a *retainer* or a *contingency* basis. *Retainer* means that an employer hires a particular recruiter to fill a specific opening over a defined time period. For its services, the search firm receives a retainer, paid partly upon acceptance of the assignment and partly at a later point agreed upon with the client. The standard retainer is about a third of the projected yearly salary, plus all search-related expenses (such as travel for the candidate or for the recruiter to meet with the candidate). Typically, retainer searches take about 90 to 120 days and are more thorough and slower than contingency-based recruitments.

Retainer searches are unique because the recruiter is paid whether or not he or she locates the best candidate, and irrespective of how long the presumably thorough search and research actually take. Working on a retainer basis removes much of the pressure from a recruiter, leaving ample time to fulfill the client's requirements. (Retained searches are usually exclusive, for at least a set period of time, so the recruiter isn't competing with other headhunters to find the best candidate soonest.)

Conversely, in *contingency* search, the recruiter receives a fee only when, and if, he or she finds the successful candidate for a client's current opening. This is the more classic sales-type orientation, in which the salesperson earns a commission only by closing the deal. Logically, the recruiter working on a contingency basis will feel more pressed for time; certainly the temptation is greater to direct larger numbers of prospective candidates to an employer with a vacant position. Contingency searches are less likely to be exclusive with one recruiter, enhancing the competitive feature. Does this mean that recruiters who work on contingency should arouse your suspicions? Absolutely not. Some of the most respected professionals in the personnel industry work on contingency, maintaining peerless ethics and conscientious work habits. There are recruiters who prefer the contingency arrangement for the greater freedom and variety it affords them.

Bob Morris, owner of a Dunhill franchise for eleven years, prefers to work on a contingency basis "because you have control of your time. If I don't feel like working on a particular project, it's up to me. Once you take someone's money as a retainer, you have an obligation—moral, ethical, legal—and they own you, in essence. They are paying you to do something. I don't like the message that creates."

As an applicant, you can assume that a corporation retains a recruiter only if that recruiter's reputation and track record are solid. It makes your own investigation simpler to encounter a recruiter whose clients all hold him or her in such high regard. You'll want to inquire a bit more thoroughly to ascertain whether a recruiter who operates only on a contingency basis is just as reputable, but most of them are.

Recruiters fill openings in virtually every industry, including high-level positions in the nonprofit sector and government. In fact, prominent search consultants have volunteered to work with the White House to fill key positions in the federal hierarchy.

No matter what field a recruiter specializes in, though, the responsibilities of the recruiting profession are consistent:

- thorough analysis of the client company
- development of job description and specifications for the position
- investigation of target industries and companies
- research to identify possible candidates for an opening
- solicitation of candidates to determine interest (if any)
- meeting with candidate for in-person screening
- performing thorough reference check of client's credentials
- presenting list of prospective candidates to employer
- arranging interviews for promising candidates
- helping negotiate salary and compensation package on behalf of the candidate

Search consultants most frequently fill openings in their local geographical area; however, they can also recruit for positions in other parts of the country, or in foreign locations. The nature of the recruiter's work does not change significantly in a more distant placement, but the candidate's activities are different in a far-flung job hunt. How can recruiters help you search for a better position in a distant area?

Richard Preston, director of development for Riverside Church in New York City, was living and working in Annapolis when he initiated a relocation effort. For eighteen months he visited New York at least one day each week and also attended conferences in Chicago and Boston, to create a higher profile in his field, fundraising. He told all the nonprofit executives he knew that he wanted to expand and would be willing to relocate. His weekly visit included a fundraising course at New York University, around which he scheduled cocktails or dinners with colleagues "and lots of conferences and meetings. I took on volunteer work to maintain high visibility in the fundraising community; it's a good way to keep yourself in tune and in touch."

Preston's work in Annapolis was on a consulting basis, so his schedule was flexible. His goal was to expand his part-time fundraising responsibilities by shifting to a broader field in his area of interest. Because he'd met and impressed so many fundraising professionals, several people recommended him to a respected headhunter who was conducting a search for Riverside Church. He got the job, which, gratifyingly, combined fundraising and community service. Preston's advice to aspiring relocators: "Be aggressive. Accept lots of invitations, and create your own opportunities." He adds, "Learn strategic use of the tax laws, especially those covering business travel, to accomplish your professional and personal objectives simultaneously."

Another transplant, economist Paul McCulley, was at his first job after Columbia Business School when he decided to move. His firm, Conoco, had been bought by Du Pont, and his corporate future looked less promising, so he phoned a well-known "economist only" recruiter to introduce himself. The recruiter looked at McCulley's résumé but felt his level of experience wasn't yet sufficient for higher-level positions. Eighteen months later, McCulley phoned again, after Conoco had announced its forthcoming move from Connecticut to Delaware. The recruiter, who had seen McCulley's letters in *The Wall Street Journal* and *The New York Times,* remembered him, asked whether McCulley planned to move south, and wanted to represent him. The recruiter took him to only two firms before E. F. Hutton, his present employer, made an attractive offer.

In 1948 Robert Half, a former C.P.A., founded a chain of employment agencies serving the finance and data processing industries. Today the firm has offices in ninety-five cities, including three in Canada, two in England, one in Israel, one in Paris, and a scheduled branch in Hong Kong. His advice for relocators is brief: "Have the skills. What have you got to make a sun-belt company want you? Do they already have lots of people nearby with those very skills?" If you've already designated a city to which you want to relocate, "subscribe to local newspapers. Get a box and a local answering service, to forward mail to you. This means you can tell companies there that you plan to move to Phoenix. Make it easy for someone to see you. Line up more than one interview when you take your vacation in your intended new city."

If you're planning to move, Half maintains, "it's better to be a specialist. For example, a lawyer-C.P.A. is a rarer breed than just an attorney, or just a C.P.A. A data processing specialist with an unusual language or hardware background will be sought after." The Robert Half network helps aspiring relocators by having a counselor in its office nearest your current home interview you and then forward all the data, with comments, to the other city's office, asking a colleague there to set up some appointments for you. A job hunter could easily look in several different cities with this sort of assistance. Foreign assignments are a little different, Half reports, noting that work permits are a key concern. (They're hard to get, and you can't get a job in a foreign country without one.)

If you're considering relocating to another city, Rhode Island recruiter Ben Furman of Positions, Inc., (speaking in 1984 dollars) points out that "location makes an important difference in terms of salary. Twenty thousand in Providence is twenty-four thousand in Boston and thirty-two thousand in New York. A degreed accountant would get ten thousand more in California than here in Providence. Hiring authorities in the West look for New England financial training because it's more thorough—we've been doing it longer!"

A recruiter's business volume is affected by several factors: the general economy, the state of a particular industry, the specific areas for which that recruiting shop is known, and the reputation of an individual recruiter or of the firm itself. As a candidate, you'll probably get more individualized attention if business is a bit slower, but it's to your advantage to seek a search firm with a steady stream of desirable openings at approximately your level.

Barbara Furman, president of the Furman Group, Ltd., explains, "Contingency volume depends on how effective you are at soliciting job orders. A retainer firm only gets orders on retainer. A recruiter who does twenty searches a year for four firms is better than a recruiter who does twenty for twenty firms. Repeat business plus knowing the company better are the key factors to look for. The sales side of executive search is getting the assignment; then I become a consultant. I won't get another assignment unless I'm a good recruiter. Ask a recruiter about clients. How many searches have they done for a particular client? Any recruiter who's not comfortable with those questions is not one you want to work with. In a chatty way, try to find out the companies, functional areas, and level of position on which this recruiter has worked."

THE CLIENTS

Who's paying the lavish fees that skilled search consultants earn? Most of the respectable profit and nonprofit corporations in America. How do they select recruiters, and what are they looking for as return on their investment?

Kathy Haskell, now an internal executive recruiter at Shearson Lehman, was a search consultant for six years before moving to the client side. "We choose based on a consultant's past performance, what we hear from American Express or other broker age firms, or on our previous experience at Shearson. Sometimes we'll give an oppor tunity to a new recruiting firm, based on how they manage their operation and the number and level of assignments they fill. We ask who will actually do our search; we want first to meet the actual headhunter, to assess ethics and integrity. Does this re cruiter have a solid sense of Shearson Lehman, as he or she will be representing the corporation to candidates? Reputation and past track record are the main factors."

Haskell's employer may give the same assignment, on a contingency basis, to sev eral recruiting firms, although if they have total confidence in a firm, the assignment is exclusive. Shearson Lehman uses search firms for positions "across the board," and Haskell has résumés on her desk a few days after making an assignment. "We may use one firm for financial analysts but go elsewhere for marketing. The bias would be toward an individual headhunter." Her employer works on both a contingency and a retainer basis, depending on the departmental budget. It will use contingency for all kinds of positions but retainer fees only for positions paying above $75,000.

INTERNATIONAL PLACEMENTS

A few recruiting shops specialize in international placements. Egon Zehnder, based in Zurich, Switzerland, is known for its searches on behalf of foreign clients. What does it look for in candidates? Fortunat Mueller-Maerki, a partner in the firm, emphasizes "the right mind-set. A candidate must have the ability to work with foreigners. Anyone who is provincial, who thinks the world is made up of beer, baseball, and bowling is not going to be happy with a foreign firm." Apart from flexibility, Egon Zehnder's ninety-eight consultants, most of whom have lived abroad during their student or professional lives, screen for experience and track record, just as other executive recruiters do for domestic companies. The firm's foreign clients seek American talent for positions in the United States, since "they need American management to run their U.S. subsidi aries." An American executive working for a foreign company will discover "the busi ness mentality and reward structure are different from those of American firms." As most foreign executives have a fair command of English, you don't necessarily need to know their native language to work for the United States branch. "The small trading nations are used to communicating in other languages."

If you're a professional in Nebraska hoping for a glamorous overseas assignment to Paris or Hong Kong, the possibilities are dim. Mueller-Maerki explains why very little actual international search exists: "It's hard for outsiders to be effective in a foreign market. They don't become part of the foreign environment. It's more a question of attitude than of language skills; you must understand that some people simply can't comprehend what you're saying." He also notes that it isn't economical to do international searches on a retainer basis.

The Bank of Tokyo, according to Vice-President and Manager of Human Resources Matt DeLuca, uses different search firms for different types of positions. "We choose an individual headhunter at a firm—and would probably follow that individual to another firm. The quality of service to us is the key; we'll use both large and small firms." The Bank of Tokyo requires written confirmation of reference checks on candidates, signed by the recruiter. The bank then performs its own verification of a candidate's credentials. DeLuca notes, "We would never do business with a firm that charged a fee to the applicant."

At its New York office the Bank of Tokyo is committed to local hiring, because of the financial advantage of using nearby talent over relocation costs. Apart from being less expensive, local hires have nearby contacts and market and cultural know-how, so they're productive faster than their Japanese counterparts would be. Only 12.5 percent of the New York staff are from Tokyo, so there's plenty of room for non-Japanese employees. The traits needed for adapting to an Oriental firm, reports DeLuca, include high self-confidence (as the Japanese don't compliment); vast energy; enthusiasm about the work; a proactive stance (formerly called being a "self starter"); intelligence; and sensitivity to different cultures. "Attitude counts more than experience. Local hires need sufficient sophistication to operate in an international climate: curiosity, maturity, adaptability, sharp interpersonal skills."

For those attracted to working at a foreign company's American office, DeLuca seeks at least three to five years of related experience. The details of an offer will vary with the candidate's qualifications. "This is a tough first spot. A more seasoned worker knows his own needs better. Bank of Tokyo wants no surprises after an individual joins the organization."

When Dan Gribbin was director of personnel at Banca Commerciale d'Italia's New York office, he used search firms for local hiring. Milan-based top management "was trying to Americanize the bank, with more local hiring, in part because of the higher cost of bringing Italian officers here combined with perks." Gribbin sought employees with "a feel for international culture, some travel exposure to help them deal with a European mentality, and some exposure to the Italian way of thinking." The associations of foreign banks were one good source of candidates; another was a headhunter Gribbin had worked with in his previous job at a large shipping company.

"Most international organizations are totally different culturally from domestic organizations. Do the officers know or respect executive search firms? They're alien to some cultures," Gribbin observes. For the manager, "coming into a foreign bank, your career is somewhat limited, for you'll never pierce the top levels. A good search firm can help you overcome that obstacle by showing you what you *can* accomplish at a foreign firm. The individual has to fit culturally, and the headhunter needs a lot of patience to deal with senior people in a foreign bank, who are wary of job hoppers. The recruiter has to navigate carefully management's suspicion about too long or too short a stint elsewhere."

If you're considering a job in a foreign firm, Gribbin raises some valuable points: "Can you work in an environment where you don't know the language everyone around you is speaking? You can be accepted 90 percent, but never 100 percent. Italians are very slow at decision making, so a non-Italian employee has an opportunity to Americanize the organization and demonstrate professional skills in a less hospitable environment. Requirements include lots of patience, tolerance for family-style management, and a great deal of seasoning. You need very good skills, but not exceptional. The atmosphere is less competitive, since you can't be promoted very far. Salaries are a little higher than at American banks; benefits are standard. You won't get lost in the shuffle in a department of twenty rather than four hundred, and there are possible foreign assignments. A smaller office means more exposure and more diversity than you'd get at a huge American bank. You can try to build up the position you're assigned, and you may be sent to headquarters in Milan for courses.

"You have to understand the nationality you'd be working with—I recommend people read *The Italians* by Luigi Barzini—and cope with more delicate office politics." The officer title is very meaningful in Italy. "At an American bank you could become an officer in three years, but it takes five years at an Italian bank," so Gribbin advises non-Italian employees to get into the mainstream after a couple of years.

Human resources consultant John Scafiddi recruits engineering, sales, and marketing staff nationally for Fujitsu America. "The company wants a combination of everything," John notes. He advertises selectively for candidates and recruits at trade shows by having an exhibit and a suite at the convention hotel. Fujitsu's stateside staff is 60 percent American, 40 percent Japanese, and moving toward more Americans. The corporate executives don't want their local employees to speak Japanese, Scafiddi reports, as "management prefers you not know what's going on. With most Japanese firms, outsiders will never reach the inner circle." Scafiddi looks intently for the right personality match, striving to avoid what he calls "the John Wayne syndrome: employees who swagger in thinking, 'Hey, I'm gonna show these guys how to do it.' It's important to be more astute, more inscrutable." He emphasizes flexibility, patience, a long-term view, and a team-player attitude for people seeking positions with Japanese firms.

"Recognize that the method of working in foreign companies will be different," Scafiddi urges applicants. "They have another language, custom, culture, and work ethic. The Japanese, for example, center their lives on their jobs. Before the interview, realize that a foreign company wants the individual's expertise in the field more than anything else." Scafiddi recently hired a twenty-five-year-old American with fiberoptics experience at a $60,000-package, including a car, because the area of knowledge was so important to Fujitsu.

Before you talk to executive recruiters about positions with foreign companies, do some background reading about the home country itself. Do these values and work ethics fit you? Have your travels ever taken you among people from this background? Was the interaction positive, or awkward and difficult? You'll want to make your own preliminary evaluation of your assimilation potential with a foreign firm before you explore it in person. A thorough or knowledgeable recruiter will also be able to give you some valuable insights into the unique features of this international corporate culture.

Chapter 2

RECRUITING A RECRUITER

SELECTING THE RIGHT RECRUITER

Gene Frank, who recruits tax professionals for Jay Heino Associates, believes that "the successful recruiter is a person who understands how to market people. You are the product." The first thing a candidate should look for, he advises, is "a headhunter who's knowledgeable about the industry and knows how to qualify assignments and candidates. Is the recruiter concerned with *your* concerns: career and life-style directions?"

"The recruiting process is a two-way street," Matt DeLuca reminds us. "The recruiter should review an applicant's credentials, and the applicant should do some homework, too. The applicant can judge the recruiter's preparation and knowledge of a position. View the recruiter as your agent."

Dunhill Personnel System, the largest national chain of specialized agencies, suggests these considerations: "Research the methods of the firm and the kind of training received by its recruiters. Is their knowledge of your business truly expert? Are they familiar with your industry, your trade publications and organizations?"

The most important issues are the reputation and track record of the individual recruiter you'll work with. Ben Furman, a Certified Personnel Consultant (C.P.C.) with the Providence office of Positions, Inc., recommends finding out how long a recruiter has been in the business. The National Association of Personnel Consultants' designation means, he points out, that "a C.P.C. has been able to support himself for at least two years!"

The single best source is a recommendation from a satisfied colleague you respect. Ronny Vance, staff attorney at an international conglomerate, met with a legal recruiter who had placed a friend at a lavish salary. The friend had phoned to ask the headhunter to meet with Vance. "Once they've placed you and earned a commission, they try to be obliging. I don't think I would have been seen by this headhunter otherwise. On paper, I wasn't coming from a great company or a good law firm or the best law school, and I wasn't Law Review, so they warned me that I might have some difficulty." She'd been out of law school less than three years at the time, and the recruiting firm sent her on a few interviews. "I liked the fact that they circulated me, instead of leaving my résumé with only one recruiter. At the first meeting I met both the headhunter who'd placed my friend and the head of the agency." Several recruiters at the firm would call her about openings. She eventually worked with three search consultants at the same office, one of whom placed her. "After I got the job, I took her to lunch so I could meet her after this phone relationship. Now if friends seek help, I'll call the recruiter and get them seen."

Wendy Reiner, manager of employee benefits at Random House, originally contacted an excellent recruiter by answering a newspaper ad. She was impressed by three features in this search consultant's policies: "She insists on the applicant coming to see her in person. She prepares you thoroughly for an interview by telling you about the corporation, the environment, details on whom you'll see and what they're like, your responsibilities, and your competition. She likes to make it a competitive situation for the candidate. And she insists you call her before and after the interview. Later, she'll phone you with feedback from the client." After nearly two years at her previous job, Reiner asked the same recruiter who'd placed her there to locate a better position, and she is enormously satisfied with the results.

Gene Frank feels it's fine to go to a library and check directories for specialists in your field, but then you'll have to investigate further. "Look for a headhunter who's not necessarily agreeable, but honest. A good one will tell you if your résumé is lousy. Someone who doesn't sincerely critique you is not helpful."

Binnie Held, a specialist in advertising executives, advises candidates to "speak to lots of colleagues, asking who's been helpful and honest. Who's been fair? accessible? returned calls? Who told you whether or not a situation was right? I assume if I've been straight and honest with candidates, they'll come back to me." Held, whose business is generated by word of mouth, is proud of being very objective. She believes job seekers should work with "more than one headhunter, but no more than two or three. All of us have different people we're close to. Not everybody has every agency, and don't believe them if they say they do. Having another headhunter means a better chance you'll hear about all the openings."

Held begins by meeting each candidate and looking at the portfolio. "Even if I like the person, I can't help if the talent isn't there. I try to get candidates the best job for this point in their career, for the kind of experience they need next. For example, someone with a lot of print experience may need diversity next. I try to steer such a person to the best next step. I've sometimes worked with a candidate for two years to improve the book or develop speculative work. I analyze their TV reels for pacing and editing." She expends an enormous amount of time and interest on each candidate.

Held cites the grapevine as a good source of an agent's credibility and reliability, warning that "some agents say they're sending your book everywhere, and it's not true. My former clients have now moved up and are creative directors, who know I'll send them just the right kind of person. A portfolio arriving with my tag is likely to be on target." After ten successful years in executive search, Held, a former stylist, observes, "Every good agent needs intuition, and knowing when to press and when to pull back. It's like being an old-fashioned marriage broker."

An M.B.A.-C.P.A. at Citibank, currently seeking a middle-management position elsewhere, detailed his central concern with a recruiter's utter confidentiality. "You don't want to find your résumé mailed to the entire *Fortune* 500. As you go further up, confidentiality becomes more important, because you don't know where the résumé is going." He'd been pleased to get referrals to two savings banks, from two different recruiters—and then discovered both leads were to the same bank. "Always get the name of the company that reads your résumé," the banker urges, "and find out whether it was liked or disliked. This is especially important when you have different versions of your résumé, or when you're using plural recruiters. If you're a middle manager, it makes you look less desirable if your résumé pours in on an opening from six different recruiters."

Staat Personnel, placing insurance industry executives since 1972, attracts candidates through two methods: personal referral from satisfied managers Staat placed, or through their heavy advertising in *The New York Times* and trade publications. Like Robert Half and specialty agencies in other fields, Staat is very receptive to new applicants but strongly prefers they have at least a year of experience in the industry.

You'll want to work with a recruiter who deals extensively with levels of salary and responsibility similar to your own. You can plan ahead, though, by introducing yourself to recruiters who can't place you just yet. Steven Ast, at the management consulting firm Brakeley John Price Jones, encourages beginners to contact him, "as long as they know no current openings exist at a suitable level. I welcome an introduction by letter (or phone), showing the writer's done some homework. I keep those, and consult that file eventually, but we'll only call when a related situation comes up." Ast remarks, "We're not immune to flattery; you can come to the office for an in-person introduction. We may not have anything at that time, but we like to put a name with a face."

Most recruiters do, in fact, accept inquiries from prospective new candidates. Letter and telephone are both acceptable, and each has its proponents among recruiters. Marshall Rice, a Connecticut-based executive search consultant, candidly explains, "I prefer letters because I can spend my time on the phone more profitably," and reports that "many good people do come in over the transom." Binnie Held likes new candidates to call her, "so I can ask about background: schooling, work history. Especially in a creative field like advertising, a résumé can't really communicate someone's potential."

Barbara Furman, a specialist in commercial and investment banking who heads her own search firm, believes that in response to a phone call, "most recruiters will put people off and ask for a résumé. But if someone really presses, I'll cave in and set up a fifteen-minute meeting. At our first meeting, I want the candidate to have a résumé and be able to talk about accomplishments. Don't say that you want to hear what your options are. The recruiter wants to hear a specific goal, such as 'I have a five-year track record and am looking for a position in multinational lending.' "

Must you mention a recognized name to get a recruiter's attention? It certainly can't hurt. Gene Frank, at Jay Heino Associates, reports, "Only 1 percent of callers *don't* mention a mutual acquaintance." Despite the frequency, says Marshall Rice, "No matter what name they drop, it doesn't take long to find out whether they have what I need. A strong name might get me to look at a résumé, but I would have looked at it anyway." Steve Ast has actually placed people who initiated contact with him, and says, "A mutual name is not relevant."

UNSOLICITED RÉSUMÉS

Many recruiting firms have a staff member designated to read unsolicited résumés. Their interest is in your qualifications and not in how you heard about them. If you have a recognized name to mention (particularly a candidate this recruiter placed success-fully, or a decision maker at one of their client companies), do so; if you haven't got one, remember the attitude shared by headhunters of every stripe or specialty: "We're not there to help the people looking for jobs," as Marshall Rice put it. They can help you today *only* if you potentially fill their current needs, so emphasize your talents and credentials rather than whom you know.

Is it worth your trouble to send unsolicited résumés? Linda Broessel, vice-president in charge of the Oram Group's executive search division, says, "I call this the chicken-soup approach: it might not help, but it sure can't hurt." Be aware that a lot of people use this approach. Windle B. Priem, managing director at Korn/Ferry International in New York, observes that although it's harder for applicants to reach retainer search firms, "Korn/Ferry gets three hundred unsolicited résumés a week in New York. The research staff opens them and sends a letter back. We have seventy professionals in New York, the search capital of the world. We screen candidates for accomplishments: position, quality of company, how fast-track, and where they went to school." Priem also raises one of the peculiarities of executive search, by mentioning, "If the writer of an unsolicited résumé is with a client company, we can't keep the résumé because that company is off limits." (In brief, one ethic of executive search stipulates that once a recruiter has placed an executive at a client company, no other executive from that company can be recruited by that search firm for some other client. This can become unwieldy, but it is an important fact of the field.)

Bill Gould, current president of both the AESC and his own firm, reports, "A typical search firm gets forty thousand unsolicited résumés a year. Out of the forty thousand, one in a thousand may be applicable to an assignment we're conducting at that point. Out of the forty we cull, we'll talk to all forty. Probably one in a hundred will end up as a candidate for search."

How do they distinguish among the forty thousand unsolicited résumés? "We look for chronology," Gould replies, specifying quality of employers and progression of re-sponsibilities. "We have a tough time with [nonchronological] résumés because it's hard to check." The president of Gould & McCoy goes on to explain that at his firm, "we destroy the rest of the unsolicited résumés rather than retain them. A person will typically be in the job market for about six months, settle into a new position, and not move again for three or four years."

Is it a good idea to send a résumé every four months, waiting for the suitable open-ing to exist at the firm you're contacting? Gould vetoes this approach. "We'd start to wonder why this job seeker is still looking." The implication is that the most talented people wouldn't stay on the job market that long. Gould notes that AESC members will not run reference checks on any individual without written permission. They do have to investigate a finalist's co-workers to learn how that candidate interacts with others and to gather other subjective information.

QUESTIONS TO ASK YOURSELF ABOUT A RECRUITER

1. Was this person recommended to you by more than one competent professional in your industry?

2. How long has the recruiter been in business? What did he or she do before? (The best recruiters often have direct experience in their area of specialization.)

3. Does the recruiter regularly make placements in a salary and title range approximating your own?

4. Are the recruiter's clients good companies? The right companies for you?

5. Was it relatively easy for you to contact this recruiter by telephone? (Accessibility and responsiveness are very important qualities in a good candidate-recruiter relationship.)

6. Is this search professional known for protecting confidential information?

7. Was your initial contact (by phone or in person) a positive one? Solid personal rapport is an essential element in good search efforts. Do you like and trust this individual to represent you to prospective future employers?

CHECKLIST OF SOURCES FOR RECRUITERS

- respected colleagues (whom you trust to be discreet)
- personnel managers at firms in your industry
- trade publications
- newspaper ads for jobs that sound appropriate
- professional directories
- professional associations
- career counselors
- college and university faculty members in related fields

Now that we've told you how to find a recruiter, the next step is developing the sales presentation of the valuable product you're offering: you.

MARKETING YOURSELF TO A SEARCH FIRM

You know what to look for in recruiters, but what will they be looking for in a prospective applicant? Agreement is universal among headhunters. "It's like that old saw about the three important features in real estate: location, location, and location," says Steven Ast. "In search, it's experience, experience, and experience."

While no one disagrees that a candidate's qualifications and background are pre-eminent, some employment specialists shared interesting perceptions. Marshall Rice has found "just lots of visibility doesn't indicate tremendous competence—it may just mean skill at politics or at gaining visibility."

Robert Half, founder of the large financial and data-processing outfit, reports his firm's only concern is "Does a candidate fill the client's specifications? If some are missing, an applicant can fill in with *quality* of experience, rather than *quantity,* or with a different academic degree that may still be relevant. Professional associations or publications are important from a career point of view, and for personal publicity, but are rarely a job requirement." Half elaborated by sketching the case of a hypothetical data-processing manager who holds a pilot's license. The aeronautical skills are unnecessary but could help the manager secure a position with an aircraft manufacturer.

Gene Frank advises on some subtle features: "With an unsolicited call, phone style is number one. The caller should be prepared to tell me who he is and what he wants. Communicate your availability with delicacy. Someone might tell me she works for a guy three years her senior, so there's little chance of a promotion. Don't say things like 'My boss comes in at seven-thirty and leaves at seven-thirty at night.' Instead, try 'He really works hard and runs a tight ship.' In case word ever gets back to your employer, you don't want it to sound like a direct statement of your intent to leave a current employer. Use the English language constructively!"

How you present your interest in a better job is crucial, especially when you're initiating contact with a recruiter. Joyce Cooper, of Advocate Search, explains her firm's view. "We're dubious about people who approach us. We seek candidates who don't *know* they want a new job. I'm usually the enticer, so any caller would have to possess the right credentials." She reflects the prevailing opinion among recruiters: that the most talented candidates are already gainfully employed. Recruiters want to work with people they see as "winners," so present a confident, success-oriented attitude at all times. When you approach a recruiter, lead with your strengths. Their concern is what you have to sell to your next employer. Gene Frank, for example, is judging a caller's phone style at the same time he's assessing this individual's "marketability for my needs. I listen for the combination of education, experience, current income level. High achievers up to the age of thirty should earn $1,000 a year [for each year of their age], and then one and a half times that up to the age of forty."

Another father of executive search, John L. Handy, warned aspiring candidates when the industry was young that "the chances of obtaining immediate results through direct communication with a recruiter are very low. Most major executive search firms receive between five hundred and one thousand unsolicited inquiries from job seekers each month. . . . Because of the limited number of positions that may be open at any given time and the precise background requirements that must be met, fewer than 3 percent of these job seekers are interviewed and considerably fewer than 1 percent will ever be referred to a client." Handy softens his discouraging news by acknowledging that "many of the best jobs in industry are not available through any other source," and continues with important information about the two most frequent mistakes made by job hunters:

1. Ignorance of the function of the executive search firm. Too often, executives contact too few recruiters, not keeping in mind that search firms work on exclusive assignments and that it is to the advantage of the individual to contact as many firms as possible, affording maximum exposure to the job market.

2. Complacency. Many executives do not allow sufficient time to secure a new job from a position of strength—being currently employed. The more successful the executive is, the more inadequately he is prepared to make a proper appraisal of his own position. . . . The top executive is not accustomed to failure, . . . [and] cannot anticipate the possibility that in the future his service to the company may no longer be essential. As a result, the more successful he has been, the more inclined he is to act with blind complacency. The top executive who prides himself on his own good business judgment does not exercise it in his own behalf, and often enters the job market unprepared, from a position of weakness.[5]

Handy's guidelines for how the farsighted executive can best present solid experience are worth reviewing. He recommends "a succinct, fact-filled dossier. . . . It should contain recent compensation information, basic biographical data, and, starting with the most recent position, a chronological job history including dates, titles held, and names of employers. Most important, the job seeker should list the dollar volume of his responsibility and his accomplishments following each position. A rule of thumb might be for the writer to reread his résumé and ask himself, 'So what?' after each sentence."

Before you actually begin telephoning recruiters, we've prepared a review of what you should make sure you've done:

ARE YOU READY FOR THE RECRUITER?

Quiz yourself: Put a check in one of the boxes following each question.

	Yes	More or less	No
1. Have you evaluated your *skills, professional assets,* and *accomplishments?*			
2. Do you have a *goal?* Is it realistic and attainable?			

---

5. From *Handbook of Executive Search.* Copyright © 1974 by Consultants News, Fitzwilliam, NH 03447.

	Yes	More or less	No
3. Can you describe the *parameters* for your next job?			
4. Do you have a *résumé* that summarizes your background to the greatest advantage?			
5. Do you know what, if anything, is *missing* or *weak* in your dossier?			
6. Have you amassed some *non-work ac-complishments* to embellish your professional image?			
7. Have you done your homework in *selecting* a recruiting firm?			

Did you answer "no" or "more or less" to any of these seven key questions? You're not ready to contact a recruiter until you can honestly respond with seven affirmatives.

Here are the reasons these considerations are so important:

1. You'll need to talk comfortably and confidently about the things you're very good at, or give anecdotal examples of challenging problems you've tackled successfully. Can you cite measurable results of your endeavors, if your work is quantifiable? Have you identified the skills you want your next job to draw upon?

2. Before you talk to a middle-management recruiter, know where you're heading. Have you looked five years ahead to assess the position or situation in which you'd like to see yourself by then? After looking at the longer term, you can backtrack to determine the interim or immediate steps. It is *not* the responsibility of the personnel person to figure out your future. It's yours, and in fact this should be meaningful and urgent enough that you'll put time and thought into being able to answer appropriate questions about your vocational aims. If it's difficult for you to anticipate your direction, preferences, or aspirations, one or two sessions with a career counselor may be a sound investment.

A personnel professional can help you most effectively if he or she has a very clear idea of where you're headed. Should your direction be too optimistic for your current value on the job market, you'll be informed of what causes the error in expectations. Personnel consultants have enough work to do to find appropriate candidates for jobs without spending extra time doing your homework for you. If you want to impress a recruiting professional with your motivation and seriousness, be prepared to indicate your own goals.

3. Do you have a minimum salary requirement? Ideally, you should get a noticeable raise over your current earnings if you're moving up in the same field. Is the kind of employer important at this stage? (For example, do you need experience in a larger or *Fortune* 500 firm now? Or would it be prudent to move to a smaller employer, so that you can take on broader responsibilities or a more powerful title?) Are you willing to relocate? Really? Where would you go—and under what circumstances? Would you consider only sun-belt locations, or are you genuinely willing to pack your possessions and go to Cheyenne or Twin Falls for an outstanding advancement opportunity? Be honest with yourself and honest with the personnel professional; neither of you will gain anything if you chase after spots you'd never accept. Let the recruiters tell you if the minimum salary you're seeking is realistic. Remember, their interest in your earnings is nearly as keen as your own, for their commission depends on your compensation.

4. If you've spent sufficient time studying your accomplishments, it should be relatively automatic to create a sales piece on paper. Most personnel consultants will give you suggestions on your résumé anyway; many will ask you to redo it in a format that can sell you better, so don't agonize indefinitely over this document. Keep in mind that employment professionals are primarily concerned with experience, so explain yours sufficiently to impress a reader. Don't overexplain, though; the purpose of a résumé is to summarize your qualifications so that the reader wants to meet you face to face. Most people don't like to read too many pages, so be brief, forceful, and selective in your content and format. (Again, if it's hard to do this on your own, seek out a competent career counselor to expedite the process. Don't agonize over something as simple as a résumé when your time could be better spent in building contacts, burnishing your credentials, or talking with experts in your field.)

5. Be prepared to overcome any objections that may be raised. Can you take on an additional project at work to increase your hands-on experience in an area? Or will you enroll in a continuing education course to supplement or update existing skills?

6. Even as a relative newcomer to the field in which you'll advance, behave like a veteran. Join the most prestigious professional groups. Subscribe to all the trade publications, and begin to contribute material to them as soon as you possibly can. There's no substitute for experience, but as you start moving upward, an excellent way to distinguish yourself from peers with similarly impressive experience is to show your savvy, versatility, and purposefulness. (Needless to say, the bank of contacts you'll be accumulating will serve you well throughout your professional life.)

7. Did you ask colleagues and former classmates to recommend professionals they respect? Is it clear to you what you would like the recruiter to do for you? Do you know exactly what to tell a personnel professional about your goals and needs?

SOME VERY IMPORTANT DON'TS

You've done careful research to locate the finest possible recruiters and have arranged first meetings with several of them to recruit one (or more) as your own search consultant. We've identified the qualities of a good headhunter; the following section provides some warnings.

Attorney Ronny Vance (not her real name) was referred by a colleague to a recruiter who agreed to see her because of the search firm's relationship with the other attorney. Vance cleared an entire afternoon to meet with the search consultants but realized quickly that all their intense questions were about her company: they were seeking inside information and news of other openings at her current law firm! "They finally said they doubted they could help me," Vance recalls with anger, advising that "if there are too many questions about the place you're leaving, rather than where you want to go, stop talking. I felt I was being exploited. A good headhunter would talk about how I see my skills and career goals, with just minor questions about my present employer."

Wendy Reiner, now manager of employee benefits at Random House, believes a headhunter actually cost her a job several years ago. "The recruiter had two other candidates he pushed more than me," she reports, "and I felt he said negative things about me to the client. Some other recruiters will send a résumé without asking you. If I went to see a headhunter and I didn't like the person, I would just take my résumé back."

An advertising agency art director had a particularly distasteful experience with a recruiter he'd known for years. The art director found out, through a mutual acquaintance, that although the headhunter had claimed he was talking to an agency in which the art director was quite interested, his portfolio had, in fact, never been sent to the desirable agency. "Because the recruiter felt I wouldn't get the associate creative director spot, he sent my book elsewhere, without telling me about this other candidate who might be better suited to the creative director position." The art director also discovered, to his deep dismay, that this recruiter "takes pieces out of the portfolio without telling the artist! Sometimes the wrong pieces end up in some other art director's book, or pieces get lost." Having learned from his unfortunate experience, this art director claims, "I'd look now for someone less well known, but who'll really work hard for me."

Another yellow light is hearing that you're a candidate in a highly confidential search—one that's unknown to top management. Consider the implications of this situation: if you join the company and are not a rapid success, will they replace *you* behind your back?

Matt DeLuca, vice-president at the Bank of Tokyo, provides some solid guidance for your recruiter recruitment. "The applicant can judge the recruiter's preparation and knowledge of a position. View the recruiter as your agent. Ask the headhunter specific questions; the more specifically a candidate defines goals and needs, the more assistance a headhunter can, and should, provide. The applicant should call the shots and raise the issues. Specify how you want feedback. Insist your résumé not go out unsolicited. Demand to discuss both position and firm before a mailing. Fire a headhunter who sends your résumé without your approval! It's important to restrict and control the amount of your exposure in the marketplace." De Luca's tip on presenting yourself to the recruiter is "Don't seem too available—it's like dating."

Chapter 3

The Preliminary Steps

As you look toward the kinds of jobs for which you wish headhunters will recruit you, plan ahead. It's never too early to map strategies for your own career.

"Create visibility within your profession," urges Gene Frank. "Within your own organization, don't be a loner. Act as a social animal. Join the proper professional organizations. Let people know, discreetly, that you might consider a new opportunity."

To make sure your name comes up when recruiters are researching for a choice position, Bill Olsen of Russell Reynolds prescribes these steps: "Be prepared for openings that may come up. Learn all the basic skills. A broad-gauged personality is important. Be a professional, which means conforming to the highest standards in your field. Build a track record. Develop a reputation; be known. Find a mentor, a champion, who will recommend you for upward openings."

One good way to create visibility is to write for professional publications, or for any widely read magazine or newspaper. However, as economist Paul McCulley discovered, "it's difficult for someone right out of the chute to get corporate permission to write over his own name. Conoco wouldn't give me approval for love or money. I had a letter published on page 2 of the Sunday [New York] *Times* business section; it identified me as an economist with a corporation in Stamford." McCulley notes an important caveat for self-promoters: "It depends on how high up you are in the firm whether you can speak for your employer. Manufacturing concerns are more reticent than financial service firms about letting lower-level employees write on their own, even for internal publications. Never be at odds with your company's public position! Remember, publications can be a nice way of attracting a recruiter in the first place."

Another good idea is to get yourself listed by name, title, and employer in every industry directory available to you.

Paula Jaye, an internal career consultant with a major international financial institution, recommends, "Try to network into a search firm, preferably via a former client or a former candidate." Networking (the process of forming an interconnected chain of contacts and resources for professional development) is a natural outgrowth of your visibility program, and while it doesn't automatically get you a top recruiter, having lots of people aware of you increases your chances of coming to the attention of premier headhunters.

SOME WORDS FOR WOMEN

Are there special concerns facing upwardly mobile professional women in the 1980s? While we've all heard about the tremendous advancement made by women in business and the professions, the fact remains that in 1985 only one *Fortune* 500 CEO was female—Katherine Graham of *The Washington Post,* who inherited the business when her husband died. How can you make sure that no lurking sex biases inhibit your corporate climb? We asked three female executive search consultants, experienced in diverse fields, to comment on the situation professional women face today.

One, who asked to remain anonymous, reported, "Women have entrenched themselves and merged into the marketplace in such a way that there's not much attention paid to sex anymore. The excitement over equal employment opportunity in the seventies has died down, and even government is not enforcing those regulations so rigorously now. There are lots of female vice-presidents in banks now, some senior vice-presidents, and practically no executive vice-presidents. My clients don't stipulate." She noted, "I could be prosecuted for accepting a search that specified 'man only' or 'woman only.'

"Most of the women I deal with make emotional decisons on career issues. They shy away from risk and are more security-driven than men. Growing up with competition, in activities like debates or sports, makes men more comfortable taking risks, whereas women are risk-averse.

"Women are less willing to travel for a year to earn a promotion. I've never heard a male candidate from one of the suburbs tell me he wouldn't work downtown, but women express reservations like that all the time. Women bad-mouth their companies more than men do—men are smart enough not to give you interpersonal dirt."

This recruiter, who's based in a large, image-conscious urban center, also noted that management women don't know how to dress! "Look like yourself," she urges, "instead of wearing a Brooks Brothers uniform. You really are pegged middle management if you come across as very preppy. Dress for the level you're aspiring to." She also warned that getting a position under affirmative action guidelines may not be a blessing. "If you're hired under E.E.O., you may never get promoted because you weren't chosen for being the best person for the job. That's not a good way to get into management."

Linda Broessel, vice-president with the Oram Group Executive Search Division, holds a different view. "Most studies show that younger women didn't have to fight the battles the earlier generation handled. So they're inclined to believe, 'No one's ever discriminated against me.' The best man for the job, as we've heard, could well be a woman. While we haven't risen so far as we should, women do get closer to the top in the softer corporate areas, like public relations or community relations, but won't move from there to CEO."

What happens when a corporation expresses discriminatory hiring wishes? "If a client tells me the company would prefer a man, I ignore it and look for the best candidate. In most of those cases, they've hired a woman. I use a soft-sell approach," reports Broessel. "I'll describe the candidate with no gender pronouns, in glowing terms, telling the client, 'I have an excellent candidate for you. This candidate has . . . and this candidate is . . . ,' finally saying, 'and her name is . . . .' The previous preference is never mentioned again."

Broessel takes a very supportive position toward other professional women. "Recruiters are usually seeking women who have worked for a number of years. We should be mentoring for those women who are not quite ready for our clients. I assume I'll be in the same business ten years from now, and I want to go back to the same individual, who may be very marketable by then. I believe very strongly in mentoring. Men have always had mentors, and we need to catch up."

Carol Palmer is president of Carol Palmer Associates, specializing in marketing positions. She finds that in her field, "women have more freedom in terms of image, since it's a less conservative area. Image is very important in certain industries, like cosmetics or fashion. Be aware of how you present yourself on a day-to-day basis, not just when you're job hunting. The cookie-cutter look of navy suits and bow ties doesn't work anymore. Adopt more sophisticated styles—not necessarily a fashion approach, but a way to reflect your individuality and personality."

"Women have been accepted more in the business world in the past ten years, so they can move on to a more expressive image. While they're becoming more forthright, many women also expect that if they do their job well, they'll be moved ahead. Men understand political aspects better; women still need to sensitize themselves to that. Your work is the most important part, from a recruiter's perspective. Being able to relate politically is very important, too. Knowing how to treat people shows awareness. I try to find out from candidates whether they know what it takes to move up in their current company. Have they taken the time to understand who's running things, and why, and what those executives' backgrounds are? If they're not aware at their own company, they won't be at a new one, either."

Palmer cites the three requisites for getting ahead: "(1) Knowing your job and doing it well; (2) understanding the corporate culture and the political environment around you; (3) looking right. You have to fit into the corporate environment, look successful, polished, and sophisticated. Be sensitive to the setting you're in, and show some individuality, selectively. Women in banking, for example, are more conservative than women in marketing, and that's reflected in their image. The marketing community tends to attract aggressive women, and there are lots of senior marketing women." Palmer also takes note of the large number of women entrepreneurs today, "who are starting their own companies because of their frustration with the corporate environment—and becoming very successful."

YOUR INITIAL APPROACH

Whether you choose to write or telephone the recruiters you've identified as strong prospects to represent you, your aims are identical: to impress the recruiters with your valuable potential for the openings they may have. Again, remember that all head-hunters view candidates in terms of current positions they're trying to fill, so target your introduction accordingly. Indicate that you know there may be nothing appropriate at the moment but that you're interested in getting acquainted with the recruiter for mutual benefit at some point in the future. You have nothing to lose by attempting to arrange an interview; some headhunters won't bother meeting a candidate until there's a possibly suitable opening available, but others are willing to slot a brief meeting just to see the person behind the résumé or telephone call. Don't be offended if you can't schedule a meeting or don't get much of a reply to your mailing—recruiters are busy trying to fill the positions that will earn them fees, and when they think you may be a successful candidate, they'll contact you.

Make it clear why you're calling this particular recruiter. "You've been recommended to me by [a particular mutual acquaintance or a personnel manager, or a professional association staff member] as one of the best recruiters in our field, and I hope my qualifications will be of interest to you." It doesn't hurt to flatter the headhunter a bit, but spend your rehearsal time sharpening your statements about your own value, because that's what a professional recruiter is trained to screen for.

Focus succinctly on your accomplishments and next goal. Following are two sample letters, received by the head of a large employment agency (with names changed for confidentiality, of course), and both on elegant, executive-sized personal letterhead:

The first is from a midwestern manager with diverse experience who supervises twenty-five employees.

Dear Mr. Smith-Jones: [the name of a search professional, *spelled correctly,* was used]

As a novice in job changing, I find myself in a peculiar position. After fifteen years in a variety of personally rewarding management positions, I am now looking for a new challenge. Your organization was recently mentioned as a top search firm, and I was hopeful you might be able to provide some assistance.

I'm enclosing my résumé to acquaint you with some highlights of my background. In reviewing it, you'll note that it includes proven success throughout.

Obviously, a résumé cannot convey the full range of my capabilities. Therefore, if my background seems to match the needs of any of your clients, or if you would be interested in at least an exploratory conversation, I would certainly be pleased to hear from you.

Sincerely,

Andrew Hardy

This second letter, confident and informative, is from an advertising manager, also living in the Midwest, who is interested in relocating. He wrote to a recruiter in a large northeastern city in which he might want to work:

Dear Mr. Smith-Jones:

Several of my associates have mentioned the quality of your search work on behalf of the advertising industry. I also understand you are well connected with corporate advertising directors. We should talk soon.

My track record as Product Advertising Manager for Test-Tube Laboratories demonstrates my exceptional advertising ability. Here's a bit of my background:

• As Product Advertising Manager for Long-Life Protein Formula and the Test-Tube Formula System, I originate and write the tactical portion of the marketing plans for these products. Once it is approved, I develop the concepts for and write individual projects in support of these plans. Projects include direct mail, ethical journal ads, sales aids, and physician premiums.

• Included in my work for Long-Life was the launch of the powder form of this product. This introduction, called the most successful in the company's history, accounted for more than $8 million in sales in the first three months.

• A look at my portfolio will show you that I have an innovative and creative approach to getting the sales message across. Both products under my advertising control have maintained a dominant share of their markets, despite rigorous competition.

While happy and reasonably well challenged where I am, I am seeking a more challenging position in a metropolitan market. Current skills, coupled with public relations experience acquired while I was a writer and editor for a *Fortune* 100 company in Chicago, should fit well in a position requiring creative leadership.

Please call me at your convenience. If possible, call me at home after 6 P.M. This will help eliminate any office gossip.

Sincerely,

Thomas Sawyer

The correspondent attached his business card, handwriting his home number on it, but chose not to enclose a résumé.

ABOUT RÉSUMÉS

Since most recruiters will take at least a quick look at a résumé, you'll probably want to enclose one. The only alternative would be a thorough, informative letter, as shown on page 32. If you're preparing a résumé to submit to executive recruiters, keep in mind their two concerns:

1. Your experience

2. Your accomplishments

Other facts, such as your educational background, are relevant and of some interest, but they won't lure recruiters to meet with you or keep your dossier on file. They'll evaluate you by your professional achievements. So emphasize these. Lead with your greatest assets. Give the reader an immediate, clear sense of your success so far. Show how you advanced to where you are now. Keep your résumé focused unwaveringly on what the recruiter cares about: your marketability to the client companies.

A résumé is simply a brief summary of your credentials and abilities. Think of it as an advertisement for yourself. Modesty has no place in a sales piece, so tout your proven accomplishments. The goal for your résumé, in this case, is to arouse a recruiter's interest in meeting you, either now or at some undetermined point in the future when a suitable opening may arise. Make sure your résumé includes all the details that will pique the recruiter's curiosity—and downplay any little item that could serve to screen you out.

What's the best way to construct your résumé to highlight your greatest assets? Three formats exist for you to choose from, and they are commonly known as the *chronological,* the *functional,* and the *combination.* Here are the positives and negatives about each one:

A *chronological* résumé simply describes your work history in reverse order, listing your current position first and moving backward to your earlier jobs. This traditional, uncontroversial layout and chronological approach work well if your work pattern has been consistently upward, with each new job a promotion carrying greater responsibility. This format lends itself well to brief recapitulations of your key achievements in each position. If you're climbing straight up the corporate ladder and want to continue in the same direction, this format may be fine. A recruiter will understand how to read it and what it reveals about your credentials. The liability is that any gap in your work history shows up very plainly as will a stint at an unimpressive company, or a deviation from your direct career path. It's almost impossible to hide any details with a chronological résumé, so choose this approach only if your track record is consistent, progressive, and continuous.

The *functional* (or *skills*) approach is more unusual and creative. It lets the subject select the particular abilities to highlight. Under each ability are listed some accomplishments that prove the individual really possesses the skills indicated. The *functional* format provides you greater control over the choice of material to include. You can omit less significant tasks or downplay the areas of responsibility in which accomplishments were relatively unimpressive. It gives you a chance to emphasize your greatest achievements and is the best way to cover any gaps in your employment history. A major caveat: because this is a less traditional format, personnel specialists are sometimes uncomfortable with it. It's trickier to decipher into the information assemblage most people are used to. Sometimes this approach arouses suspicion that the résumé writer has something to hide. But if you're comfortable with this format and feel that it points up your assets unmistakably, go ahead and use it. Should you get no response from a dozen recruiters, try another format and see whether it yields a better reaction.

The *combination* format, as the label suggests, puts together chronological order and an emphasis on skills. It includes names and dates of employment in addition to stressing important competencies. This approach works well for professionals who have had a variety of promotions, all with the same company, and for people who'd like to downplay a gap in work history. Again, this is a somewhat untraditional approach, so people may be a little uncomfortable with it. Your résumé is the first thing a recruiter will see about you, so it's important that you be comfortable with its reflection of your style and personality.

No matter which format you choose, it helps the reader of your unsolicited résumé if you start with a brief summary at the top or a statement of your professional objective. The difference between a summary and an objective is that one looks at where you've been while the other calls attention to where you're heading. Select the approach that makes the stronger sales pitch about you, from a recruiter's perspective.

We've included a sample of each résumé format so that you can react to all three and get a sense of which one might express your image best. While we are speaking of image, as you're trying to pierce the middle ranks of American business, make sure you present yourself with good taste, professionalism, poise, and appropriateness at all times. This means that your résumé has to be flawlessly spelled; attractive, with neat, clean design; well worded; and on very good paper. For an executive position, don't try anything offbeat, like colored paper or colored ink. Stick to white, beige, or gray pages, with subdued colors on them, in standard business sizes. (If you're in one of the "creative" or glamour fields, such as advertising, media, or marketing, you're less likely to offend people with unusual-looking printed matter. However, this is still the first glimpse of you that anyone's getting, and you don't know the personal taste or style of the individual to whom you're directing your mailing. Why risk putting someone off at this initial juncture?) Don't abbreviate, and stay away from slang or excessive trade jargon. Use active verbs to communicate authority, accomplishment, and strength. Find synonyms instead of overworking the same terms.

Sample Functional Résumé

ROBERT L. STEVENSON
1000 East Blank Drive
Chicago, Illinois 60606
312-555-7892

SUMMARY: fourteen years of middle-management experience, in a variety of positions: Director of Human Resources, Personnel Administrator, Accounting Supervisor, Training Director, Department Supervisor responsible for direct management of 25 employees.

SELECTED ACCOMPLISHMENTS

Management: Direction and budget control of volunteer services. Coordinated over-all personnel functions, policies, and procedures. Supervised managers, benefits administrators, secretaries, and production employees. Affirmative action officer; benefits manager. Ensured sound, equitable, and consistent personnel administration. Developed recommendations for Board of Directors' consideration. Recruited, developed, and motivated employees. Prepared area budget; ensured conformance. Monitored personnel budget.

Communications: Developed and wrote policies, employee handbooks, supervisor guides, benefits package brochures, and individual benefit flyers. Devised situational tests and administered work samples. Liaison between employer and employees. Active in customer relations. Counseled employees.

Program Development: Centralized personnel functions, records. Implemented job description and classification system. Created wage and salary administration program. Centralized confirmation of staffing requirements and recruiting. Combined approval of all personnel status and pay changes to comply with both in-house policy and government regulations. Helped initiate operation for lower-level producers.

EDUCATION

University of Chicago, Chicago, Illinois   1972
    Master of Arts, Personnel Psychology

University of Wisconsin, Madison, Wisconsin   1969
    Bachelor of Arts. Major: Accounting, Minor: Business Administration

PROFESSIONAL MEMBERSHIPS

The American Society for Personnel Administration
Vocational Evaluation and Work Adjustment Association
Great Lakes Personnel Association

As you can see, this sample omits all mention of employers, dates of employment, and kinds of firm for which Stevenson performed the tasks he describes. Compare his résumé (which is wholly fictional, since we made him up), with the classic chronological résumé.

Sample Chronological Résumé

ELIZABETH S. JONES
632 Columbus Avenue
New York, N.Y. 10024
212-555-6543

Professional Objective: Position in Operations Management with worldwide financial institution, drawing upon my six years of experience in international banking and my fluent Japanese and English.

EMPLOYMENT EXPERIENCE: Canadian Imperial Bank of Commerce,
                          January 1977 to present

Positions Held:

April 1982 to present: Assistant Branch Manager,
                          Tokyo, Japan

                          Responsibilities: Supervision of all internal
                          operational functions relating to a wholesale banking
                          unit. Liaison with local correspondent banks.
                          Supervision of compensation review process for all
                          local personnel. Regular client meetings with
                          Japanese customers.

July 1981 to March 1982:   International Bank Management
                              Training Program,
                          Toronto, Canada

April 1980 to July 1981:   Administration Officer,
                          Commercial Banking Branch,
                          Toronto, Canada

April 1979 to March 1980: Domestic Bank Management
                              Training Program,
                          Toronto, Canada

EDUCATION

> Qualified as Fellow of the Institute of Canadian Bankers, December, 1979.
>
> Bachelor of Arts, International Affairs (Honors)
>
> Queen's University, Kingston, Canada, May 1976

COMMUNITY INVOLVEMENT

> Treasurer, Tokyo Community Counseling Service, May 1983 to present.
> Member, Canadian Chamber of Commerce, Tokyo, April 1982 to present.
> Membership Secretary, Tokyo American Club, Tokyo, April 1982 to present.

Citizenship: Canadian

This is a clear, simple, concise summary of Jones' upward progress at her bank and serves to communicate her effectiveness and promotion potential. The format presumes the reader understands the duties of each position Elizabeth held and therefore omits the details. (If you want to expand or vary your past responsibilities, try a more flexible format.)

Two résumés in combination format follow.

Combination Résumé 1

MARTIN TROQUE   8 Jones Street   Dallas, Texas 75275

214-555-9290

<u>Goal</u>: A challenging position in international marketing management, utilizing my eight years of experience in foreign transactions, augmented by fluent French, German, Spanish, and English.

ACCOMPLISHMENTS

Marketing and Sales

Researched domestic market for import potential. Followed up with direct sales presentations to prospective customers.

Acquired new accounts for lace and fabric importer: Polo/Ralph Lauren; Calvin Klein; Adolfo; Perry Ellis Sportswear; Sakowitz; Stanley Blacker; Fernando Sanchez; Halston; Mary McFadden; Armani.

Helped plan clients' co-op advertising for trade publications.

Originated 35 of 40 accounts I managed.

International Transactions

Established links with other import firms in Europe.

Instructed customers in procedures for importing or exporting.

Arranged all phases of importing, shipping, and tracking of goods.

Communications and Customer Service

Constant contact, by telephone or personal visit, with customers.

Served as Account Executive for firms I had solicited and targeted.

Dealt comfortably with diverse cultures and languages: conversant in French, German, Spanish, English. (Now studying Chinese.)

Public relations and promotional work with French and German Chambers of Commerce, and fashion publications.

Gave presentations to French Embassy and West German Chamber of Commerce.

EMPLOYMENT HISTORY

1979-1985   Account Executive, *Rogers Corporation,*
Dallas, Texas

1976-1979   Assistant to Vice-President, *Vaugiron, S.A.,*
Brussels, Belgium

EDUCATION

1983   Southern Methodist University, Dallas, Texas
Bachelor of Science
Major: Marketing and International Business

1978-79   Institute of Translators and Interpreters
Brussels, Belgium
Major: English and German

      Troque's résumé gives him the opportunity to focus on the accomplishments that point most specifically toward his next area of interest. He substantiates his experience by specifying when and where he's been working and gives an understandable statement of his intention for the immediate future.

      Our final sample, also in a combination format, allows the candidate to explain his two jobs (at the same advertising agency) in enough detail to show his versatility and impressive advancement.

Combination Résumé 2

PAUL MORTON
511 Van Gogh Terrace
Tarzana, California 91357
818-555-9089

Summary Of Qualifications: Strong communications and mathematical skills. Creative thinker, able to implement promotion campaigns effectively. Experience in wide variety of product categories; specialty in sports promotions. Develop strategy, implementation, and budget for consumer and trade promotion, tailored to meet each client's objectives. Report directly to Senior Vice-President for Promotion Services.

EMPLOYMENT EXPERIENCE

January 1980 to April 1981
Assistant Promotion Account Executive, Young & Rubicam, Inc.

May 1981 to present
Promotion Account Executive, Young & Rubicam, Inc.

Account Assignments

Toyota Motor Sales, Toyota Dealers Association
General Mills (Cereals: Cheerios, Total, etc.)
Florida Department of Citrus
Shulton (Old Spice, Lady's Choice)
Olympia Breweries
Merck Sharp & Dohme (agricultural)
Peter Paul Cadbury
Popsicle Industries
Blue Bell (Wrangler Jeans)
Ciba-Geigy (home and garden)
Megatron Electronics

MAJOR ACCOMPLISHMENTS

Wrote and presented position paper at Y & R International conference on use of sports-related programs as promotional vehicle. (Document later distributed to 37 Y & R affiliates, worldwide.)

FLORIDA CITRUS developed $8.5MM 3-year consumer/trade promotion program. Plan includes 10 major events which will comprise bulk of client's national promotional activities for years 1983-1985.

TOYOTA MOTOR SALES and DEALER ASSOCIATIONS created and implemented consumer/trade promotions in six West Coast markets, designed to augment client's TV sports sponsorships (including California Angels, Los Angeles Dodgers, Oakland A's). Major innovation was inclusion of television stations and sports teams as "promotion partners," sharing costs previously absorbed totally by the client.

GENERAL MILLS organized client's projected sponsorship of bicycling events aimed at creating national impact via package-back promotions, point-of-sale visibility, and tie-in partnerships with cosponsors.

EDUCATION

M.B.A., Major in Marketing and Market Research
  University of California at Los Angeles, 1979

B.A., Major in Economics
  Williams College, Williamstown, Massachusetts, 1977

ADDITIONAL ACTIVITIES

- former 12th-ranked Scrabble player in the United States
- co-organizer, Advertising Volleyball League, 1981
- designer of original needlework art

You can omit from your résumé all personal references, such as marital status, number and ages of children, or leisure activities. The hobby section, though, is an eye-catching section of Morton's résumé because his activities outside of work are unusual and interesting. If your spare-time pursuits are biking, jogging, travel, and movies, don't even mention them, because no one will notice such a list. Once again, recruiters are looking at your experience, not your leisure activities. While it can only help to present yourself as versatile, well rounded, healthy, and team-oriented or endowed with leadership abilities, these are still not the aspects to focus on.

YOUR INTERVIEW WITH THE RECRUITER

So the strategy's worked thus far, and you're preparing for a first meeeting with a reputable headhunter with whom your telephone rapport, at least, has been good. Here are some helpful hints as you prepare yourself for that encounter.

Joe Bartol, a former headhunter, emphasizes, "Look for a job while you're working! Anticipate your needs to plan for your future. Even if you're leaving a phone number of your previous employer, it will soon be obvious as just a message center, spreading the image that you've been dismissed. You can use a headhunter to learn your real value in the job market even if there's no position for you right then. To succeed economically, move within your own industry. Keep raising your plateau by changing jobs, which raises your starting level at the next position. Most importantly, stop being viewed as you *were* instead of as you *are.*" Bartol, now director of the Department of Banking and Finance at a large private university, is advising that you manage and direct the impression your recruiter will form during the interview.

"The successful applicant," according to Gene Frank at Jay Heino Associates, "is not necessarily the best qualified, but the one who is able to create the impression in the employer's eyes of these three points: that you're agreeable and will be supportive of your boss and never be a back-stabber; that the position is exactly the type of opportunity you're seeking, and that your education and experience mean you can make a significant contribution to the new company; that you're not joining your next employer with an eye toward leaving." You have to communicate your loyalty as an employee to the recruiter who will represent you, as they need to believe you'll be able to make the appropriate impression on prospective employers.

John L. Handy, founder of Handy Associates, with offices worldwide, and former head of recruiting at McKinsey & Company, explained, "For a top-level executive position, the recruiter is looking for a business leader with two basic qualities: the money-making instinct and administrative ability. Administrative ability includes, but goes beyond, executive ability, and the personal attributes that make for administrative success are drive, responsibility, the ability to think, the ability to communicate, and the ability to get along with people."

Handy advises that if a candidate was fired or had great difficulty with a previous position, "he should be frank with the interviewer but at the same time be objective and not dwell on the past. A person is going to be judged on what he is doing and not on what he could have done if conditions had been different in the past. . . . What is important for the recruiter to know is what you did do under the conditions you were faced with at the time."

Handy also offers his six key points to remember in an interview with a recruiter (or possible employer, for that matter). They're as relevant today as they were in the early seventies when he formulated them:

1.   Your appearance must be standard, neat and orderly. Give the impression of one who wants to get things done. . . .

2.   Don't appear overconfident. . . or too relaxed, as a casual, slow approach suggests a lack of discipline . . . and an overfriendly nature not normally suited to the job at hand. Strike a middle course in demeanor.

3.   Be specific about achievements, using numbers wherever possible. These are the critical areas upon which decisions are made.

4. [Be] honest and direct. . . . A recruiter will soon learn if your interest in a position is authentic or if you are shopping for offers to provide leverage with your own employer. He will also discover if you have withheld vital information.

5. . . . Maintain a proper perspective throughout the negotiating stage. Don't wait until the final negotiations are under way to change your requirements. (For example, making additional monetary demands or deciding that location is a problem.)

6. Don't. . . negotiate directly with the client yourself. Let your recruiter handle the details, once you have fully informed him of the requirements and negotiable items. Not only is he likely to do better than you can but the risk of a strained situation with the new employer is minimized.[6]

You can't miss if you keep all of John Handy's suggestions firmly in mind. And we'd like to leave you with one final, crisp reiteration of the executive recruiter's perspective; it is, after all, a discriminatory specialty, offering the most talented and successful professionals an opportunity for even greater achievement. "We're not dealing with mediocrity," says Windle B. Priem, managing director of the National Financial Services Search Division at Korn/Ferry International, "not at this level."

---

6. From *Handbook of Executive Search.* Copyright © 1974 by Consultants News, Fitzwilliam, NH 03447.

PART II

THE SEARCH FIRMS

Chapter Four

USING THIS DIRECTORY

THE BIG SIX

This directory of executive search firms and specialized employment agencies has been carefully arranged in two sections: a geographical listing by state and then a breakdown by thirty-one occupational areas.

We have included firms that will work with individuals who now earn up to $40,000. Our aim is to provide you with a large number of professional services that can accelerate your career progress. However, no book about executive search would be complete without the Big Six, the six top search firms in the world. These companies place executives earning more than $50,000. While such high-level shops may not be interested in you right now, we want you to know who they are:

Korn/Ferry International—headquartered in Los Angeles
Heidrick & Struggles—based in Chicago
Spencer Stuart & Associates—main office in New York City
Russell Reynolds Associates—based in New York City
Boyden Associates—headquartered in New York City
Egon Zehnder International—based in Zurich, Switzerland

Each of the Big Six has offices in most major American cities, and they all operate internationally. Any Big Six firm in your area will be listed in the Business Yellow Pages under "Executive Search."

DIRECTORY: COMPANIES LISTED BY STATE

In this first section we have arranged hundreds of search firms and specialized employment agencies geographically. The states are listed in alphabetical order, and the companies are then arranged alphabetically within each state. In every entry you will find a company name, an address, and, in most cases, a telephone number. These addresses and phone numbers are as up to date as it was humanly possible to make them, but you should be advised that we cannot guarantee their accuracy beyond January of 1986.

Most search firms and employment agencies specialize in particular industries or occupations, as we have noted. For these companies we have inserted code letters indicating the area(s) of specialization on the line following the telephone number. Your guide to these code letters can be found on the page facing this one.

If a company belongs to either the National Association of Personnel Consultants or the Association of Executive Search Consultants, the designation "NAPC" or "AESC" appears at the end of the entry.

Entries for firms with branches in other countries have a line reading "foreign affiliates" and a listing of the cities in which these overseas offices are located.

DIRECTORY: COMPANIES LISTED BY SPECIALIZATION

In the second section of this directory we have grouped search firms and employment agencies according to the occupations or industries in which they specialize. Under each of the thirty-one occupational headings are the names and cities of firms whose recruiting emphasizes this type of work. You can then refer to the geographical listings of the first section for the full details on how to reach a firm in your occupational area. Under each of the thirty-one specializations, entries are arranged in alphabetical order by the name of the search firm or employment agency.

CODES FOR SPECIALTY FIELDS

Accounting	a	Office Administration	o
Advertising	A	Personnel	pe
Architecture	ar	Pharmaceuticals	ph
Banking	b	Printing and Packaging	pp
Computers	c	Public Relations	P
Construction	C	Publishing	pu
Engineering	e	Purchasing	p
Finance	f	Real Estate	re
General Management	g	Research and Development	r
Health Care/Hospitals	H	Retail	R
Hotel and Restaurant	hr	Sales	s
Insurance	i	Science and Technology	S
Legal	l	Securities and Investments	se
Manufacturing	M	Telecommunications	T
Marketing	m	Transportation	t
Nonprofit	n		

Chapter Five

COMPANIES LISTED BY STATE

ALABAMA

Career Personnel Service
2421 Presidents Drive Building "B"
Montgomery, AL 36116
205-277-2460
g; H; ph; s; S
NAPC

Cruit Executive Search
P.O. Box 59353
Birmingham, AL 35259
205-870-8170
a; e
NAPC

Diversified Personnel Consultants
P.O. Box 19003
Birmingham, AL 35219
205-942-1115
NAPC

Dunhill of Montgomery
500 East Boulevard, Suite 301
Montgomery, AL 36117
205-279-0494
NAPC

Gary W. Little and Associates
1 Riverchase Office Plaza, Suite 106
Birmingham, AL 35244
205-987-7989
hr
NAPC

Longs Personnel Service
P.O. Box 16704
Mobile, AL 36616
205-476-4080
e; s
NAPC

Murkett Associates
801 South Perry
Montgomery, AL 36101
205-265-5531
foreign affiliate: London

Placement Experts
944 Central Bank Building
Huntsville, AL 35801
205-539-2467
e; M
NAPC

Sales Consultants—Birmingham
2 Office Park Circle
Birmingham, AL 35223
205-871-1128
g; H; s
NAPC

ALASKA

Alaska Executive Search, Inc.
821 North Street, Suite 204
Anchorage, AK 99501
907-276-5707
a; c; o; pe

Culp & Associates
3301 C Street
Anchorage, AK 99502
907-563-2190

North Employment Agency
519 West Fourth Avenue
Anchorage, AK 99501
907-277-8682
g
NAPC

ARIZONA

Far Western Placement Services
4744 North Central
Phoenix, AZ 85012
602-264-1025
e; s
NAPC

Great Southwestern Personnel Co.
2747 East Camelback Road
Phoenix, AZ 85016
602-242-3792
b; S
NAPC

Paul C. Green & Associates, Ltd.
Box 1448
Green Valley, AZ 85614
602-625-6232
f; i; m

Hans & Associates, Inc.
3408 West Denton
Phoenix, AZ 85017
602-973-7795
H; hr

Harris & U'Ren, Inc.
101 North First Avenue
Phoenix, AZ 85003
602-257-1072
b; e; S
AESC

Keyth Hart & Associates, Inc.
7102 E. Sylvane Street
Tucson, AZ 85710
602-886-1029
l

A. R. Hutton Agency
350 West 16th Street, #408
Yuma, AZ 85364
602-782-2549
e; S
NAPC

International ExecuSearch, Ltd.
10830 North 71st Place, #104
Scottsdale, AZ 85254
602-991-5000
e; M
NAPC

Kingston & Associates
101 North Wilmot Street, #210
Tucson, AZ 85710
602-745-2345
a; b; f; re; s
NAPC

National Hospitality Associates, Inc.
610 West Broadway
Suite 202
Tempe, AZ 85282
602-438-0985
A; g; hr; s

William H. Nenstiel & Associates, Inc.
6710 East Camelback Suite 228
Scottsdale, AZ 85251
602-949-5164
a; f; g; M; m; pp

Richard E. Nosky & Associates
7510 East 1st Street
Scottsdale, AZ 85251
602-947-9785
c; S

PPS Consultants
1525 North Central Avenue
Suite 101
Phoenix, AZ 85004
602-252-5764
c; e; l; T

William Snyder Associates
7302 East 22nd Street
Tucson, AZ 85710
602-298-8989
g; T
NAPC

Tirocchi, Wright & Associates, Inc.
3300 North Central Avenue
Phoenix, AZ 85012
602-279-7411

Western Personnel Associates, Inc.
316 East Flower
Phoenix, AZ 85012
602-264-0766
a; e; f; g; pe; r; s
NAPC

ARKANSAS

Dunhill Personnel—Little Rock
2024 Arkansas Valley Drive, #704
Little Rock, AR 72212
501-225-8080
a; e
NAPC

Executive Recruiters
14 Office Park Drive
Little Rock, AR 72211
501-224-7000
a; f

Gold Card Recruiters
351 Washington, Suite 224
Camden, AR 71701
501-836-5414
e; S
NAPC

CALIFORNIA

Accountants Unlimited Personnel Services
10920 Wilshire Boulevard, #800
Los Angeles, CA 90010
213-208-1600
a

Accounting Management Resources
550 North Parkcenter Drive, #203
Santa Ana, CA 92705
714-558-0702
a

Accounting Resources International
3101 Town Center Drive, Suite 200
Laguna Niguel, CA 92677
714-495-3730
a; b; f; re

Jeffrey C. Adams & Co., Inc.
233 Sansome Street, Suite 904
San Francisco, CA 94104
415-421-4700
a; f; m; pe

The Advisory Group
4370 Alpine Road
Portola Valley, CA 94025
415-851-2015
c

Allied Search
2001 Union Street, #300
San Francisco, CA 94123
415-921-1971
g; hr; T
NAPC

Amato & Associates, Inc.
465 California Street, Suite 701
San Francisco, CA 94104
415-781-7664
i

American Executive Search Services, Inc.
7045 Via Valverde
San Jose, CA 95135
408-725-1200
g; M; m

American Executive Search Services, Inc.
3350 Scott Boulevard, Building 24
Santa Clara, CA 95051
408-496-6872
g; M; m; pp

American Research Institute
5199 Pacific Coast Highway, Suite 202
Long Beach, CA 90804
213-498-7644
pp; r; S; T

Anderson, Johnston & Roberts Agency, Inc.
Box 8385
Newport Beach, CA 92660
714-760-5075
re

Anderson, Johnston & Roberts Agency, Inc.
2938 Daimler Street
Santa Ana, CA 92705
714-760-5075
re

Apple One Personnel Service
101 Central
Glendale, CA 91203
213-240-8230
i

Apple One Personnel Service
1400 Hacienda
La Puente, CA 91744
213-918-8345
i

Apple One Personnel Service
1250 Westwood
Los Angeles, CA 90024
213-475-9461
i

Apple One Personnel Service
3323 Wilshire Boulevard
Los Angeles, CA 90010
213-383-8710
i

Apple One Personnel Service
18538 Hawthorne
Torrance, CA 90504
213-542-8534
i

Apple One Personnel Service
5955 DeSoto
West Hollywood, CA 90069
213-703-7711
i

Aristocrat Personnel Services
540 Golden Circle Drive, #104
Santa Ana, CA 91423
714-550-9131
a

Armstrong & Associates
11140 Los Alamitos Boulevard, Suite 202
Los Alamitos, CA 90720
213-594-6977
a; c; e; f; g; M; m

Associated Business Consultants, Inc.
1 Wilshire Boulevard, Suite 1210
Los Angeles, CA 90017
213-689-1112
M

Barry & Co.
900 Wilshire Boulevard
Los Angeles, CA 90017
213-620-1590
e; g; m; p

Ted Bavly Associates, Inc.
369 San Miguel Drive, Suite 160
Newport Beach, CA 92660
714-760-1313
l

The Baxter Group
11 Amber Sky Drive
Rancho Palos Verdes, CA 90274
213-541-1499
a; b; f

Rick Beedle Associates, Inc.
5301 Laurel Canyon Boulevard, Suite 219
North Hollywood, CA 91607
818-785-9929
a; c; e; f; l

J. W. Bell & Co.
1 Civic Plaza, Suite 270
Newport Beach, CA 92660
714-833-9700
C; re

Belzano, Deane & Associates
2102 Business Center Drive, Suite 203
Irvine, CA 92715
714-752-1244
c; g; H; r

Bench Ltd.
116 North Robertson Boulevard, Suite 705
Los Angeles, CA 90048
213-652-1177
l

Benson McBride & Associates Agency, Inc.
9100 Wilshire Boulevard, #442
Beverly Hills, CA 90212
213-276-6339
a

Bialla & Associates, Inc.
631 Bridgeway
Sausalito, CA 94965
415-332-7111
A; m

Billington, Fox & Ellis, Inc.
44 Montgomery Street
San Francisco, CA 94104
415-788-1723
g
AESC
foreign affiliates: Brussels, Dusseldorf,
    London, Paris

Blaine & Associates, Inc.
16055 Ventura Boulevard, Suite 1024
Encino, CA 91436
818-981-9940
a; c; f; M
NAPC

J. L. Bohart & Co.
Box 132
San Mateo, CA 94401
415-571-7788
g; M; R

The Bradford Group, Inc.
28183 La Cadena Drive, Suite 101
Laguna Hills, CA 92653
714-951-0476
hr

Brown-Bernardy, Inc.
12011 San Vincente Boulevard, Suite 512
Los Angeles, CA 90049
213-476-9947
A; m; P

California Legal Search
319 Elm Street, Suite 205
San Diego, CA 92101
619-232-1298
l

Douglas Campbell & Associates, Inc.
2700 North Main Street, Suite 508
Santa Ana, CA 92701
714-835-1152
M; pp

Career Enterprises Agency
1165 East San Antonio Drive, Suite A-1
Long Beach, CA 90807
213-422-1154
c; T

Career Specialists
4600 El Camino Real, #206
Los Altos, CA 94022
415-941-3200
e; s; T
NAPC

CDH & Associates
19712 MacArthur Boulevard, Suite 105
Irvine, CA 92715
714-848-0788
g; m; s; T

C/E Search Construction Engineering
74947 Highway 111, Suite 204
Indian Wells, CA 92210
619-568-3060
C

Cole International
1400 Shattuck Avenue, Suite 8
Berkeley, CA 94709
415-540-0213
g; H; s

Colton Bernard Inc.
417 Spruce Street
San Francisco, CA 94118
415-386-7400
M

The Computer Resources Group, Inc.
303 Sacramento Street
San Francisco, CA 94111
415-398-3535
c; o

The Computer Resources Group, Inc.
1990 North California Boulevard
Walnut Creek, CA 94596
415-945-0676
c; o

Concept Corp.
Box 575
Sausalito, CA 94966
415-332-7373
g; H; M; m; pp; r

Mabel Cook & Associates
P.O. Box 2998
Northridge, CA 91323
231-349-2811
l

Coopers & Lybrand
1000 West Sixth Street
Los Angeles, CA 90017
213-481-1000
a; f

Corporate Career Consultants
244 California Street
San Francisco, CA 94111
415-421-4541
a; f; g; M; r

Corporate Service Group, Ltd.
500 Sutter Street, Suite 901
San Francisco, CA 94102
415-391-0430
a; f; g; M; m; pe

Crown, Michaels & Associates, Inc.
2029 Century Park East, Suite 600
Los Angeles, CA 90067
213-556-8838
a; f; g; o

Robert W. Dingman Co., Inc.
32131 West Lindero Canyon Road
Westlake Village, CA 91360
213-991-5950
e

Druthers Agency
4676 Admiralty Way, #601
Marina Del Rey, CA 90291
213-822-3313
H
NAPC

E.D.P. World, Inc.
600 Montgomery Street
San Francisco, CA 94111
415-788-7800
a; c; e; f; M

Emco Personnel Service
23121 La Cadena Drive, Suite 1-1
Laguna Hills, CA 92653
714-855-0314
b
NAPC

Evans Associates, Inc.
44 Montgomery Street
San Francisco, CA 94104
415-989-6174
a; f; g; m; o

Executive Resources
582 Market Street, Suite 218
San Francisco, CA 94104
415-543-0321

Raymond L. Extract & Associates
21031 Ventura Boulevard, Suite 405
Woodland Hills, CA 91364
818-999-5155

Foster & Associates, Inc.
One Market Plaza Stewart Street Tower
San Francisco, CA 94105
415-777-0330
a; c; C; f; g; M; m
AESC

Fox-Morris Associates, Inc.
601 Montgomery Street, Suite 615
San Francisco, CA 94111
415-392-4353
l

Edward Gaylord & Associates
Box 503
Mill Valley, CA 94942
415-383-4811
a; f; g; o

General Employment Enterprises
39175 Liberty Street, #229
Fremont, CA 94538
415-797-5680
e; M
NAPC

General Employment Enterprises
2471 East Bayshore Road, #510
Palo Alto, CA 94303
415-494-3444
a; e; g
NAPC

General Employment Enterprises
Del Amo Financial Center, #665
Torrance, CA 90503
213-540-9151
e; M
NAPC

General Employment Enterprises
5930 Vareil, Suite 1
Woodland Hills, CA 91367
818-703-6908
e; g

General Employment Enterprises, Inc.
3699 Wilshire Boulevard, #850
Los Angeles, CA 90010
213-386-4630
c

Genovese & Co. Management Consultants
1880 Century Park East
Los Angeles, CA 90067
213-277-7421
e; g; M; m

GMR, Inc.
11901 Sunset Boulevard, Suite 108
Los Angeles, CA 90049
213-472-2092
e

Barry Goldberg & Associates, Inc.
2135 Benedict Canyon Drive
Beverly Hills, CA 90210
213-749-4436
l

S. Gorlick & Associates
17910 Sky Park Circle #108
Irvine, CA 92714
714-261-7261
s
NAPC

Gottschalk & Associates, Inc.
146 Sand Hill Circle
Menlo Park, CA 94025
415-323-3774
l

E. W. Green & Associates
225 Stevens Avenue, Suite 204
Solana Beach, CA 92075
619-481-8841
M; T

Groenekamp & Associates
Box 2308
Beverly Hills, CA 90213
213-855-0119

The Gruen Co.
5686 Maxwelton Road
Oakland, CA 94618
415-635-9303
c; e; m; r; T

**Robert Half of Los Angeles Personnel
Service**
3600 Wilshire Boulevard
Los Angeles, CA 90010
213-386-6805
c

Robert Half of Orange County
1600 Dove
Newport Beach, CA 92660
714-476-8925
a; f

Robert Half of Northern California
111 Pine
San Francisco, CA 94111
415-434-1900
f

Harmon Anderson International
5655 Linden Canyon Road, #325
Westlake Village, CA 91362
805-889-5522
e; m
NAPC

Harreus & Strotz, Inc.
600 Montgomery Street
31st floor
San Francisco, CA 94111
415-461-9100
A; m

Keyth Hart & Associates, Inc.
8300 Tampa Avenue
Suite J
Northridge, CA 91324
213-873-2807
l

Health Care Executive Search
3771 Sundale Road
Suite 4
Lafayette, CA 94549
415-283-5420
H; pe

Health Link Systems, Inc.
6325 Topanga Canyon
Suite 410
Woodland Hills, CA 91367
818-704-4707
H

Hergenrather & Co.
3435 Wilshire Boulevard
Los Angeles, CA 90010
213-385-0181

HiTech Consulting Group
1801 Avenue of the Stars, #601
Los Angeles, CA 90067
213-556-1628
a; b; c; f; m; s

Holderman Partners, Ltd.
220 Montgomery Street
Suite 428
San Francisco, CA 94104
415-788-6664
l

Horizon Associates
322 Broadway
Redondo Beach, CA 90277
213-540-3231
M; r

Horton Associates, Inc.
Box 9
Helendale, CA 92342
619-243-4453
c; g; m; s

Houck, Meng & Co.
6151 West Century Boulevard, Suite 506
Los Angeles, CA 90045
213-624-8088

Hytex Engineering
3662 Katella, #224
Los Alamitos, CA 90720
213-493-3554
e

Inaba Consultants
14542 Ventura Boulevard, #208
Irvine, CA 91403
818-906-1288
H
NAPC

Information Resources Group
2239 Townsgate Road, Suite 206
Westlake Village, CA 91361
805-496-7802
c; T

Input Search Agency
23161 Lake Center
El Toro, CA 92630
714-855-4999
c

Input Search Agency
23161 Lake Center Drive #203
Lake Forest, CA 92630
714-855-4999
T
NAPC

Input Search Agency
5757 Wilshire Boulevard, #493
Los Angeles, CA 90036
213-938-9137
c; T
NAPC

Insurance Placement
3757 Wilshire Freeway
Los Angeles, CA 90048
213-385-4306
i

Insurance Recruitment Agency
11777 San Vicente Boulevard, #905
Los Angeles, CA 90049
213-207-2133
i

International Staffing Consultants, Inc.
4667 MacArthur Boulevard, Suite 306
Newport Beach, CA 92260
714-752-6228
c; e; l; M; T

A. G. Johnson & Co., Inc.
19762 MacArthur Boulevard, Suite 300
Irvine, CA 92715
714-752-1140
a; f; g

JPM & Associates
4621 Teller Avenue, Suite 110
Los Angeles, CA 92660
714-553-0311
e
NAPC

JPM Associates, DBA
635 Camino De Los Mares, #210
San Clemente, CA 92672
714-496-2000
e; s; S; se
NAPC

Howard L. Karr & Associates, Inc.
1777 Borel Place, #408
San Mateo, CA 94402
415-956-5277
a; f; g; o; pe

Kass/Abell & Associates
10642 Santa Monica Boulevard, Suite 201
Los Angeles, CA 90025
213-475-4666
l

Keith Management Company, Inc.
9302 Wilshire Boulevard, Suite 208
Beverly Hills, CA 90210
213-274-8664
l

King & Associates, Inc.
20300 Ventura Boulevard, Suite 250
Woodland Hills, CA 91364
818-887-3234
H

Kuhnmuench & Cook Associates
77 West Las Tunas Drive
Arcadia, CA 91006
818-445-1961
C; e; g; M; m

Marvin Laba & Associates
6255 Sunset Boulevard
Los Angeles, CA 90028
213-464-1355
m; R

Paul W. Larson Associates, Inc.
31877 Del Obispo, Suite 213
San Juan Capistrano, CA 92675
714-493-6500
g; M; m; r; S

John Lawrence Agency of Los Angeles
20446 Nordhoff Street
Chatsworth, CA 91311
213-999-2430
g; i
NAPC

Lawsearch Inc.
16000 Ventura Boulevard
Encino, CA 91436
818-986-9511
l

Lee, Jackson & Bowe
9401 Wilshire Boulevard, Suite 1120
Beverly Hills, CA 90212
213-275-0171
l

Alan Lewis Associates
341 South Cedros
Solana Beach, CA 92075
619-259-0955
b; g
NAPC

Charles R. Lister International Inc.
Box 4347
Carmel-by-the-Sea, CA 93921
408-624-2995
S

Ernest L. Loen & Associates
2330 West Third Street
Los Angeles, CA 90057
213-388-3354

Lyman & Co.
102 North Brand Boulevard,
   Suite 412/Box 10368
Glendale, CA 91203
818-240-7624
a; b; f; g; l; m; o
NAPC

McCormack & Farrow
211 East Ocean Boulevard
Long Beach, CA 90802
213-435-1100
a; b; f; g; pe; S

McMorrow Associates, Inc.
1925 Century Park East, Suite 1120
Los Angeles, CA 90067
213-556-0158
l

Joseph J. McTaggart
Box 1104
Campbell, CA 95009
408-578-1221

Robert A. Major & Associates
680 Beach Street, Suite 492
San Francisco, CA 94109
415-441-2063
l

Management Decisions Agency
13455 Ventura Boulevard, #233
Sherman Oaks, CA 91423
818-788-6660
c

Management Recruiters Midwest
325 East Hillcrest Drive, #160
Thousand Oaks, CA 91360
714-493-1140
e; R; s; T
NAPC

**Management Resources Executive
   Recruiters**
6475-B Pacific Coast Highway, Suite 324
Long Beach, CA 90803
213-493-4445
c; o

Thomas Mangum Co.
930 Colorado Boulevard
Los Angeles, CA 90041
213-259-0600
g; M; m; pe; r

Marshall Group
1100 Quail Street #117
Los Angeles, CA 92660
714-476-0200
e; H; M; m; ph
NAPC

Mason Concepts Agency, Inc.
6380 Wilshire Boulevard, #1000
Los Angeles, CA 90048
213-655-7555
a; c

Midcom Agency
1940 North Tustin, #117
Orange, CA 92665
714-998-6041
e
NAPC

Bill Miller & Associates
P.O. Box 28271
San Diego, CA 92128
714-487-2455
g; H
NAPC

Miller-Hanna & Associates
10850 Wilshire Boulevard
Los Angeles, CA 90010
213-475-7711
ar

Mini-Systems Associates
634 Venice Boulevard
Marina Del Rey, CA 90291
213-822-0573
c

Mini-Systems Associates
3931 MacArthur Boulevard, #101,
 P.O. #1940
Newport Beach, CA 92658
714-752-5420
c

J. R. Morrison & Associates, Inc.
600 Montgomery Street, 35th floor
San Francisco, CA 94111
415-956-3260
a; f; g; M; m; pe

Herbert H. Moss, Inc.
2963 Orella Circle
Palm Springs, CA 92262
619-320-0289
g; M; m; ph; p

MSL International Consultants, Ltd.
50 California Street, Suite 2400
San Francisco, CA 94111
415-543-3950
g

National Recruiters Corporation
22801 Ventura Boulevard
Woodland Hills, CA 91364
818-792-8000
s

Nation-Wide Recruiting, Inc.
5365D White Oak Avenue
Encino, CA 91316
818-996-5050
g; m; s

Gary Nelson & Associates, Inc.
10050 North Wolfe Road
Cupertino, CA 95014
408-255-7400
c; e; f; M; S
NAPC

Gary Nelson & Associates, Inc.
4270 Redwood Highway
San Rafael, CA 94913
415-479-5101
a; c; f; M

NHS Legal Search Consultants, Inc.
1 Wilshire Boulevard, Penthouse Suite
Los Angeles, CA 90017
213-489-6818
l

Paul Norsell & Associates, Inc.
6200 Canyon Rim Road, Suite 108C
Anaheim, CA 92807
714-974-9460
a; f; g; M; m; r

Paul Norsell & Associates, Inc.
9841 Airport Boulevard, Suite 720
Los Angeles, CA 90045
213-645-7751
a; f; g; M; m; r

Ott & Hansen, Inc.
136 South Oak Knoll
Pasadena, CA 91101
818-578-0551
e

Robert Ottke Associates
1000 Quail Street, Suite 290
Newport Beach, CA 92660
714-752-0932
ph; S

Paramount Personnel Service
2150 Franklin Street, #550
Oakland, CA 94612
415-893-5466
a; b; e
NAPC

Perry-White & Associates, Inc.
3333 Wilshire Boulevard, Suite 609
Los Angeles, CA 90010
213-384-8800
c; e

Perry-White & Associates, Inc.
465 California Street, Suite 815
San Francisco, CA 94104
415-981-7000
c; e; S

Perry-White & Associates, Inc.
3150 De La Cruz Boulevard, Suite 101
Santa Clara, CA 95050
408-970-9600
c; e; T

Pierce Associates, Inc.
601 Montgomery Street, Suite 1117
San Francisco, CA 94111
415-421-9440
c; m; s; T

Pinsker and Shattuck, Inc.
100 Bush Street
San Francisco, CA 94104
415-421-6264
H; S
AESC

Pinsker and Shattuck, Inc.
P.O. Box 1235
Saratoga, CA 95070
408-867-5161
H; S
AESC

Pro, Inc.
7726 Girard Avenue
La Jolla, CA 92037
619-454-1193
i; S
NAPC

Pro Select
4238 Holt Boulevard
Montclair, CA 91763
714-625-2386
pp
NAPC

Proctor & Davis
2811 Wilshire Boulevard, Suite 590
Santa Monica, CA 90403
213-829-4721
a; c; e; f; M; m

Purcell Employment Systems
3660 Wilshire Boulevard, #610
Los Angeles, CA 90010
213-380-4550
e; g; S
NAPC

Pursuant Legal Consultants
383 South Palm Canyon Drive
Palm Springs, CA 92262
619-322-1486
l

L. J. Quinn & Associates, Inc.
1156 East Green Street, Suite 101
Pasadena, CA 91106
818-793-6044

Real Estate Executive Search, Inc.
1303 Jefferson Street, Suite 600B
Napa, CA 94559
707-253-9260
re

The Recruiting Group
24861 Alicia Parkway, Suite C-206
Laguna Hills, CA 92653
714-768-4212
e

Redden & Associates
201 South Lake Avenue, Suite 707
Pasadena, CA 91101
818-792-1931

Redlands Employment Agency
Redlands Plaza, Suite 222, P.O. Box 190
Redlands, CA 92373
714-793-3351
g
NAPC

The Pamela Reeve Agency, Inc.
9000 Sunset Boulevard, Suite 501
Los Angeles, CA 90069
213-273-4950
A; m

Reichelt & Associates, Inc.
1633 Westwood Boulevard
Los Angeles, CA 90024
213-478-2591
A; m; P

Rivera Legal Search Consultants, Inc.
2001 Wilshire Boulevard, Suite 600
Santa Monica, CA 90403
213-829-1869
l

Riviera Executive Services
2082 Business Center Drive
Irvine, CA 92715
714-833-9410

Rollins & Co.
8060 La Jolla Shores Drive
La Jolla, CA 92037
619-459-2911
M

Lowell N. Ross & Associates
Box 629
Corte Madera, CA 94925
415-924-6511
c; e; r; S; T

Roth Young—Los Angeles
6133 Bristol Parkway, Suite 100
Fox Hills, CA 90230
213-670-0521
hr; M; R; s
NAPC

St. Clair International
5335 Middlefield Road
Menlo Park, CA 94025
415-325-8480
g; i; m

Sales Consultants Encino
16133 Ventura Boulevard
Encino, CA 91436
818-986-7550
s

Search Division
404 North LaCienga Boulevard
Los Angeles, CA 90048
213-652-3315
T; t

Search Tech Associates
23801 Calabasas Road, Suite 2050
Calabasas, CA 91302
818-704-5373
e; m; s; S

Search West
16133 Ventura Boulevard
Encino, CA 91436
818-986-6300

Search West
1875 Century Park East, Suite 1025
Los Angeles, CA 90067
213-930-1313

Search West
5900 Wilshire Boulevard, Suite 201
Los Angeles, CA 90036
213-930-1313

Search West
337 Vineyard Avenue
Suite 200
Ontario, CA 91764
714-986-1966
c

Search West
1701 Bank America Tower
Orange, CA 92668
714-634-4300

Search West
2 Embarcadero Center
Suite 1670
San Francisco, CA 94111
415-788-1770

Search West
100 North Citrus Avenue
West Covina, CA 91790
818-967-0551

Search West
2900 Townsgate
Westlake Village, CA 91361
805-496-6811

Seaton/Russo Inc.
9744 Wilshire Boulevard
Suite 205
Beverly Hills, CA 90212
213-550-6171
l

The September Group
11611 San Vincente Boulevard, #840
Los Angeles, CA 90049
213-207-0444
b

Sequent Personnel Services
444 Castro Street
Suite 1020
Mountain View, CA 94041
415-964-4000
b; e
NAPC

Charles Sharp & Associates
10920 Wilshire Boulevard, Suite 1110
Los Angeles, CA 90024
213-824-0700
A; m; P

Siegel & Bishop, Inc.
1770 San Jose Avenue
San Francisco, CA 94112
415-239-1016
e; M; m; r; T

Siegel Shotland & Associates
16311 Ventura Boulevard, Suite 1110
Encino, CA 91436
818-995-1501
a; f; M; m; pe

Simon & Ryan, Inc.
235 Montgomery Street, Suite 1004
San Francisco, CA 94104
415-956-3550
b; f

Smith, Goerss & Ferneborg, Inc.
25 Ecker Street, Suite 600
San Francisco, CA 94105
415-543-4181

Carolyn Smith Paschal International
1237 Camino del Mar, Suite C506
Del Mar, CA 92014
619-587-1366
A; f; m; n; P

A. William Smyth, Inc.
P.O. Box 380
Ross, CA 94957
415-457-8383
R

Sollmar Incorporated
P.O. Box 155
Tustin, CA 92681
714-832-1220
g; M; m; pe; r

Source Finance
1875 Century Park East
Century City, CA 90067
213-203-9911
a; f

Source Finance
444 South Flower Street
Los Angeles, CA 90017
213-688-0082
a; f

Source Finance
2061 Landings Drive
Mountain View, CA 94043
415-969-4990
a; f

Source Finance
4299 MacArthur Boulevard
Newport Beach, CA 92660
714-955-3800
a; f

Source Finance
50 California Street
San Francisco, CA 94111
415-956-4740
a; f

Source Finance
15643 Sherman Way
Van Nuys, CA 91406
818-781-7200
a; f

Source Finance
1900 North California Boulevard
Walnut Creek, CA 94596
415-945-8484
a; f

Southern Personnel Services
72261 Highway 111, #206
Palm Desert, CA 92260
714-340-1612
a; hr
NAPC

Paul Stafford Associates, Ltd.
115 Sansome Street, Suite 1204
San Francisco, CA 94104
415-788-0544
g; hr
AESC

Stephens & Associates
4365 Mission Bay Drive, Suite 1
San Diego, CA 92109
619-270-8800
re

The Stevenson Group, Inc.
2030 East Fourth Avenue
Santa Ana, CA 92705
714-547-0143

Streeter & Associates
3250 Wilshire Boulevard, Suite 900
Los Angeles, CA 90010
213-480-1022
a; c; f

W. J. Stuart & Co.
2201 Outpost Drive
Los Angeles, CA 90068
213-851-8601
c; e; T

Sun Valley Personnel Agency
190 North Wiget Lane, P.O. Box 4520
Walnut Creek, CA 94596
415-933-0100
e; s
NAPC

Systematics Agency
3660 Wilshire Boulevard
Los Angeles, CA 90025
213-487-1020
c

Systems Careers
558 Sacramento Street, Suite 400
San Francisco, CA 94111
415-434-4770
c

Tanzi Executive Search
110 West C Street, Suite 1407
San Diego, CA 92101
619-233-0584
g; m

Tanzi Executive Search
110 Sutter Street, Suite 612
San Francisco, CA 94104
415-391-9991
g; m

Richard Theobald & Associates
675 Mariners Island Boulevard, Suite 107
San Mateo, CA 94404
415-570-5200
a; f; g; m; o; pe

Torretto & Associates, Inc.
Box 265—307 Bridgeway
Sausalito, CA 94965
415-332-9420
c; C; f; H; ph; R; S; t

The Trattner Network
7807 Wren Lane
Citrus Heights, CA 95610
916-965-1616
c; e; m; s; S

Trotter, Mitchell, Larsen & Zilliacus
523 West Sixth Street
Los Angeles, CA 90014
213-489-7120
g

Trotter, Mitchell, Larsen & Zilliacus
3613 West MacArthur Boulevard, Suite 612
Santa Ana, CA 92704
714-720-9070
g

Thomas L. Trout & Associates, Inc.
30423 Canwood Street, Suite 123
Agoura Hills, CA 91301
818-706-1980

Varo & Lund Corp.
1800 North Highland Avenue, Suite 406
Los Angeles, CA 90028
213-469-3109
e; g; M; m; r

Vine Associates, Inc.
10850 Riverside Drive, 600C S. Building
North Hollywood, CA 91602
818-906-3368
g; m; pe

Vlcek & Company
1100 Quail Street, Suite 208
Los Angeles, CA 92660
714-752-0661
e; m; S
NAPC

Waldorf Associates, Inc.
660 Gretna Green, Suite 100
Los Angeles, CA 90049
213-476-4777
l

Sally Walters Placement Agency
115 Sansome Street, Suite 1005
San Francisco, CA 94104
415-981-1414
e
NAPC

The Ward Consulting Group, Inc.
586 North First Street, Suite 261
San Jose, CA 95112
408-986-8611

Ward Howell International Inc.
10100 Santa Monica Boulevard
Los Angeles, CA 90067
213-553-6638

Ward Howell International Inc.
3 Embarcadero Center, Suite 1060
San Francisco, CA 94111
415-398-3900

Wells International
1900 Avenue of the Stars, Suite 850
Los Angeles, CA 90067
213-553-0200
l

Western Personnel Agency
625 Market Street, Suite 1200
San Francisco, CA 94105
415-982-4880

Wheeler Associates
533 Sutter Street, Suite 1130
San Francisco, CA 94102
415-330-7394
g
NAPC

Betty White Agency
365 Esplanade Drive, #206
Oxnard, CA 93030
805-485-8333
g
NAPC

Whitman Stone Associates
505 City Parkway West, #1000
Orange, CA 92668
714-634-2261
e; S

Wilkinson and Ives, Inc.
23 Altarinda Road, Suite 101
Orinda, CA 94563
415-254-2770
c; f; g; i; S; t
AESC

Wilkinson and Ives, Inc.
601 California Street; Suite 1809
La Canada, CA 91011
818-790-9657
f

The Winchester Group
951 Mariners Island Boulevard, Suite 230
San Mateo, CA 94404
415-570-5627
g

Winguth, Schweichler Associates, Inc.
24 California Street, Suite 750
San Francisco, CA 94111
415-495-8255
a; f; g; M; m; pe

Winship Associates
220 Montgomery Street, Suite 318
San Francisco, CA 94104
415-781-8180
l

XXCAL
2001 South Barrington Avenue, #114
Los Angeles, CA 90025
213-477-2902
e; T
NAPC

Yelverton & Company
353 Sacramento Street
San Francisco, CA 94111
415-981-6060
b; S; T
AESC

Arthur Young Executive Resource Consultants
515 South Flower Street, 24th floor
Los Angeles, CA 90071
213-977-3473
g
AESC

Arthur Young Executive Resource Consultants
1 Post Street, 29th floor
San Francisco, CA 94104
415-393-2746
g
AESC

Ziskind, Greene & Associates
8912 Burton Way
Beverly Hills, CA 90211
213-274-7202
l

Ziskind, Greene & Associates
1750 Montgomery Street
San Francisco, CA 94111
415-391-2310
l

The Zivic Group
517 Washington Street, Suite 201
San Francisco, CA 94111
415-421-2325
a; e; f; g; pe

COLORADO

Accounting Resources International
5650 South Syracuse Circle, Suite 204
Englewood, CO 80111
303-779-4260
a

Allied Careers, Inc.
9175 East Kenyon Avenue, #201
Denver, CO 80237
303-771-0332
s
NAPC

William B. Arnold Associates, Inc.
1776 South Jackson Street
Denver, CO 80210
303-759-9941

Barclays Recruiting Services, Inc.
4155 East Jewell Avenue, Suite 908
Denver, CO 80222
303-759-2828
b; f; i; M; s
NAPC

Buxton & Associates
1763 Vine Street
Denver, CO 80206
303-377-4862
b; g
NAPC

Careers Ltd.
1390 Logan, Suite 204
Denver, CO 80203
303-832-5200
b; e; s
NAPC

Dimarchi & Associates
P.O. Box 996
Denver, CO 80201
303-443-8100
g
NAPC

Dunhill of Fort Collins
2120 South College Avenue, #3
Fort Collins, CO 80525
303-221-5630
b; e
NAPC

S. Ronald Gaston & Associates
P.O. Box 2527
Littleton, CO 80161
303-699-1780
hr

Greene & Associates
695 South Colorado Boulevard, #290
Denver, CO 80222
303-698-2292
c

Health Industry Consultants, Inc.
7353 South Alton Way, Penthouse
Englewood, CO 80112
303-850-7611
e; g; H; M; m; o; ph; r

John Heckers & Associates
8795 Ralston Road
Aruada, CO 80002
303-422-8072
b; c
NAPC

Jorgenson Associates
5271 South Quebec Street, Suite 100
Englewood, CO 80111
303-779-4447
e
NAPC

Karam Associates
2121 South Oneida Street, Suite 612
Denver, CO 80224
303-623-2882
a; f; g; M; m; pe

Kearney: Executive Search Group
7951 East Maplewood Avenue, Suite 220
Englewood, CO 80111
303-572-6175
H; t
AESC

Kenex Consultants
3025 South Parker Road, Penthouse Suite
Aurora, CO 80014
303-696-8490
a; c; e
NAPC

Lyons/Aspen Consultants Group
295 West Hampden Avenue
Englewood, CO 80110
303-761-3011
M; p
NAPC

MPI Associates
1919 14th Street, Suite 701
Boulder, CO 80302
303-443-1302
c; e; r

Phillips Personnel Search
1675 Broadway, Suite 2280
Denver, CO 80202
303-893-1850
a; e; l; s
NAPC

PMG, Inc.
6000 East Evans Avenue, Building 2
 Suite 400
Denver, CO 80222
303-759-9313

Riley Recruiting Enterprises
1410 High Street, Suite 300
Denver, CO 80218
302-388-1467
b; se
NAPC

Rocky Mountain Recruiters
1430 Larimer Square, #210
Denver, CO 80202
303-628-9400
e
NAPC

Scully & Associates
6285 Lehman Drive, Suite D-202
Colorado Springs, CO 80918
303-594-0106
c; e
NAPC

Source Finance
7720 East Belleview Avenue
Englewood, CO 80111
303-298-8181
a; f

CONNECTICUT

Alexander & Zier Associates
14 Ascolese Road
Trumbull, CT 06611
203-268-9553
c; S

Amity Consultants, Inc.
2505 Black Rock Turnpike
Fairfield, CT 06430
203-372-4316
a; b; c; M; s; S; T
NAPC

Auden Associates, Inc.
505 Main Street, P.O. Box 1077
Middletown, CT 06457
203-344-9847
a; e; g
NAPC

Availability of Hartford
179 Allyn Street
Hartford, CT 06103
203-247-5566
a; e
NAPC

Bailey Employment Service
20 East Main Street
Waterbury, CT 06702
203-756-8958
a; e
NAPC

Bentley & Evans International, Inc.
30 Tower Lane, Avon Park South
Avon, CT 06011
203-674-8701

The Best People
1786 Bedford Street
Stamford, CT 06905
203-348-5919
i
NAPC

Brakeley, John Price Jones, Inc.
1600 Summer Street
Stamford, CT 06905
203-348-8100
n

William H. Brawley Associates
Box 486
107 Cherry Street
New Canaan, CT 06840
203-966-5697
a; f

Breck Lardner Associates, Inc.
Box 611
Essex, CT 06426
203-767-2143

The Breen Group, Inc.
3780 Whitney Avenue
Hamden, CT 06518
203-288-7461
c; f

Breitmayer Associates
38 Fair Street
Guilford, CT 06437
203-453-8778
f; g; M; m

Breitmayer Associates
300 Broad Street
Stamford, CT 06901
203-324-6063

D.A.K. Brown & Associates
191 Post Road West
Westport, CT 06880
203-226-8658

Business Personnel Associates
61A Wells Street
Glastonbury, CT 06033
203-659-3511
c; e; i
NAPC

Jaci Carroll Personnel Service
37 Leavenworth Street, P.O. Box 1525
Waterbury, CT 06721
203-574-4838
b; e
NAPC

Center for Health Care Personnel
936 Silas Deane Highway
Wethersfield, CT 06109
203-278-3067
H; S
NAPC

Richard Clark Associates
45 South Main Street
Fairfield, CT 06017
203-236-6886
b; c; e; i; M
NAPC

Corporate Resource Group
457 Castle Avenue
Fairfield, CT 06430
203-787-5791
a; e
NAPC

Corporate Resource Group
60 Washington Street
Hartford, CT 06106
203-547-0900
a; c; e; g; H
NAPC

Corporate Search & Placement
P.O. Box 839
Orange, CT 06477
203-874-6699
e; g
NAPC

Craighead Associates, Inc.
3 Landmark Square
Stamford, CT 06901
203-325-0066
a; f; M; m; pe

Data Management Resources
100 Prospect Street
Stamford, CT 06901
203-324-4358
c; g; T
NAPC

David-Kris Associates
225 Main Street, P.O. Box 5051
Westport, CT 06881
203-227-4206
a; f

Diversified Employment Services
531 Whalley Avenue
New Haven, CT 06511
203-397-2500
e
NAPC

Dunhill of Greater Stamford
213 Danbury Road
Wilton, CT 06897
203-762-7722
m; s
NAPC

Dunsmore & Associates, Ltd.
87 Whitfield Street, P.O. Box 588
Guilford, CT 06437
203-453-3942
g; m
NAPC

Employment Opportunities
213 Main Street
Danbury, CT 06810
203-792-9536
b; e; g; ph; s
NAPC

Engineering Search Associates
99 Durham Road
Madison, CT 06443
203-245-1983
e
NAPC

Equinox Management Corp.
83 East Avenue
Norwalk, CT 06851
203-846-8111
b; c; f; H

Executive Recruiters
630 Oakwood Avenue
Fairfield, CT 06110
203-521-7400
NAPC

Executive Register, Inc.
34 Mill Plain Road
Danbury, CT 06810
203-743-5542
a; c; e; f; M
NAPC

Executive Resources
Route 5—Squire Hill Road
New Milford, CT 06776
203-355-3737
m; S; T

Executive Search
1 Landmark Square
Stamford, CT 06901
203-327-5100
a; f

Fairfield Whitney
88 Ryders Lane, Suite 213
Stratford, CT 06497
203-377-8900
a; c; e
NAPC

Fanning Personnel
18 Asylum Street, Suite 203
Hartford, CT 06103
203-247-3303
l

Fortune Personnel Consultants
400 Main Street
Stamford, CT 06901
203-324-1313
a; c; e
NAPC

George W. Fotis & Associates, Inc.
170 Mason Street
Greenwich, CT 06830
203-661-1081
pe

B. Goodwin, Ltd.
Box 340
Fairfield, CT 06430
203-255-9401
a; f; M; pe; r

Maxwell Gould Associates
44 Avonwood Road, Laurelside 316
Avon, CT 06001
203-674-1491

Halbrecht Associates, Inc.
1200 Summer Street
Stamford, CT 06905
203-327-5630

K. M. Harrison Associates, Inc.
P.O. Box 11174
Greenwich, CT 06830
203-431-4300
l

Herz, Stewart & Company
1200 Summer Street
Stamford, CT 06905
203-324-5400
g
NAPC

Higbee Associates, Inc.
151 Rowayton Avenue
Rowayton, CT 06853
203-853-7600
a; f; l; m; P

Hipp Waters Office Personnel
43 Greenwich Avenue
Greenwich, CT 06830
203-661-6010
NAPC

Hipp Waters Professional Recruiters
707 Summer Street
Stamford, CT 06901
203-357-8400
a; e; m; s
NAPC

Hire Counseling and Personnel Service
15-H Hillcrest Avenue
Fairfield, CT 06110
203-522-0307
g
NAPC

Human Resource Consultants Ltd.
15 Lewis Street, Suite 503
Hartford, CT 06103
203-522-0400
e
NAPC

Indusearch
100 Market Square
Newington, CT 06111
203-667-1685
e; M
NAPC

Industrial Recruiters Associates, Inc.
630 Oakwood Avenue
West Hartford, CT 06110
203-278-3643
M; m; r

Interquest, Incorporated
270 Farmington Avenue, Suite 305
Farmington, CT 06032
203-674-1500
l

Kensington Management Consultants, Inc.
25 Third Street
Stamford, CT 06905
203-327-9860

KGC Associates
100 Connecticut Boulevard
East Hartford, CT 06108
203-528-1728
e; f; i
NAPC

Kinkead Associates
1 Financial Plaza
Hartford, CT 06103
203-246-1901
a; c; e; i; m
NAPC

Lou Klein Associates
4695 Main Street
Bridgeport, CT 06606
203-374-5588
e
NAPC

Lamay Associates, Inc.
1111 East Putnam Avenue
Riverside, CT 06878
203-637-8440
m

Lambert Associates
21 Charles Street, Court Office Building
Westport, CT 06880
203-226-6622

Gilbert Lane Personnel
2880 Bixwell Avenue
Hamden, CT 06518
203-281-3984
a; e
NAPC

Gilbert Lane Personnel
750 Main Street, #1110
Hartford, CT 06103
203-278-7700
a; e; i
NAPC

Arthur J. Langdon
750 Main Street
Hartford, CT 06103
203-724-3441
c; e; i
NAPC

Leon Lawrence Personnel
4697 Main Street
Bridgeport, CT 06606
203-371-8177
b; e
NAPC

W. R. Lawry, Inc.
P.O. Box 832
Simsbury, CT 06070
203-651-0281
e; g
NAPC

Samuel F. Leigh Associates, Inc.
322 Noroton Avenue
Darien, CT 06820
203-655-7276
ph; pp

Leonard Associates
56 Fairview Drive
Rocky Hill, CT 06067
203-563-2272
f; i
NAPC

Arthur Lyle Associates, Inc.
300 Broad Street
Stamford, CT 06901
203-964-0046
a; f

Lynn Associates
231 Farmington Avenue
Farmington, CT 06032
203-677-5556
H; i; ph
NAPC

Management Recruiters—Fairfield
15 Bank Street
Fairfield, CT 06901
203-324-2232
NAPC

Management Recruiters—Hamden
2911 Dixwell Avenue
Hamden, CT 06518
203-248-0770
e
NAPC

Management Search & Associates
10 Bay Street
Westport, CT 06880
203-227-3524
a; f; M; m; pe

Mason Associates
1 Hoyt Street
Norwalk, CT 06851
203-853-7775
c; M; m; r
NAPC

Midgette Consultants, Inc.
182 Grand Street
Suite 419
Waterbury, CT 06702
203-575-0010
c; S

MRG Search & Placement
900 Chapel Street
Suite 515
New Haven, CT 06510
203-624-0161
a; f; M; m; P

Nicastro Associates
246 Post Road East
Westport, CT 06880
203-226-6945
e
NAPC

People Management Inc.
10 Station Street
Simsbury, CT 06070
203-651-3581
e; M; m; r; S

Barry Persky & Company, Inc.
830 Post Road East
Westport, CT 06880
203-226-7833

The Personnel Laboratory
733 Summer Street
Stamford, CT 06901
203-325-4348
pe

Power Industry Personnel
1064 Poq Road
Groton, CT 06340
203-446-9930
e
NAPC

Professional Computer Personnel
111 West Main Street
Waterbury, CT 06702
203-575-1651
c; e
NAPC

Professional Employment Registry
2 Stony Hill Road
Bethel, CT 06801
203-743-3050
g
NAPC

Quality Control Recruiters
P.O. Box 1900
Bristol, CT 06010
203-582-0003
e; H
NAPC

Quinn Associates, Ltd.
33 King Street
Stratford, CT 06497
203-386-1300
e
NAPC

QVSCC Employment Connection
94 South Main Street
Brooklyn, CT 06239
203-774-9590
g
NAPC

Redmond & Associates, Inc.
57 North Street, Suite 307
Danbury, CT 06810
203-797-9766
a; f; M; m; pe

Research Technologies
490 Old Toll Road
Madison, CT 06443
203-421-3088
e; g; M; T
NAPC

Retail Personnel Associates
P.O. Box 923
Glastonbury, CT 06033
203-659-3207
R
NAPC

Retail Recruiters
1850 Silas Deane Highway
Rocky Hill, CT 06067
203-721-9550
hr; R
NAPC

Reynolds Technical Services
3638 Main Street, P.O. Box 661
Stratford, CT 06497
203-375-1953
e
NAPC

Marshall Rice
Box 1053
Weston, CT 06883
203-222-0677
n

Ridgefield Search International
224 Barlow Mountain Road
Ridgefield, CT 06877
203-438-8000
f; M; m; pe; r; s

RJS Associates
241 Asylum Street
Hartford, CT 06103
203-278-5840
e; m
NAPC

Roche Associates
Box 1353
Stamford, CT 06094
203-348-3833
a; f; g; M; s; T

Rogers, Slade & Hill, Inc.
17 Wilmot Lane
Riverside, CT 06878
203-637-8600

Sanford Rose Associates of Hartford
340 Broad Street
Windsor, CT 06095
203-683-0205
e; H; M
NAPC

Sales Consultants of Hartford
1800 Silas Deane Highway
Hartford, CT 06067
203-563-2301
g; m; s
NAPC

Sales Consultants—New Haven
1800 Silas Deane Highway
Rocky Hill, CT 06067
203-563-2301
g; m; s

William A. Sharon & Associates
P.O. Box 758
Essex, CT 06426
203-767-0903
m

Howard W. Smith Associates
101 Pearl Street
Hartford, CT 06103
203-549-2060
a; f; g; o; pe

Smyth Dawson Associates
100 Prospect Street, Century Plaza
Stamford, CT 06901
203-358-0010
a; f; g

Specialized Search Associates
100 Melrose Square
Greenwich, CT 06830
203-629-8811
C; g; m; s

Spectra Professional Search
419 Whalley Avenue
New Haven, CT 06511
203-288-2803
e
NAPC

Staub, Warmbold & Associates, Inc.
1600 Summer Street
Stamford, CT 06905
203-358-0055

The Technical Group
361 Post Road West
Westport, CT 06880
203-222-1281
e

Technical Search Associates
P.O. Box 2149
Danbury, CT 06810
203-794-0757
e;T
NAPC

Tidewater Group, Inc.
66 Crescent Street
Stamford, CT 06906
203-327-4406
g

Uni/Search of New Haven
264 Amity Road
Woodbridge, CT 06525
203-389-5341
e; M
NAPC

Vannah/Rowe, Inc.
11 Mountain Avenue, P.O. Box 514
Bethel, CT 06002
203-243-0424
g
NAPC

Vantage Careers, Inc.
777 Summer Street
Stamford, CT 06904
203-357-7977
a; c; f; pe

Vezan-West & Co.
1000 Framington Avenue
West Hartford, CT 06107
203-233-9804
e; g; M; pe; r

Ward Howell International Inc.
1 East Putnam Avenue
Greenwich, CT 06830
203-629-2994

Ward Liebell Associates, Inc.
35 Field Point Road
Greenwich, CT 06830
203-622-0787
A; m

John H. Warner Associates, Inc.
37 Lewis Street, Suite 10
Hartford, CT 06103
203-522-9251
a; f; g; M; pe

Weatherby Associates, Inc.
25 Van Zant Street
Norwalk, CT 06855
203-866-1144

Winchester Consultants, Inc.
Box 1334
New Canaan, CT 06840
203-972-0011
g; m; r

Zackrison Associates, Inc.
88 Beach Road
Fairfield, CT 06430
203-255-5401
c; e; f; M; m; pe
NAPC

Zackrison Associates, Inc.
1275 Summer Street
Stamford, CT 06905
203-348-6965
c; e; f; M; m; pe

Zackrison Associates, Inc.
630 Oakwood Avenue
West Hartford CT 06110
203-527-3406
c; e; f; M; m; pe

Ellie Mack Associates
3411 Silverside Road
Wilmington, DE 19810
302-478-6955
a; e
NAPC

**National Employment Consultants—
  Brandywine, Inc.**
1016 Delaware Avenue
Wilmington, DE 19806
302-654-4441
l

The Placers, Inc.
2000 Pennsylvania Avenue, Suite 201
Wilmington, DE 19806
302-575-1414
a; b; e; f; H; R; se
NAPC

DELAWARE

The Barry Companies
820 Washington Street
Wilmington, DE 19801
302-571-8000
g
NAPC

Robert Half of Wilmington
Brandywood Plaza, Foulk & Grubb Roads
Wilmington, DE 19810
302-475-4500
a; b
NAPC

DISTRICT OF COLUMBIA

Dan Buckley & Associates, Inc.
1050 Connecticut Avenue, N.W., #300
Washington, DC 20036
202-296-1120
g; l
NAPC

The Counselors Consultant
1030 15th Street, N.W., Suite 720
Washington, DC 20005
202-682-1520
l

Dunhill—Legal
1518 K Street, N.W., Suite 410
Washington, DC 20005
202-783-9172
l

Jacquelyn Finn & Susan Schneider Associates, Inc.
1624 Eye Street, N.W., Suite 822
Washington, DC 20006
202-822-8400
l

Garofolo, Curtiss & Company
1730 Rhode Island Avenue, N.W., Suite 417
Washington, DC 20036
202-822-0070
H; i; n
AESC

Linda Goldsman, Ltd.
1750 K Street, N.W., Suite 380
Washington, DC 20006
202-785-3575
l

Holtzman & Associates
4801 Massachusetts Avenue, N.W., #447
Washington, DC 20016
202-363-9503
b
NAPC

Interface Group, Ltd.
1230 31st Street, N.W.
Washington, DC 20007
202-342-7200
l; M

The Interface Group, Inc.
3238 Prospect Street, N.W.
Washington, DC 20007
202-893-7223
l; pe

Janus Consultants, Inc.
1212 Potomac Street, N.W.
Washington, DC 20007
202-333-0100
c; m; T

Paul Johnson Associates
1900 M Street, N.W., Suite 1002
Washington, DC 20036
202-429-0098
c; l

Thomas E. Kenney
1211 Connecticut Avenue, N.W.
Washington, DC 20036
202-466-5245
l

Ross MacAskills Associates, Inc.
1600 L Street, N.W., Suite 612
Washington, DC 20036
202-659-8055
c; C; f; H; M; m; n; pe; S

Management Recruiters
2020 K Street, N.W., Suite 350
Washington, DC 20006
202-466-5300
a; b
NAPC

Susan C. Miller Associates, Inc.
1919 Pennsylvania Avenue, N.W., Suite 300
Washington, DC 20006
202-659-9800
l

MSL International Consultants, Inc.
1110 Vermont Avenue, N.W.
Washington, DC 20005
202-467-6405

The NRI Group
2000 L Street, N.W., 607
Washington, DC 20036
202-452-0505
c; f; l
NAPC

NRI Legal
1901 Pennsylvania Avenue, N.W.
Washington, DC 20006
202-466-2160
l

R. H. Perry & Associates, Inc.
2607 31st Street, N.W.
Washington, DC 20008
202-965-6464

Don Richard
1717 K Street, N.W. #1000
Washington, DC 20006
202-463-7210
a

Source Finance
1800 K Street, Suite 540
Washington, DC 20006
202-822-0100
f

Paul Stafford Associates, Ltd.
888 17th Street, N.W.
Washington, DC 20006
202-331-0090
AESC

Tabor Search Group, Inc.
315 Pennsylvania Avenue S.E., Suite 402
Washington, DC 20003
202-547-9335
n

Tech Careers
2550 M Street, N.W., Suite 405-E
Washington, DC 20037
202-775-8081
c

Technical Recruiters
1120 G Street, N.W., Suite 300
Washington, DC 20005
202-626-4637
c

Thomas, Whelan Associates, Inc.
1835 K Street, N.W., Suite 300
Washington, DC 20006
202-833-8980
a; f

P. T. Unger Associates
1900 L Street, N.W., Suite 205
Washington, DC 20036
202-463-6110
e; T

Washington Legal Search
1100 17th Street, N.W., #1000
Washington, DC 20036
202-775-8400
l

Washington Legal Search, Inc.
1050 Connecticut Avenue, N.W., Suite 300
Washington, DC 20036
202-429-6526
l

Wells International
1110 Vermont Avenue, N.W.
Washington, DC 20005
202-331-1910
l

**Arthur Young/Executive Resource
 Consultants**
1025 Connecticut Avenue, N.W., Suite 1100
Washington, DC 20036
202-838-7190
AESC

FLORIDA

ACI
3101 Maguire Boulevard, #200
Orlando, FL 32803
305-894-6551
a; e; s
NAPC

Advantage Personnel Agency
7861 Bird Road
Miami, FL 33155
305-264-7060
a; b; e; g; s
NAPC

Atlantic Personnel
670 North Courtnay Parkway
Merritt Island, FL 32953
305-452-0006
e; hr
NAPC

Bales Sales Recruiters
2016 Gulf Life Tower
Jacksonville, FL 32207
904-398-9080
s
NAPC

**Benson & Associates Personnel
  & Management Consultants**
800 West Cypress Creek Road, #208
Fort Lauderdale, FL 33309
305-491-5004
A; b; e; s; se
NAPC

Blake & Associates
303 S.E. 17th Street
Fort Lauderdale, FL 33316
305-467-8103
b
NAPC

BMR Associates
2500 Hollywood Boulevard, #310
Hollywood, FL 33020
305-921-4585
g; r
NAPC

Bowker, Brown & Co.
2451 Brickell Avenue
Miami, FL 33129
305-858-3400
g; t

R. L. Brown & Associates
1620 South Federal Highway, #800
Pompano Beach, FL 33062
305-946-4682
e; g; H; hr
NAPC

Capital Medical Placement Agency
P.O. Box 13266
Tallahassee, FL 32317
904-877-9018
H
NAPC

Circare
6660 Biscayne Boulevard, #101
Miami, FL 33138
305-757-6655
a; i
NAPC

Clemo, Evans & Co., Inc.
3500 East Fletcher Avenue
Tampa, FL 33612
813-962-6992

Corporate Advisors Inc.
250 N.E. 27th Street
Miami, FL 33137
305-573-7753
a; b; f; g; o
NAPC

Corporate Staffing Group
655 Ulmerton Road, Suite 9-A
Largo, FL 33541
813-586-6666
g; T
NAPC

W. J. Derden Consultants
P.O. Box 12745
Tallahassee, FL 32317
904-893-1161
m
NAPC

Dorison & Company
134 Madeira Avenue, Suite 100
Coral Gables, FL 33134
305-443-5733
a; f; g; M; m

Dunhill of Greater Jackson
5285 Galazie, Suite "F"
Jacksonville, FL 39206
601-981-3151
a; e
NAPC

Dunhill of St. Petersburg
3151 Third Avenue North, #327W
St. Petersburg, FL 33713
813-823-5295
e; g
NAPC

Gwen Dycus, Inc.
P.O. Box 1889
Winter Park, FL 32790
305-678-7007
A; P; re; R

R. E. Eckert & Associates, Inc.
200 Gulf Life Tower
Jacksonville, FL 32207
904-353-5302

Executive Career Development
1305 U.S. 19 South, Suite 404
Clearwater, FL 33546
813-536-4737
m; s
NAPC

Executive Manning Corporation
Suite 405, 3000 NE 30th Place
Fort Lauderdale, FL 33306
305-561-5100

Harry E. Fear & Associates
Deer Creek Country Club, Box 8645
Deerfield Beach, FL 33441
305-421-3337
H

Fleming Associates
8390 N.W. 53rd Street, Suite 314
Miami, FL 33166
305-592-0081
f; H; M
AESC

Fleming Associates
1343 Main Street, Suite 407
Sarasota, FL 33577
813-366-7979
f; H; M
AESC

Florapersonnel
P.O. Box 1732
Deland, FL 32721
904-738-5151
p; s
NAPC

The Foster McKay Group
4919 Memorial Highway
Tampa, FL 33614
813-884-7790
a; f

Geller Associates
1110 Brickell Avenue, #430
Miami, FL 33131
305-371-3355
b
NAPC

Robert Gette
400 Beach Road
Tequesta, FL 33458
305-746-6240

Griffith & Werner, Inc.
5740 Hollywood Boulevard, Suite 200
Hollywood, FL 33021
305-963-1300
a; f; g; M; m; pe

Hardwick Resources
2280 U.S. 19 North, #113 Executive
Clearwater, FL 33575
813-797-4477
m; ph; s
NAPC

Hastings & Hastings
1201 Brickell Avenue
Miami, FL 33131
305-374-2255
a; A

Henrietta's Personnel Service
150 S.E. Second Avenue, #1003
Miami, FL 33131
305-373-7373
b
NAPC

Hones and Company
3949 Evans Avenue, Suite 205
Fort Myers, FL 33901
813-936-3121
a; e
NAPC

Lamalie Associates, Inc.
13920 North Dale Mabry
Tampa, FL 33618
813-961-7494
g
AESC

R. H. Larsen & Associates, Inc.
1040 Bayview Drive, Suite 330
Fort Lauderdale, FL 33304
305-561-8102

Mina Latham
10250 Collins Avenue, Bal Harbour Square
Bal Harbour, FL 33154
305-868-8660
b; f

Alan Lerner Associates
855 South Federal Highway
Boca Raton, FL 33432
305-392-1890
R

McGuire Executive Search
8049 Hook Circle
Orlando, FL 32819
305-876-4426
hr

Markett Personnel
P.O. Box 162-211
Miami, FL 33116
305-386-0005
g
NAPC

Main Hurdman
2000 Palm Beach Lakes Boulevard
Suite 1000
West Palm Beach, FL 33409
305-471-9666
hr; re

MD Resources, Inc.
7385 Galloway Road, Suite 200
Miami, FL 33173
305-271-9213
g; H; pe

Meads & Associates
5150 Florida Avenue, P.O. Box 6896
Lakeland, FL 33807
813-644-0411

Medical Recruiters of America
3421 West Cypress Street
Tampa, FL 33607
813-872-0202
a; f; g; H; m; o; pe

Richard Mowell Associates, Inc.
2016 Delta Boulevard
Tallahassee, FL 32303
904-386-6171
c; f; g; i; pe; re

Murphy Employment Service
4950 West Kennedy Boulevard, #607
Tampa, FL 33609
813-875-1099
g; s
NAPC

NPF Associates, Ltd.
3300 University Drive, #514
Coral Springs, FL 33065
305-753-8560
g; pe
NAPC

Personnel Center
919 N.W. 13th Street, P.O. Box 1111
Gainesville, FL 32602
904-372-6377
e; H; s
NAPC

Personnel Pool of America
P.O. Box 359000
Fort Lauderdale, FL 33335
305-764-2200
H

Peyser Associates, Inc.
100 N.W. 37th Avenue
Miami, FL 33125
305-665-5606
a; f; M; m

Pickett Professional Placement
1213 A Hodges Drive
Tallahassee, FL 32308
904-656-1842
H
NAPC

The PMS Group
9200 South Dadeland Boulevard, Suite 516
Miami, FL 33156
305-667-6100

Professional Health Care Service
P.O. Box 8623
Fort Lauderdale, FL 33310
305-524-7444
H
NAPC

Professional Personnel Consultants—Tampa
1211 North Westshore Boulevard, Suite 314
Tampa, FL 33607
813-877-7008
a; b; e; g
NAPC

Retail Recruiters, Spectra Professional Search
2550 West Oakland Park Boulevard, #109
Fort Lauderdale, FL 33311
305-731-2300
e; H; R
NAPC

Ropes Associates, Inc.
1 Financial Plaza, Suite 1404
Fort Lauderdale, FL 33394
305-525-6600
b; c; C; hr; re
AESC

Royal Recruiters
600 Corporate Drive, Suite 410
Fort Lauderdale, FL 33334
305-771-6030
H; s
NAPC

Leo J. Shea Associates, Inc.
1901 Brickell Avenue, Suite BPH 3
Miami, FL 33129
305-285-0997
g; i; pe; P

Tasa, Inc.
2199 Ponce de Leon Boulevard, Suite 201
Coral Gables, FL 33134
305-448-0100
g
AESC

Dennis Wynn Associates, Inc.
1325 Snell Isle Boulevard, N.E., Suite 205C
St. Petersburg, FL 33704
813-823-2042
c; g; o; T

GEORGIA

Advancement Concepts
4405 International Boulevard, #C-106
Norcross, GA 30093
404-925-8570
c; s
NAPC

Advantage Executive Search
2965 Flowers Road South, #211
Atlanta, GA 30341
404-458-6158
g
NAPC

Agri-Personnel
5120 Old Bill Cook Road
Atlanta, GA 30349
404-768-5701
e; g
NAPC

Albany Personnel Service
235 Roosevelt Boulevard, Suite 216
Albany, GA 31701
912-439-2231
e; R; s; T
NAPC

Allied Search
6244 Crooked Creek Road, N.W., #C
Norcross, GA 30092
404-446-9100
g; M
NAPC

Anderson, Graham & Stewart
P.O. Box 1311
Marietta, GA 30061
404-943-3851
g; M; s
NAPC

Arista Corporation
One Exchange Place, #1236
Atlanta, GA 30338
404-458-2774
e; s
NAPC

Beall International, Inc.
5500 Interstate North Parkway, Suite 470
Atlanta, GA 30328
404-953-1062
g

Bellon & Hughes, Inc.
3169 Maple Drive, N.E.
Atlanta, GA 30305
404-881-1153
l

Berkley and Associates
1827 Powers Ferry Road, Building #20
Atlanta, GA 30339
404-956-0305
P; s
NAPC

Berman Associates
209 14th Street, Suite 307
Atlanta, GA 30309
404-992-5362
c; e; o; S; T

Blackshaw & Olmstead
134 Peachtree Street, N.W., Suite 1700
Atlanta, GA 30303
404-525-6700
g

Bowman & Associates, Inc.
Box 450149
Atlanta, GA 30345
404-974-9768
H

Rick Brank & Associates
3664 Salem Trail
Lithonia, GA 30058
404-987-9131
g
NAPC

M. L. Carter & Associates
P.O. Box 48148
Atlanta, GA 30362
404-455-6035
c; H

Claremont-Branan
2900 Chamblee-Tucker Road, Building 7
Atlanta, GA 30341
404-451-1983
e
NAPC

Clark Associates, Inc.
2220 Parklake Drive, Suite 160
Atlanta, GA 30345
404-493-3910
a; f; M; pe; p

Coker, Tyler & Co.
1835 Savoy Drive, Suite 205
Atlanta, GA 30341
404-451-7991
a; H; pe; ph
NAPC

Computer Network Resources
1835 Savoy Drive, #315
Atlanta, GA 30341
404-451-6100
c; i
NAPC

Delta Resource Group, Ltd.
1827 Powers Ferry Road, Building 11
Marietta, GA 30067
404-952-1169
a; f

Dimmerling & Associates
2900 Paces Ferry Road, #D-250
Atlanta, GA 30339
404-433-0863
e; M; m
NAPC

Dotson Benefield & Associates, Inc.
2295 Parklake Drive, N.E., Suite 190
Atlanta, GA 30345
404-493-1441
c; e; f; s; t

Drum/Companies, Inc.
211 Perimeter Center Parkway, Suite 1080
Atlanta, GA 30346
404-395-1780
c; o

Dunhill of Atlanta
3475 Lenox Road, N.E., Suite 785
Atlanta, GA 30326
404-261-3751
R; s
NAPC

EDP Research
4300 Paran Walk, N.W.
Atlanta, GA 30327
404-821-2188
NAPC

Fleming Associates
2625 Cumberland Parkway, N.W., Suite 290
Atlanta, GA 30339
404-435-2547
a; f; M
AESC

Garrett Associates, Inc.
100 Galleria Parkway, N.W., Suite 675
Atlanta, GA 30339
404-955-2774
a; f; g; H; o; pe

Houchins & Associates, Inc.
250 Piedmont Avenue, N.E., Suite 101
Atlanta, GA 30308
404-588-0060
a; g; H; M; m

Robert Howe & Associates
2971 Flowers Road, South, Suite 171
Atlanta, GA 30341
404-455-6618
a; f; M; m; pe

Industry Consultants
3 Dunwoody Park, Suite 114
Atlanta, GA 30338
404-458-8148
g; M; pp; r

Insurance Personnel Resources
8097-B Rosewell Road
Atlanta, GA 30338
404-396-7500
i
NAPC

Lamalie Associates, Inc.
3340 Peachtree Road, N.E.
Atlanta, GA 30026
404-237-6324
g
AESC

Gilbert Lane Associates
2840 Mount Wilkinson Parkway, #110
Atlanta, GA 30339
404-434-2300
a; e; f; M; m; pe; r

J. Lee & Associates
P.O. Box 28334
Atlanta, GA 30358
404-327-5628
m; s
NAPC

Lovewell & Associates, Inc.
100 Colony Square
Atlanta, GA 30361
404-436-9999
A; m; P

MacFarlane & Co., Inc.
450 One Park Place
Atlanta, GA 30318
404-352-2290
g; m; o; pe

Went MacKenzie
4920 Winters Chapel Road
Atlanta, GA 30360
404-396-1292
g; T
NAPC

McMahon & Associates
P.O. Box 1656
Stone Mountain, GA 30086
404-296-2468
e; i; s
NAPC

Bob Maddox Associates
3390 Peachtree Road, N.E., Suite 1025
Atlanta, GA 30326
404-231-0558
m; s

Mahony Associates
6065 Roswell Road, N.E., #1355
Atlanta, GA 30328
404-457-5501
e; g; s
NAPC

Management Search
400 Perimeter Center, Territory, #820
Atlanta, GA 30346
404-396-2494
g

James Mercer & Associates, Inc.
P.O. Box 888656
Atlanta, GA 30356
404-396-9060
m; o; r

MSL International Consultants, Ltd.
1770 The Exchange, Suite 250
Atlanta, GA 30339
404-955-9550
g

Niermann Personnel Service
1331 Citizens Parkway, #105
Morrow, GA 30260
404-996-6170
a; i
NAPC

OMNI Executive Search, Inc.
6800 Roswell Road, Suite 2B
Atlanta, GA 30328
404-394-1200
g; m; r

Parker Page Associates
2951 Flowers Road South
Atlanta, GA 30341
404-455-0502
g; i
NAPC

Roth Young of Atlanta
1190 West Druid Hills Drive, T-75
Atlanta, GA 30359
404-329-0088
g; hr; R
NAPC

Savannah Personnel Consultants
115 Oglethorpe Professional Center
Savannah, GA 31406
912-352-2273
e; g; s
NAPC

Schuyler Associates, Ltd.
1945 The Exchange, Suite 310
Atlanta, GA 30339
404-952-1992
f; H; T

James F. Smith & Associates
4651 Roswell Road, N.E., Suite B102
Atlanta, GA 30342
404-256-6408
M; m; pe

Source Finance
233 Peachtree Street, N.E.
Atlanta, GA 30303
404-523-7000
a; f

Spectra Professional Search
41 Perimeter Center East, N.E., Suite 610
Atlanta, GA 30346
404-391-9661
R
NAPC

Status, Inc.
3330 Peachtree Road, N.E., Tower Place
Atlanta, GA 30326
404-233-8600
g; s
NAPC

Stumbaugh Associates, Inc.
4319 Covington Highway, Suite 3202
Atlanta, GA 30035
404-288-5450
g; M; pe; pp

Thalatta Corp.
P.O. Box 76643
Atlanta, GA 30358
404-396-1725

Thomas-Pond Enterprises
1530 Dunwoody Village Parkway
Atlanta, GA 30338
404-394-5046

Toar Enterprises
P.O. Box 767096
Roswell, GA 30076
404-992-4526
a; g
NAPC

Waterford, Inc.
2900 Paces Ferry Road, N.W., Suite D-150
Atlanta, GA 30339
404-435-2916

R. M. Whiteside Company
5775 Peachtree-Dunwoody Road, N.E.
Atlanta, GA 30342
404-252-5245

Whitlow and Associates
3390 Peachtree Road, N.E.
Atlanta, GA 30326
404-262-2566
b; e
NAPC

Whittaker & Associates, Inc.
2675 Cumberland Parkway, N.W., Suite 263
Atlanta, GA 30339
404-434-3779
a; e; hr; M; m; R
NAPC

Zay, Champagne, Boyer & Company
101 Marietta Tower, Suite 3600
Atlanta, GA 30303
404-588-0550

HAWAII

Robert T. Guard & Associates, Inc.
820 Mililani Street, Suite 714
Honolulu, HI 96813
808-536-2338
g

Security Jobs Corporation
737 Bishop Street, #1575
Honolulu, HI 96813
808-521-7828
g; hr; s
NAPC

ILLINOIS

Administrative Resources
188 Industrial Drive
Elmhurst, IL 60126
312-530-8388
c

Agra Placements, Ltd.
220 North Kickapoo Street
Lincoln, IL 62656
217-735-4373
g; m; s
NAPC

Allerton, Heinze & Associates, Inc.
208 South LaSalle Street
Chicago, IL 60602
312-263-1075

A.R.C. Consultants
P.O. Box 324
Lake Bluff, IL 60044
312-234-8500

Artists Counselor & Placement Service
333 North Michigan Avenue, #622
Chicago, IL 60601
312-726-8679
m; pp
NAPC

E. J. Ashton & Associates, Ltd.
3223 North Frontage Road, Suite 2313
Arlington Heights, IL 60004
312-577-7900
a; f; g; i; o
NAPC

D. P. Baiocchi Associates, Inc.
150 North Wacker Drive, Suite 2440
Chicago, IL 60606
312-443-0070

Banner Personnel Service
7 West Madison, #1100
Chicago, IL 60602
312-641-6456
e; g; H; i; M; m; pp; T

Barnett-Matthews & Associates
321 Grand Avenue
Waukegan, IL 60085
312-244-6500

Richard Beers & Associates, Ltd.
Box 7
Glenview, IL 60025
312-729-4430
f; g; M; m; pe

John Bell & Associates, Inc.
875 North Michigan Avenue, Suite 1524
Chicago, IL 60611
312-440-0989
a; f; M

Benton, Schneider & Associates, Inc.
Park Plaza, 100 Park Place
Naperville, IL 60540
312-357-3131
a; c; f; g; M; m

Billington, Fox & Ellis, Inc.
20 North Wacker Drive
Chicago, IL 60606
312-236-5000
g
AESC

Britt Associates, Inc.
53 West Jackson Boulevard
Chicago, IL 60604
312-427-9450
M; m; pp
NAPC

Bryant Associates, Inc.
875 North Michigan Avenue, Suite 1524
Chicago, IL 60611
312-649-0700
a; f; M; m; pe
NAPC

Cadillac Associates, Inc.
32 West Randolph Street
Chicago, IL 60601
312-346-9400

Caprio & Associates, Inc.
2625 Butterfield Road
Oak Brook, IL 60521
312-920-1450
M; m; pp; pu; r

Neal Carden & Associates
620 West Roosevelt Road
Suite 2A
Wheaton, IL 60187
312-665-3932
l

Career Link
1926 Waukegan
Glenview, IL 60025
312-562-5465
NAPC

Joseph Chandler & Associates, Inc.
19 West Chicago Avenue
Hinsdale, IL 60521
312-323-2274

Clapp, Kleffer & Associates, Ltd.
666 North Lake Shore Drive
Suite 1322
Chicago, IL 60611
312-951-1370
H

Darryl Clausing & Associates
655 Center Road
P.O. Box 454
Frankfort, IL 60423
815-469-3153
e; M

The Clayton Group, Inc.
1 South 450 Summit Avenue
Oakbrook Terrace, IL 60181
312-953-2299
c; m; s

The Concord Group, Ltd.
512 Division Street
Barrington, IL 60010
312-382-6420
a; c; f; g; hr; s

Coopers & Lybrand
222 South Riverside Plaza
Chicago, IL 60606
312-559-5500
b

Corporate Environment, Ltd.
457 Coventry Lane, Suite 124
Crystal Lake, IL 60014
815-455-6070
g; M; m; r; S

Corporate Search Group, Inc.
2711 West 183rd Street
Homewood, IL 60430
312-957-4520
c; r; T

Allan Cox & Associates
410 North Michigan Avenue
Chicago, IL 60611
312-644-2360

Davidson Consultants
616 Enterprise Drive
Oak Brook, IL 60521
312-920-1330

William S. DeFuniak, Inc.
211 West Chicago Avenue, Suite 215
Hinsdale, IL 60521
312-887-9790
a; c; f; o; s

Paul DeRivera
150 West Wacker Drive, Suite 775
Chicago, IL 60606
312-786-6062
e

Ned E. Dickey and Associates
P.O. Box 1598
Rockford, IL 61110
815-968-1883
g; M; m; s

Ditch & Associates, International
625 North Michigan Avenue, Suite 500
Chicago, IL 60611
312-266-1095

E. M. Donahue Associates, Inc.
3 First National Plaza, Suite 1400
Chicago, IL 60602
312-782-6156

Downer & Starbuck
5286 Gingeridge Lane
Rockford, IL 61111
815-654-7860
M

J. H. Dugan & Co.
1 Magnificent Mile, Suite 1400
Chicago, IL 60611
312-751-1566
g; M; m; s

Dynamic Search Systems, Inc.
3201 North Frontage Road, Suite 103
Arlington Heights, IL 60004
312-259-3444
c; o; T

Dyna-Search
175 West Jackson Boulevard, Suite 1864
Chicago, IL 60604
312-939-0600
c; e; M; o; pp

Eastman & Beaudine, Inc.
111 West Monroe Street
Chicago, IL 60603
312-726-8195

Edwards & Sowers, Inc.
875 North Michigan Avenue
Chicago, IL 60611
312-266-1100
a; c; f; o; pe

Elliott, Pfisterer, Chinetti Associates, Inc.
20 North Wacker Drive
Chicago, IL 60606
312-332-6682

E.S.Q. Legal Search, Ltd.
77 West Washington Street, Suite 712
Chicago, IL 60602
312-372-5730
l

Estar Execu/Search, Ltd.
1 East Northwest Highway
Palatine, IL 60067
312-934-8883
a; f; g; pe

Executive Recruiting Consultants, Inc.
2510 Dempster, Suite 110
Des Plaines, IL 60016
312-296-4800
c; e; o

Fairchild, Gould & Associates
P.O. Box 769
Rockford, IL 61105
815-968-1841
g
NAPC

George Fee Associates
345 North Canal Street
Chicago, IL 60606
312-454-1600
l

Flinn Consultants, Inc.
394 Prospect Avenue
Highland Park, IL 60035
312-433-7830
a; f; g; M; m; pe

Stephen Fox Associates, Inc.
4712 North Sabath
McHenry, IL 60050
815-344-4000

Edmund A. Frank & Associates
11045 West Roosevelt Road
Westchester, IL 60153
312-562-5181
f; g

Gaffney Management Consultants
2850 Golf Road, 10 Gould Center, Suite 704
Rolling Meadows, IL 60008
312-640-8130

General Employment Enterprises
150 South Wacker Drive, #512
Chicago, IL 60606
312-782-1024
e; g
NAPC

General Employment Enterprises
900 Jorie Boulevard, #144
Oak Brook, IL 60521
312-986-1009
e; i; M; s; T
NAPC

General Employment Enterprises, Inc.
350 Shuman
Naperville, IL 60540
312-983-1233
a; c; o

Gleason Associates, Inc.
2210 Prudential Plaza
Chicago, IL 60601
312-565-0050

Robert Half, Inc.
35 East Wacker Drive
Chicago, IL 60601
312-782-6930
a; c; f; o

D. N. Hall & Associates
5901 North Cicero Avenue
Chicago, IL 60646
312-777-7100
g; i
NAPC

The Heidrick Partners, Inc.
20 North Wacker Drive, Suite 4000
Chicago, IL 60606
312-845-9700
g
AESC

Higgins & Co.
108 Wilmot Road
Deerfield, IL 60015
312-940-0675

Hilton Research Associates
415 East Golf Road, Suite 107
Arlington Heights, IL 60005
312-228-7710

W. Warner Hinman & Co.
875 North Michigan Avenue, Suite 1812
Chicago, IL 60611
312-951-8010
c; g; o; T

The Hite Company
36 South Wabash, Suite 900
Chicago, IL 60603
312-856-1011
g; pe; re

Hodge-Cronin and Associates, Inc.
9575 West Higgins Road, Suite 904
Rosemont, IL 60018
312-692-2041
g
AESC

Daniel D. Howard Associates, Inc.
307 North Michigan Avenue
Chicago, IL 60601
312-372-7041
pe

Human Resources
P.O. Box 301
Geneseo, IL 61254
309-944-4606
NAPC

John Imber Associates, Ltd.
2000 Algonquin Road
Schaumburg, IL 60172
312-397-3090

International Management Services, Inc.
216 Higgins Road
Park Ridge, IL 60068
312-698-2800

Robert J. Irmen Associates
211 West Chicago Avenue
Hinsdale, IL 60521
312-325-8220
g; M; m; pp

Jacobson Associates
221 North La Salle Street
Chicago, IL 60625
312-726-1578
l

JAMAR Personnel Service
508 R.I. Bank Building
Rock Island, IL 61201
309-786-4441
e; hr; s; se
NAPC

J.D. Limited Enterprise
20370 Rand Road
Palatine, IL 60074
312-438-3855
l

John H. Johnson & Associates, Inc.
332 South Michigan Avenue
Chicago, IL 60604
312-663-4176

Johnson & Genrich, Inc.
5481 North Milwaukee Avenue
Chicago, IL 60630
312-792-2323
e; g; M; r; s

Johnston & Associates
322 Carriage Hill Road
Naperville, IL 60565
312-369-2777
c; T

Kearney: Executive Search Group
222 South Riverside Plaza
Chicago, IL 60606
312-648-0111
AESC
foreign affiliates: Amsterdam, Brussels,
  Dusseldorf; London

Peter A. Kechik & Associates
P.O. Box 294
Park Ridge, IL 60068
312-823-9725

Kennedy and Company
20 North Wacker Drive
Chicago, IL 60606
312-372-0099
b; i; re; se

Jack Kennedy Associates, Inc.
233 East Wacker Drive, Suite 4001
Chicago, IL 60601
312-565-0551
A; m

Ketchum, Inc. Executive Recruiting Service
2411 Prudential Plaza
Chicago, IL 60601
312-321-1166
g; n; P

James M. Kittleman & Associates, Inc.
209 South LaSalle Street
Chicago, IL 60604
312-236-0473
a; f

Knorps Computer Consultants, Inc.
Box 406
Winnetka, IL 60093
312-446-8889
c; o; T

Knudsen & Co.
1211 West 22nd Street, Suite 900
Oak Brook, IL 60521
312-789-8960
c; S; T

Kolden & Associates, Ltd.
1211 West 22nd Street
Oak Brook, IL 60521
312-986-9110

Kuehne & Co., Inc.
2 North LaSalle Street, Suite 1900
Chicago, IL 60602
312-346-5145
g

Kunzer Associates, Ltd.
208 South LaSalle Street
Chicago, IL 60604
312-641-0010
a; c; f; g; m; pe; r
AESC

Lamalie Associates, Inc.
120 South Riverside Plaza
Chicago, IL 60606
312-454-0525
g
AESC

Lamson, Griffiths Associates, Inc.
1 East Northwest Highway
Palatine, IL 60067
312-991-4070
H

Lascio Associates
1001 Ogden Avenue, Suite 204
Downers Grove, IL 60515
312-971-1701

Lauer, Sbarbaro Associates, Inc.
1 North LaSalle Street, Suite 1230
Chicago, IL 60602
312-372-7050
g
foreign affiliate: Zurich

James H. Lowry & Associates
303 East Wacker Drive
Chicago, IL 60601
312-861-1800
M; m

McSherry & Associates
307 North Michigan Avenue
Chicago, IL 60601
312-332-1333
a; c; f; g; T

Management Search, Inc.
664 North Michigan Avenue, Suite 1010
Chicago, IL 60611
312-426-7700
a; c; e; f

Manplan Consultants
222 Wisconsin Avenue, Suite 306
Lake Forest, IL 60045
312-234-4288

Edwin Martin & Associates
20 North Wacker Drive
Chicago, IL 60606
312-726-3573
g

**Matthews Professional Employment
  Services, Inc.**
321 Grand Avenue
Waukegan, IL 60085
312-244-6500
ph
NAPC

George S. May International Company
111 South Washington Street
Park Ridge, IL 60068
800-323-9230
s

The Mendheim Co., Inc.
6055 North Lincoln Avenue
Chicago, IL 60659
312-973-6969
g

Menzel, Robinson, Baldwin, Inc.
550 West Campus Drive
Arlington Heights, IL 60004
312-394-4303

Metricor, Inc.
1 South 450 Summit Avenue
Oakbrook Terrace, IL 60181
312-953-1800
a; c; f; g; o

Modern Employment Service
7 West Madison Street, Suite 602
Chicago, IL 60602
312-782-3960
g
NAPC

MSL International Consultants, Ltd.
1 East Wacker Drive, Suite 3600
Chicago, IL 60601
312-321-0080
g

Mullins & Associates
P.O. Box 887
Barrington, IL 60010
312-382-1800
e

Murphy Employment Service
1301 West 22nd Street, Suite 911A
Oak Brook, IL 60521
312-655-2011
NAPC

Newpher & Co., Inc.
2215 York Road, Suite 202
Oak Brook, IL 60521
312-789-8181

Ronald Norris & Associates
8457 East Prairie Road
Skokie, IL 60076
312-679-6074
f

David North Associates
532 Eugenie Street
Chicago, IL 60614
312-951-2766

C. J. Noty & Associates
332 South Michigan Avenue
Chicago, IL 60604
312-663-5330

Oberlander & Co., Inc.
233 East State Street, P.O. Box 789
Geneva, IL 60134
312-232-2601

John Paisios, Ltd.
2222 Kensington Court
Oak Brook, IL 60521
312-655-1080

Peat Marwick Mitchell & Co.
303 East Wacker Drive
Chicago, IL 60606
312-938-1000

The Personnel Center
201 West Springfield, #308
Champaign, IL 61820
217-356-7535
g
NAPC

Pinkerton & Associates, Inc.
625 North Michigan Avenue, Suite 500
Chicago, IL 60611
312-266-8669
a; f; g; M; m; pe

Polytechnical Consultants, Inc.
2525 West Peterson Avenue
Chicago, IL 60659
312-262-9000
e; S

Professional Executive Consultants
3000 Dundee, Suite 418
Northbrook, IL 60062
312-564-3900
e; g; M; m; s
NAPC

The Protech Group
2 North Riverside Plaza, #2400
Chicago, IL 60606
312-559-1990
e; g
NAPC

The R & L Group
1309 North Rand Road
Arlington Heights, IL 60004
312-392-1340
c; M; r

Rambert & Co., Inc.
11 North Skokie Highway
Lake Bluff, IL 60044
312-234-2780
g; r

Richard/Allen/Winter, Ltd.
222 Wisconsin Avenue
Suite 303
Lake Forest, IL 60045
312-295-2222

Ridenour & Associates
230 North Michigan Avenue
Suite 2212
Chicago, IL 60601
312-444-1160
a; m

Robertson, Spoerlein & Wengert
10 South Riverside Plaza
Chicago, IL 60606
312-930-1958
c; e; g; M; m; pe

Bea Rosenbaum, Executive Recruiter
1111 Lake Cook Road
Buffalo Grove, IL 60090
312-541-6990

Keith Ross & Associates, Inc.
150 North Wacker Drive
Suite 1733
Chicago, IL 60606
312-558-1850

Williams Roth & Kruger, Inc.
101 North Wacker Drive, Suite 675
Chicago, IL 60606
312-977-0800

James Russell, Medical Search Consultants
211 Prospect Road, P.O. Box 427
Bloomington, IL 61701
309-663-9467
g; H
NAPC

Sales & Management Search, Inc.
10 South Riverside Plaza
Chicago, IL 60606
312-930-1111
a; f; g; m; s

Samuelson Associates
3 First National Plaza, Suite 2025
Chicago, IL 60602
312-263-0033
l

Scott/Hubbard Associates
Box 9131-HW
Winnetka, IL 60093
312-446-5495
m; p

Search Source Inc.
Box 1228
Granite City, IL 62040
618-797-1900
a; f; M; m; pe

Search Specialists, Inc.
1500 Ravinia Avenue
Orland Park, IL 60462
312-460-9557
e

David Shane & Associates
1383 North Henderson Street, Suite A
Galesburg, IL 61404
309-343-1208
M

Raymond James Smith & Associates
10 West Main Street
Cary, IL 60013
312-639-8250
l

Stephen R. Smith & Co., Inc.
221 North LaSalle Street
Chicago, IL 60601
312-726-3182

Paul Stafford Associates, Ltd.
222 South Riverside Plaza
Chicago, IL 60606
312-454-0942
g; hr
AESC

Stevens, Thurow & Associates, Inc.
100 West Monroe Street
Chicago, IL 60603
312-332-6277
pe; s

John J. Sudlow & Co.
625 North Michigan Avenue, Suite 500
Chicago, IL 60611
312-944-5127
a; f; g; M; m; pe

Sullivan Associates
20 North Wacker Drive
Chicago, IL 60606
312-348-2244
l

Synergistics Associates, Ltd.
320 North Michigan Avenue, Suite 1002
Chicago, IL 60601
312-346-8782
a; c; f; g; T

Systems Network Assistance
523 "A" North Milwaukee Avenue
Glenview, IL 60048
312-367-1286
g; s
NAPC

Roy Talman & Associates
203 North Wabash, Suite 1120
Chicago, IL 60601
312-630-0130
e

Tesar-Reynes, Inc.
360 North Michigan Avenue
Chicago, IL 60601
312-661-0700
A; m

Thai, Inc.
133 East Cook Avenue
Libertyville, IL 60048
312-680-7177
l

Ray Travaglio & Associates, Inc.
1936-42 Augusta Boulevard
Chicago, IL 60622
312-252-0900

Tully & Hobart, Inc.
333 North Michigan Avenue
Chicago, IL 60601
312-332-4545
AESC

VanMaldegiam Associates, Inc.
20 North Wacker Drive
Chicago, IL 60606
312-648-0807
a; f; g; m; pe

Ward Howell International, Inc.
20 North Wacker Drive, Suite 2920
Chicago, IL 60606
312-236-2211

Warren & Associates
P.O. Box 173
Geneseo, IL 61254
309-441-5700
a; b
NAPC

Wells International
150 North Michigan Avenue, Suite 2900
Chicago, IL 60601
312-642-6000
l

Westcott Associates, Inc.
Prudential Plaza
Chicago, IL 60601
312-856-1700

David J. White & Associates, Inc.
205 West Wacker Drive, Suite 1522
Chicago, IL 60606
312-670-0404
a; f; l; pe

E. N. Wilkins and Company, Inc.
7131 Sears Tower
Chicago, IL 60606
312-930-1036
a; f; g; H; M; m; r
AESC

Wills & Company
333 North Michigan Avenue, #812
Chicago, IL 60601
312-236-5356
g
NAPC

Witt Associates, Inc.
1415 West 22nd Street
Oak Brook, IL 60521
312-325-5070
a; f; g; H; m; o; pe
AESC

Woltz & Associates, Inc.
199 South Addison Road
Wood Dale, IL 60191
312-860-9090
g; pe; s

The Woodward Group
35 East Wacker Drive
Chicago, IL 60601
312-726-5682
a; f; g; m

Wunderlich & Associates, Inc.
120 Oak Brook Center, #204
Oak Brook, IL 60521
312-789-8600
a; f

Wytmar & Company, Inc.
10 South Riverside Plaza
Chicago, IL 60606
312-236-1350
H

Xagas & Associates
701 East State Street
Geneva, IL 60134
312-232-7044
e; H; i; m
NAPC

Arthur Young Executive Resource Consultants
1 IBM Plaza, 36th floor
Chicago, IL 60611
312-645-3065
g
AESC

INDIANA

Agra Placements, Ltd.
16 East Fifth Street, Berkshire Court
Peru, IN 46970
317-472-1988
g; m; s
NAPC

Alexander & Associates, Inc.
700 East Beardsley, P.O. Box 30
Elkhart, IN 46515
219-264-9629
M; S; t
NAPC

Bone Personnel
2008 Fort Wayne North Bank Building
Fort Wayne, IN 46802
219-424-4466
g
NAPC

Career Consultants
107 North Pennsylvania
Indianapolis, IN 46204
317-639-5601
e; g; hr; s
NAPC

Careers Unlimited
1238 South Main
Elkhart, IN 46516
219-293-0659
e; g; i; m
NAPC

Chevigny Personnel Agency
100 West 79th Avenue
Merrillville, IN 46410
219-769-4880
e; H; M; R; s
NAPC

Fleming Associates
1428 Franklin Street, P.O. Box 604
Columbus, IN 47202
812-376-9061
a; f; M
AESC

National Recruiting Service
Box 218
Dyer, IN 46311
219-865-2373
g; M

Ramming & Bennett, Inc.
5640 Professional Circle, Suite A8
Indianapolis, IN 46241
317-247-1240

Robert Sage Recruiting
26586 Windsor Avenue
Elkhart, IN 46514
219-264-1126
NAPC

IOWA

Agra Placements, Ltd.
1200 35th Street, #210
West Des Moines, IA 50265
515-225-6562
g; m; s
NAPC

Agri-Associates
215 Brenton Bank Building/1606 Brady
  Street
Davenport, IA 52803
319-323-3677
g; M; m; ph; s
NAPC

City & National Employment
504 Jefferson, P.O. Box 83
Waterloo, IA 50704
319-232-6641
a; e
NAPC

Dunhill of Cedar Rapids
119 Third Street, N.E., 121 Professional Park
Cedar Rapids, IA 52401
319-366-8273
e; m; s
NAPC

Executive Resources, Ltd.
4515 Fleur Drive
Des Moines, IA 50321
515-287-6880
a; b
NAPC

J. D. Limited Enterprise
3807 Glen Oaks Boulevard
Sioux City, IA 51104
712-239-1660
l

Job Finders/Jobs Temporary
2203 Grand Avenue
Des Moines, IA 50312
515-243-7576
e; g; H; s
NAPC

E. A. Keepy—National Recruiters
601 Brady Street, #303, P.O. Box 576
Davenport, IA 52805
319-323-6364
e; s
NAPC

Key Employment Services
1001 Office Park Road, Suite 320
West Des Moines, IA 50265
515-224-0446
a; b; e; R; s
NAPC

Pharmacists Exchange
206 Sixth Avenue, Suite 1103
Des Moines, IA 50309
515-244-2300
ph
NAPC

The Recruiter
4900 University Avenue, Suite 220
Des Moines, IA 50311
515-243-5414
e; g; m
NAPC

KANSAS

Associated Personnel Technicians, Inc.
1650 East Central
Wichita, KS 67214
316-264-0681
m; pe

Bossler/Brown & Associates
1035 South Topeka Boulevard
Topeka, KA 66612
913-234-5626
a; M
NAPC

Crippin, Inc.
9209 West 110th Street
Overland Park, KS 66210
913-451-1288
g; M; m; o; pe

Lee & Burgess Associates, Inc.
4500 College Boulevard, Suite 310
Overland Park, KS 66211
913-345-0500

Stoneburner Associates, Inc.
10000 West 75th Street, King's Cove
Shawnee Mission, KS 66204
913-432-0055
c; e; pe

KENTUCKY

Fleming Associates
10172 Linn Station Road, Suite 450
Louisville, KY 40220
502-426-3500
f; H; M
AESC

Mike Lawson Personnel
P.O. Box 17222
Louisville, KY 40217
502-634-1662
e; i
NAPC

J. C. Malone Associates
1941 Bishop Lane, Suite 100
Louisville, KY 40218
502-456-2380
a; b; e; M; m

Gordon Mulvey & Associates
4801 Sherburn Lane, #201, P.O. Box 6823
Louisville, KY 40207
502-897-5371
e; g;
NAPC

LOUISIANA

Alan & Associates Employee Search
2625 Line Avenue, Gamble Professional Plaza
Shreveport, LA 71104
318-424-2626
a; M; s
NAPC

Aviation Personnel International
Box 6846
New Orleans, LA 70174
504-392-3456
t

A. D. Boudreaux & Associates
6960 Martin Drive, Suite B
New Orleans, LA 70126
504-245-1930
e
NAPC

Corporate Consultants
806 Perdido, Suite 205
New Orleans, LA 70112
504-523-5442
a; b; e; hr
NAPC

Creative Career Corporation
200 Carondelet Street, #100
New Orleans, LA 70130
504-522-7180
a; b
NAPC

Jerry Demaso & Associates
2800 Veterans Boulevard, Suite 104
Metairie, LA 70002
504-833-0061
a; b; c; f; i; pe
NAPC

Driggers & Blackwell Personnel
320 Neal Street
Ruston, LA 71270
318-251-0244
b; g
NAPC

Kenneth Evans & Associates
611 Gravier Street, Suite 910
New Orleans, LA 70130
504-522-7957
a; b
NAPC

Executive Locators of America
P.O. Box 1337, 3124 49th Street
Metairie, LA 70004
504-838-8262
a; A; b; g; M; m; P; R; s
NAPC

Fleming Associates
3900 North Causeway Boulevard, Suite 770
Metairie, LA 70002
504-831-3797
a; f; M
AESC

Robert Half
P.O. Box 57629
New Orleans, LA 70157
504-835-4296
f

Legal Headhunters, Inc.
2121 Ridgelake Drive, Suite 104
Metairie, LA 70001
504-833-5111
l

Network Affiliates, Ltd.
3500 North Causeway, #160
Metairie, LA 70002
504-837-8712
b; g; i
NAPC

Walters & Associates
3350 Ridgelake Drive, #240
Metairie, LA 70002
504-837-7930
b
NAPC

MAINE

Ames & Wyand Associates, Inc.
84 Main Street, Suite A
Brunswick, ME 04011
207-729-5158
M; pp

The Bartlett Agency
P.O. Box 1666, 1115 Lisbon Street
Lewiston, ME 04240
207-786-0134
a; e
NAPC

Executive Search of New England, Inc.
3 Canal Plaza
Portland, ME 04112
207-772-4677

Kuebler Associates
2 Monument Square, Executive Office Center
Portland, ME 04101
207-774-9100
e; g; m
NAPC

Northern Consultants, Inc.
17 Western Avenue, Box 220
Hampden, ME 04444
207-862-2323
H; M

Professional Placement Services
P.O. Box 2446
Augusta, ME 04330
207-623-4833
b; g
NAPC

Rogers & Seymour, Inc.
94 Auburn Street
Portland, ME 04103
207-797-2191
a; b; c; f; o

Romac & Associates, Inc.
3 Canal Plaza, P.O. Box 7469 DTS
Portland, ME 04112
207-773-6387
a; b; c; f; se
NAPC

MARYLAND

Mark Allen Associates
5 Riggs Avenue, #2
Severna Park, MD 21146
301-544-0444
e; g
NAPC

AMD Associates
P.O. Box 6699
Silver Spring, MD 20906
301-871-6926
e; T
NAPC

Charles A. Binswanger Associates
P.O. Box 5325
Baltimore, MD 21209
301-433-6610
pp; r

Brandjes Associates
5 North Calvert Street, 1031 Munsey Building
Baltimore, MD 21202
301-547-6886
b

Calvert Group
4550 Montgomery Avenue
Bethesda, MD 20814
301-951-4820

Career Consultants
515 East Joppa Road
Towson, MD 21204
301-821-5100
s

Clark, Clark & Clark Associates
7338 Baltimore Boulevard
College Park, MD 20740
301-864-1117
e; g; m; s; T
NAPC

CMZ Recruiting
2360 West Joppa Road
Lutherville, MD 21093
301-583-7426
i

Commonwealth Personnel
6110 Executive Boulevard, #835
Rockville, MD 20852
301-231-0055
e; T
NAPC

Conaway Legal Search
209 East Fayette Street
Baltimore, MD 21202
301-539-1234
l

Conaway Personnel Associates, Inc.
209 East Fayette Street
Baltimore, MD 21202
301-539-1234
f; l; pe

Cross Country Consultants, Inc.
16 West 25th Street
Baltimore, MD 21218
301-889-2994
c; e; f; M; r

Dynamac Corporation Personnel Department
11140 Rockville Pike
Rockville, MD 20852
301-468-2500

Employment Unlimited Agency
1750 Eastern Avenue
Baltimore, MD 21231
301-327-6900
e; g; M; m; pe; s

Executive Recruiters
7315 Wisconsin Avenue, #333E
Bethesda, MD 20814
301-986-8815
hr; R
NAPC

A. G. Fishkin & Associates, Inc.
6121 Executive Boulevard
Rockville, MD 20852
301-770-4944
a; c; f; g; ;m; s; T
NAPC

Ford Employment Agency
Empire Towers Building, Suite 408
Glen Burnie, MD 21061
301-766-4090
g

Fox Morris
Mercantile Towson Building
Baltimore, MD 21204
301-296-4500
a; e; s

Futures Personnel Services
601 Oxford Building, 8600 LaSalle Road
Baltimore, MD 21204
301-321-1984
a; b; e; H; i; M; ph; R; s
NAPC

Gabriel & Bowie Associates, Ltd.
Route 175 & Gambrills Road, P.O. Box 21160
Baltimore, MD 21228
301-987-6670
c; g
NAPC

Holland & Associates
Jefferson Building
Towson, MD 21204
301-296-6900
a; f

Intelcom Professional Services
Wilde Lake Village Green, #240
Columbia, MD 21044
301-596-1133
e; g
NAPC

JDG Associates, Ltd.
1700 Research Boulevard
Rockville, MD 20850
301-340-2210
c; o; T

E. G. Jones Associates, Ltd.
5400 Scott Adam Road, Suite 308
Cockeysville, MD 21030
301-279-0200 or 667-6001

M. D. Mattes & Associates
30 East Padonia Road, #203, P.O.Box 291
Timonium, MD 21093
301-252-8071
a; e; M
NAPC

MBC Systems Ltd.
744 Dulaney Valley Court, #11
Towson, MD 21204
301-583-8600
R; s
NAPC

Michaels, Patrick, O'Brien & Williams, Inc.
5565 Sterrett Place, Suite 510
Columbia, MD 21044
301-995-1044
a; f

Kors; Marlar; Savage & Associates
2060 West Street, Suite 200
Annapolis, MD 21401
301-224-4545
e; f; H; n; r

Perry Newton Associates
932 Hungerford Drive, #23, P.O. Box 1158
Rockville, MD 20850
301-340-3360
g; R
NAPC

The NRI Group
1700 East Gude Drive
Rockville, MD 20850
301-424-9330
a; f; l; o; T
NAPC

The NRI Group
6100 Executive Boulevard, #709
Rockville, MD 20852
301-881-9070
a; e; f; hr; l; o; T
NAPC

Paul-Tittle Associates, Inc.
8720 Georgia Avenue, Suite 900
Silver Spring, MD 20910
301-585-7600
c; o; T

Retail Recruiters/Spectra Search
6110 Executive Boulevard, #1065
Rockville, MD 20852
301-231-8150
R
NAPC

Don Richard
7927 Jones Branch Drive, #400
Bethesda, MD 20814
301-652-1182
a

Ken Richardson
7501 Democracy Boulevard, Suite B11
Bethesda, MD 20817
301-365-2116
b; g; se
NAPC

Salesworld Inc.
802 Gleneagles Street, Suite 209
Towson, MD 21204
301-296-5600
s

Silver Employment Agency
524 Dolphin Street
Baltimore, MD 21217
301-669-1721
a

SysTech Organization
2825 Cub Hill Road
Baltimore, MD 21234
301-665-6033
b; c; g
NAPC

Target Search
932 Hungerford Drive, Suite 7B
Rockville, MD 20850
301-340-7009
e; g
NAPC

Tech Search
11428 Rockville Pike
Rockville, MD 20852
301-984-6282
e
NAPC

C. J. Vincent Associates, Inc.
2000 Century Plaza
Columbia, MD 21044
301-997-8590
c; e; s
NAPC

Wallach Associates, Inc.
6101 Executive Boulevard, Suite 380
Rockville, MD 20852
301-231-9000
e; S
NAPC

MASSACHUSETTS

Ackerman Associates, Inc.
60 State Street, 33rd floor
Boston, MA 02109
617-720-4981
l

Thomas R. Aldrich & Associates
Gateway, 288 Littleton Road
Westford, MA 01886
617-692-8732
g; M; m; pe; pp; s

American Executive Management, Inc.
30 Federal Street
Salem, MA 01970
617-744-5923
e; C

Andover Personnel, Inc.
1 Elm Square
Andover, MA 01810
617-475-8833

Arancio Associates
542 High Rock Street
Needham, MA 02192
617-449-4436
M; t

Ashworth Consultants
92 State Street
Boston, MA 02109
617-720-0350
f; i; M; m; re; R

Asquith & Jackson Associates, Inc.
586 Boston Road, Box 326
Weston, MA 02193
617-891-0310

Aubin International, Inc.
303 Wyman Street, Suite 300
Waltham, MA 02154
617-890-1722
e; M; r; S

David T. Barry Associates
572 Washington Street
Wellesley, MA 02181
617-235-1520

Nathan Barry Associates, Inc.
301 Union Wharf
Boston, MA 02109
617-227-6067
a; c; f; g; H; m; r; s

BFH Associates
P.O. Box 358
Sharon, MA 02067
617-668-0960
a; c; e
NAPC

Bostonian Personnel Co., Inc.
6 Faneuil Hall Marketplace, 3rd floor
Boston, MA 02109
617-367-8771
l

Bowen & Berndt, Inc.
15 Depot Square
Lexington, MA 02173
617-862-8850

Dr. Will G. Bowman, Inc.
560 Wellesley Street
Weston, MA 02193
617-431-7494
S

Thomas A. Buffim Associates
1 Post Office Square
Boston, MA 02109
617-423-4100
AESC

Career Dynamics, Inc.
8 Newcomb Road
Melrose, MA 02176
617-662-0922
e; g; M; m

Carpenter Consultants, Inc.
824 Boylston Street
Chestnut Hill, MA 02167
617-731-3730
e; g; M; m
NAPC

CIS Personnel Services
711 Boylston Street
Boston, MA 02116
617-266-1000
NAPC

Computer Security Placement Service, Inc.
1 Computer Drive, Box 204-D
Northborough, MA 01532
617-393-7803
c

Consultant Group—Langlois & Associates, Inc.
109 Highland Avenue
Needham, MA 02194
617-332-8808
a; f; g; H; o
NAPC

Timothy D. Crowe, Jr.
26 Higate Road, Suite 101
Chelmsford, MA 01824
617-256-2008
M

Daly & Co., Inc.
575 Boylston Street
Boston, MA 02116
617-262-2800
a; f; M

Robert H. Davidson Associates
151 Providence Highway
Norwood, MA 02062
617-769-8350
a; f; g; hr; M; m; pe; r
NAPC

DeLoughrey & Co.
273 Washington Street
Wellesley Hills, MA 02181
617-237-3336
m; s

Donegan Associates, Inc.
244 Willow Street
Yarmouthport, MA 02675
617-362-8146
c

Double M Executive Placement Service, Inc.
160 Speen Street
Framingham, MA 01701
617-272-1912
NAPC

Dumont Kiradjieff & Moriarty
79 Milk Street
Boston, MA 02109
617-451-9212
f; i; M; m; o; pe

Eastern Employment Service
18 Tremont Street
Boston, MA 02108
617-523-7622

The Elliott Company, Inc.
100 Unicorn Park
Woburn, MA 01801
617-938-6050
a; g; M; m

Don Ellis Personnel
101 Tremont Street
Boston, MA 02108
617-357-8243
i

Emerson Professionals
12 New England Executive Park
Burlington, MA 01803
617-861-0808
a; f
NAPC

The Engineers Index
133 Federal Street
Boston, MA 02110
617-482-2800
a; c; f

Executive Selection
303 Wyman Street, Suite 300
Waltham, MA 02154
617-890-0402
NAPC

Fanning Personnel of Boston
376 Boylston Street, 2nd floor
Boston, MA 02116
617-261-8400
a; b; f; i
NAPC

Folger & Company, Inc.
214 Lewis Wharf
Boston, MA 02110
617-227-5900

Ford & Ford
850 Providence Highway, Box 597
Dedham, MA 02026
617-329-5600
a; e; f; M; pe; R
NAPC

Fortune Personnel Consultants—Boston
44 Mall Road
Boston, MA 01803
617-273-3020
a; e
NAPC

A. O. Frost, Staffing Consultant
P.O. Box 2633
Springfield, MA 01101
413-782-5084
b; e
NAPC

Garofolo, Curtiss & Company
65 East India Row, Harbor Towers, Suite 3-G
Boston, MA 02110
617-227-0260
H; i; n
AESC

Gather, Inc.
P.O. Box 10
Chartley, MA 02712
617-226-2348
e; g; H; s
NAPC

Gillard Associates
1 Fuller Place
Dedham, MA 02026
617-329-4731
l

Glou International
400 Hunnewell Avenue, Box 601
Needham MA 02192
617-449-3310

Robert J. Grace Associates
P.O. Box 339, 745 High Street
Westwood, MA 02090
617-329-0188
e
NAPC

Robert Half of Boston
100 Summer Street, Suite 2905
Boston, MA 02110
617-423-1200
a; b; c; f
NAPC

Robert Half
430 Bedford Street
Lexington, MA 02173
617-862-1000
a; c; f

Robert Half
1125 Mechanics Bank Tower
Worcester, MA 01608
617-755-9000
a; c; f

Harper Associates
1618 Main Street
Springfield, MA 01103
413-781-1785

Hayden & Refo, Inc.
10 High Street
Boston, MA 02110
617-482-2444
a; f; g; m; o; pe

T. J. Hayes Associates
2 Geneva Avenue
Assonet, MA 02702
617-644-2350
e; M
NAPC

Hilton Research Associates
10 Tower Office Park
Woburn, MA 01801
617-933-4760
H

Hipp Waters Professional Recruiting
50 Milk Street
Boston, MA 02109
617-267-8300
a; e; f
NAPC

**Insurance Personnel, Martin Grant
 Associates**
65 Franklin Street
Boston, MA 02110
617-357-5380
i
NAPC

JNB Associates, Inc.
75 Federal Street
Boston, MA 02110
617-720-8243
b; f

Hubert L. Kelly, Personnel Consultants
51 Asselin Street
Chicopee, MA 01020
413-593-5793
M
NAPC

Kelly, Sullivan & Co., Inc.
125 Pearl Street/The International House
Boston, MA 02110
617-542-6696

John J. Kennedy Associates
35 Bedford Street, Suite 4
Lexington, MA 02173
617-863-8860

Ketchum, Inc. Executive Recruiting Service
1 Post Office Square
Boston, MA 02109
617-482-6060
n

Kimball Shaw Associates, Inc.
3 Pleasant Street
Hingham, MA 02043
617-749-5574
H

Robert Kleven & Co., Inc.
50 Milk Street, 15th floor
Boston, MA 02109
617-861-1020 or 542-7667
c; e; pe; r; S

Robert Kleven & Co., Inc.
181 Bedford Street
Lexington, MA 02173
617-861-1020
g; M; pe; r

Lane Employment Service
370 Main Street, Suite 820
Worcester, MA 01608
617-757-5678
e; T
NAPC

Gilbert Lane Personnel Service
1500 Main Street
Springfield, MA 01115
413-733-2133
b; e
NAPC

Larsen Personnel
1492 Highland Avenue
Needham, MA 02192
617-449-3840
e; M
NAPC

Leahy & Company
88 Broad Street, Suite 301
Boston, MA 02110
617-423-4489
a; b; f

Alan Lerner Associates
200 Boylston Street
Chestnut Hill, MA 02167
617-964-7722
R

McInturff & Associates, Inc.
209 West Central Street
Natick, MA 01760
617-237-0220
M; p

Management Resource Associates
7 Wheeling Avenue
Woburn, MA 01801
617-933-1600
e; m; pe
NAPC

F. L. Mannix & Co., Inc.
33 Broad Street
Boston, MA 02109
617-523-3549
c; S

MBA Associates, Inc.
79 Milk Street
Boston, MA 02109
617-338-1257
c; f; i; M; re

Morgan & Associates
1500 Main Street, P.O. Box 15727
Springfield, MA 01115
413-734-0769
e; M
NAPC

Morgan-Webber, Inc.
Union Wharf Box 214
Boston, MA 02109
617-227-1155

Multi Processing, Inc.
1 Militia Drive
Lexington, MA 02173
617-861-6300
c; S

Multi Technology Inc.
869 Concord Street
Framingham, MA 01701
617-875-5466
e; m; s

Nagler & Co., Inc.
65 William Street
Wellesley Hills, MA 02181
617-431-1330

Nationwide Business Service
145 State Street
Springfield, MA 01103
413-732-4104
e
NAPC

New Dimensions
444 Washington Street
Woburn, MA 01801
617-933-1313
e
NAPC

New England Legal Search, Inc.
286 Beacon Street
Boston, MA 02116
617-266-6068
l

O'Grady Associates, Inc.
81 Commonwealth Avenue
West Concord, MA 01742
617-369-4210
s; m

Organization Resources, Inc.
63 Atlantic Avenue
Boston, MA 02110
617-742-8970

Parker, Eldridge, Sholl & Gordon, Inc.
440 Totten Pond Road, Suite 3
Waltham, MA 02154
617-244-5355

Robert Pencarski & Company
250 Providence Highway
Dedham, MA 02026
617-329-5430
e; M
NAPC

Perry-White & Associates, Inc.
300 Bear Hill Road
Waltham, MA 02154
617-890-6500
e; S

Personnel Management Associates
61 Commerce Way
Woburn, MA 01801
617-938-8010
m
NAPC

Power & Co.
79 Milk Street
Boston, MA 02109
617-338-1255
C; re

Norman Powers Associates, Inc.
Box 3221
Saxonville, MA 01701
617-877-2025
c; e; pe; r

Prime Selection
28 Edgehill Road, P.O. Box 85
Waltham, MA 02254
617-894-9360
g
NAPC

Professional Placement Group
33 Broad Street, Suite 410
Boston, MA 02109
617-523-3576
b; f; i; M; re; se

Professional Recruiters Inc.
23 Midstate Drive
Auburn, MA 01501
617-832-5757
b; c; f; M
NAPC

Rita Personnel—West Massachusetts
1243 Main Street
Springfield, MA 01103
413-781-3262
a; e; g
NAPC

E. J. Rhodes, Inc.
10 Speen Street
Framingham, MA 01701
617-879-2603
a; c; f; g; M
NAPC
foreign affiliate: London

Rogers & Sands Inc.
8 N.E. Executive Park
Burlington, MA 02108
617-229-2640
f; H; i; M; re
NAPC

Romac
126 High Street, 6th floor
Boston, MA 02110
617-482-2856
a; b; f

Romac
20 Walnut Street
Wellesley, MA 02181
617-239-0900
a; b; f

Louis Rudzinsky Associates, Inc.
394 Lowell Street, Suite 17
Lexington, MA 02173
617-862-6727
a; f; g; M; m; pe; S

Sales Consultants of Boston
155 Middlesex Turnpike
Boston, MA 01803
617-273-1430
m; s

Sales Consultants of Wellesley
1 Washington Street, Suite 212
Wellesley, MA 02181
617-235-7700
g; m; s
NAPC

George D. Sandel Associates
Box 588
Waltham, MA 02254
617-890-0713

Robert M. Sandoe & Associates
29 Newbury Street
Boston, MA 02116
617-262-5380

SCI
390 Main Street, #620
Worcester, MA 01608
617-754-8499
NAPC

Scott-Wayne Associates, Inc.
545 Boylston Street, 10th floor
Boston, MA 02116
617-267-6505

Selected Executives Inc.
959 Park Square Building
Boston, MA 02116
617-426-3100

Slovin Personnel Associates
9 Mason Street
Worcester, MA 01609
617-853-4289
c; S

The Software Alliance
385 Elliot Street
Newton, MA 02164
617-965-2808
c
NAPC

S.P.I. Personnel Consultants
60 William Street, Suite G-30
Wellesley, MA 02181
617-235-4670
f; i
NAPC

Alan R. Stone, Esq., Attorney Placement Consultants, Inc.
121 Mount Vernon Street
Boston, MA 02108
617-227-3838
l

Technical Support Etc.
117 Upland Road
Marlboro, MA 01752
617-485-0935
e; M
NAPC

Technology Profiles, Inc.
400 West Cummings Park, Suite 2900
Woburn, MA 01801
617-935-8555
c

Travis & Co., Inc.
20 Walnut Street
Wellesley Hills, MA 02181
617-235-4267

Weston Consultants, Inc.
Box 216
Weston, MA 02193
617-890-3750

Joel H. Wilensky Associates, Inc.
P.O. Box 155
Sudbury, MA 01776
617-443-5176
R

Winter, Wyman & Company
19 Crosby Drive
Bedford, MA 01730
617-890-7000
a; f; M; pe; p

Winter, Wyman & Company
50 Milk Street, 15th floor
Boston, MA 02109
617-542-5000

Winter, Wyman & Company
124 Mount Auburn Street, Suite 200
Cambridge, MA 02138
617-235-8505

Woodson Associates
30 Main Street, Suite 13
Ashland, MA 01721
617-881-5650
e; S
NAPC

Xavier Associates, Inc.
1350 Belmont Street
Brockton, MA 02401
617-584-9414
l; pe

Yorkshire Consulting Group, Inc.
381 Elliot Street
Newton Upper Falls, MA 02164
617-965-6700
i; m

MICHIGAN

B. Hans Becker Associates
3155 West Big Beaver Road, #210
Troy, MI 48084
313-643-6650
NAPC

G. A. Burns Associates, Inc.
77 Monroe Center
Suite 1104
Grand Rapids, MI 49503
616-454-3222
g; H

Continental Search Associates
139 West Maple, P.O. Box 413
Birmingham, MI 48012
313-644-4506
e; g
NAPC

Dunhill of Troy
755 West Big Beaver Road, #423
Troy, MI 48084
313-362-3115
g
NAPC

Elwell & Associates, Inc.
2155 Jackson Road
Suite 200
Ann Arbor, MI 48103
313-662-8775

Harper Associates
15659 West 10 Mile Road
Southfield, MI 48075
313-557-1700
f; H; hr

Henry Labus Personnel, Inc.
820 Ford Building
Detroit, MI 48226
313-962-4461
a; b; l
NAPC

Littman Associates
2525 Crooks Road
Troy, MI 48084
313-649-1150
g; T
NAPC

Ludot Personnel Services
3000 Town Center, Suite 1707
Southfield, MI 48075
313-353-9720
e; g
NAPC

Stephen W. Matson Associates, Inc.
954 North Hunter Boulevard
Birmingham, MI 48011
313-540-1662
A; M

Personnel Director Associates
111 South Main Street, Suite 350
Ann Arbor, MI 48104
313-769-0924
e; g
NAPC

Professional Personnel Consultants
19189 West 10 Mile Road
Southfield, MI 48075
313-357-4810
a; b; e; g; M; m
NAPC

Sales Executives, Inc.
755 West Big Beaver Road, Suite 2107
Troy, MI 48084
313-362-1900
M; m; s
NAPC

Scope Services, Inc.
2095 Niles
St. Joseph, MI 49085
616-983-1554
c; M
NAPC

Thomas-Pond Enterprises
21700 Greenfield Road, Suite 440
Oak Park, MI 48237
313-968-0040

Upton Management Services, Inc.
2100 West Big Beaver Road, Suite 208
Troy, MI 48084
313-362-1015

Duane I. Wilson Associates, Inc.
954 North Hunter Boulevard
Birmingham, MI 48011
313-647-3234
a; f; M; m; o

MINNESOTA

Accounting Personnel Minnesota
5354 Cedar Lake Road, #104
Minneapolis, MN 55416
612-544-1005
a; b
NAPC

Agri-Business Services
1751 West Country Road B., Box 13168
St. Paul, MN 55113
612-631-0570
b; e; s
NAPC

Andcor Companies
600 South County Road #575
Minneapolis, MN 55426
612-546-0966
b; g
NAPC

James Bangert Associates, Inc.
1212 Wayzata Boulevard
Wayzata, MN 55391
612-475-3454
a; c; C; f; M; R

Computer People
5353 Wayzata Boulevard, #604
Minneapolis, MN 55416
612-542-8520
c
NAPC

Corporate Resources, Inc.
Shelard Plaza North, Suite 310
Minneapolis, MN 55426
612-546-4430
c; M; r; S

Electronics Systems Personnel Agency
121 South Eighth Street
Minneapolis, MN 55402
612-338-6714
e;
NAPC

Ells Personnel Systems
1129 Plymouth Building
Minneapolis, MN 55402
612-333-1131
b; g; s
NAPC

Employment Specialists
7200 France Avenue South
Minneapolis, MN 55435
612-831-6444
e; i
NAPC

Russ Fallstad and Associates
7515 Wayzata Boulevard, Westbrook Building
Minneapolis, MN 55426
612-546-5007
e; M
NAPC

Barbara Jensen Employment
7101 York Avenue South
Edina, MN 55435
612-831-4438
i
NAPC

McNitt Personnel Bureau
Seventh & Second Avenue South, 602 Baker
  Building
Minneapolis, MN 55402
612-339-5533
a; A; g

Maetzold Associates, Inc.
3822 County Road, #73
Minnetonka, MN 55343
612-933-7505
a; f; g; M; m; pe

Management Search Inc.
400 Shelard Plaza South, Suite 366
Minneapolis, MN 55426
612-546-2541
a; c; f; g; m; pe

Harry D. Parkhurst & Associates, Inc.
7515 Wayzata Boulevard
Minneapolis, MN 55426
612-546-3455
g; M; r; S

Roth Young Personnel of Minneapolis
4530 West 77th Street, Suite 250
Edina, MN 55435
612-831-6655
A; e; g; H; m; R; s
NAPC

Robert Sirny & Associates
8120 Penn Avenue South
Minneapolis, MN 55431
612-884-1004
l

Peter Van Leer & Associates
1212 Wayzata Boulevard
Wayzata, MN 55391
612-473-3793
i

Walker Recruitment
125 North Plaza, Gamble Center
Minneapolis, MN 55416
612-546-3700
A; g; m; pe; R

Arthur Young Executive Resource
  Consultants
1000 Pillsbury Center
Minneapolis, MN 54402
612-343-1000
AESC

Steven Yungerberg Associates, Inc.
1022 IDS Center, 80 South Eighth Street
Minneapolis, MN 55402
612-332-5313

MISSISSIPPI

Buzhardt Associates
5420 1-55 North, Suite H
Jackson, MS 39211
601-981-5425
a; f; g; ;M; m; pe

Resource Staffing Group
633 North State Street, #402
Jackson, MS 39201
601-354-4475
NAPC

M. D. Treadway & Company
9369 Goodman Road
Olive Branch, MS 38654
601-895-4106
e; M
NAPC

Jim Woodson & Associates
2679 Insurance Center Drive, Suite D3
Jackson, MS 39216
601-362-8298
a; e; M
NAPC

MISSOURI

Associated Ventures
1534 St. Ives
Dellwood, MO 63136
314-867-7357
m; s
NAPC

Ron Ball & Associates
330 West 47th Street, Suite 219
Kansas City, MO 64112
816-941-3550

Belle Oaks of America
1212 McGee, 2nd floor
Kansas City, MO 64106
816-421-7181
a; g; s
NAPC

R. L. Booton & Associates
11500 Olive Boulevard, Suite 230
St. Louis, MO 63141
314-432-5580
a; f

Grant Cooper & Associates, Inc.
2388 Schuetz Road, Suite 40
St. Louis, MO 63146
314-567-4690

Davis Company
408 Olive Street, #333
St. Louis, MO 63102
314-241-7100
a
NAPC

Dice Cowger & Associates
12555 Manchester, Suite 830
St. Louis, MO 63131
314-821-5151
pe

Dorsey Love & Associates
4255 South Glenstone, P.O. Box 4387GS
Springfield, MO 65804
417-883-1212
b
NAPC

Executive Career Consultants
111 North Taylor Avenue
St. Louis, MO 63122
314-965-3939
g
NAPC

Executive Resource
1010 Collingwood Drive
St. Louis, MO 63132
314-993-3232
e
NAPC

Gordon, Cook & Associates
34 North Brentwood, Suite 208
Clayton, MO 63105
314-725-1400
a; e; M
NAPC

HDB Inc.
300 Ozark Trail Drive, #101
St. Louis, MO 63011
314-391-7799
T
NAPC

Holohan Group, Ltd.
9807 Wild Deer Road
St. Louis, MO 63124
314-821-3225

Huntress Real Estate Executive Search, Inc.
P.O. Box 8667
Kansas City, MO 64114
816-381-8128
re

Huxtable Associates, Inc.
P.O. Box 621
Bridgeton, MO 63044
314-928-4205
a; f; g; M; m; pe

Kendall and Davis Company
408 Olive Street, #333
St. Louis, MO 63102
314-241-2832
e; M
NAPC

Kincannon & Reed
200 South Hanley
St. Louis, MO 63105
314-727-1960

Michael Latas & Associates, Inc.
1311 Lindbergh Plaza Center
St. Louis, MO 63132
314-993-6500
C; f; i; M; R

Lawrence-Leiter & Co.
427 West 12th Street
Kansas City, MO 64105
816-474-8340

Frank Lockett Associates
818 Olive Street, Suite 762
St. Louis, MO 63101
314-231-9336

R.E.A. Associates
11906 Manchester Road
St. Louis, MO 63131
314-965-1470

Recruiting Consultants
11605 Studt Avenue
St. Louis, MO 63141
314-991-5088
NAPC

Regency Recruiters
1102 Grand
Kansas City, MO 64106
816-842-3860
b

Richard R. Rosche
3115 South Grand Avenue, #602
St. Louis, MO 63163
314-771-1615
e; T
NAPC

Roth Young Personnel
120 South Central, #212
St. Louis, MO 63105
314-726-0500
H; hr; M; m; R
NAPC

Charles Russ Associates, Inc.
1820 West 91st Place
Kansas City, MO 64114
816-523-4001
a; f; M; m; pe

Sales Recruiters of Kansas City
1125 Grand Avenue, Suite 2002
Kansas City, MO 64106
816-471-1010
e; s
NAPC

S. J. Associates
5865 Hampton Avenue, Suite "B"
St. Louis, MO 63109
314-481-2715
s
NAPC

NEBRASKA

Eggers Personnel & Consulting
11272 Elm Street, Eggers Plaza
Omaha, NB 68144
402-333-3480
a; b; e; g; R; s
NAPC

Personnel Search
1126 South 72nd Street
Omaha, NB 68124
402-397-2980
b; e; s
NAPC

Professional Recruiters
6818 Grover
Omaha, NB 68106
402-397-2885
e

Staff America
2120 South 72nd Street, Suite 900
Omaha, NB 68124
402-391-2065
NAPC

NEVADA

Delaney & Associates
1700 East Desert Inn Road, #301
Las Vegas, NV 89109
702-737-5500
g
NAPC

Western Executive Consultants
1205 Smith Street
Las Vegas, NV 89108
702-646-1926
e; g
NAPC

NEW HAMPSHIRE

Availability Personnel Consultants
169 South River Road
Bedford, NH 03102
603-669-4440
f; i; M; re
NAPC

Barger & Sargent, Inc.
5 Warren Street
Concord, NH 03301
603-224-7753
b; i; M; m
AESC

Craig's Criterion
P.O. Box 700
Contoocook, NH 03229
603-669-8810
a; e
NAPC

Exeter Associates, Inc.
820 Lafayette Road, P.O. Box 4979
Hampton, NH 03842
603-926-6712
c

Fortune Personnel Consultants
505 West Hollis Street, #208
Nashua, NH 03062
603-880-4900
e; T
NAPC

International Personnel Consultants, Inc.
Wheeler Professional Park, Box 887
Hanover, NH 03755
603-643-2412
c; e

James H. Kennedy
15 Collins Pond Trail
Fitzwilliam, NH 03447
603-585-2200
e; g

Preferred Positions
157 Main Dunstable Road
Nashua, NH 03060
603-889-0112
e; M
NAPC

NEW JERSEY

Aaron Engineering Agency
11 West Passaic
Rochelle Park, NJ 07662
201-845-6011
e

ACME Agency
915 Clifton Avenue
Clifton, NJ 07013
201-779-8790
e

Alberta-Smyth Personnel Agency, Inc.
2444 Morris Avenue
Union, NJ 07083
201-686-6610
a; b; f

Associated Business Consultants, Inc.
43 North Main Street
P.O. Box 246
Medford, NJ 08055
609-953-8600
c; H; M; r; s

William Alder Associates
117 Fort Lee Road
Leonia, NJ 07605
201-262-9060
M

Arthur Personnel
8 Forest Avenue, Suite 100
Caldwell, NJ 07006
201-226-4555
a; f; g; M; m; pe

Baker Scott & Company
1259 Route 46
Parsippany, NJ 07054
201-272-3355
a; g; T

Barone Associates
57 Green Street
Woodbridge, NJ 07095
201-634-4300
C; e; M; m

Gary S. Bell Associates, Inc.
393 Crescent Avenue
Wyckoff, NJ 07481
201-891-5900
g; H; M; m; r; S

Brandon Associates
2175 Lemoine Avenue
Fort Lee, NJ 07024
201-461-5544
i; se

Brentwood Organization
1280 Route 46, Box A-5
Parsippany, NJ 07054
201-335-8700
NAPC

BRJ Associates, Inc.
615 Sherwood Parkway
Mountainside, NJ 07092
201-233-6000
l; M; m; r

Career Center
210 River Street
Hackensack, NJ 07601
201-342-1777
g
NAPC

Career Path
1156 East Ridgewood Avenue
Ridgewood, NJ 07450
201-652-2500
e; g
NAPC

Christensen & Montgomery
250 Madison Avenue
Morristown, NJ 07960
201-540-1444
f; H; M; re
AESC

Citizens Employment Service
217 Main Street
Fort Lee, NJ 07024
201-947-9233
g; i; M
NAPC

Consultants, Inc.
1441 Kearney Drive, P.O. Box 1938
North Brunswick, NJ 08902
201-297-0861
e; M; r; T

Curry, Telleri, Ziegler, Inc.
At The Castle, 433 River Road
Highland Park, NJ 08904
201-828-3883
ph

Data Finders, Inc.
140 Sylvan Avenue
Englewood Cliffs, NJ 07632
201-947-6002
c; e

The Dean Group
1973 Springfield Avenue
Maplewood, NJ 07040
201-763-3898
a; f; g; H; M; m; pe

Deven Associates, Inc.
3 Claridge Drive
Verona, NJ 07044
201-239-5500
f; i; M; re; R

R. M. Donaldson Personnel
14 Commerce Drive
Cranford, NJ 07016
201-272-0500
a; f; g; m; pe

Dunhill of Paramus
East 28th Fairview Terrace
Paramus, NJ 07652
201-845-0610
m; H
NAPC

Eastern Executive Associates
881 Allwood Road
Clifton, NJ 07012
201-777-6900
c; M; r; T

Henry H. Eskay
24 Hutton Avenue
West Orange, NJ 07052
201-731-3968
g; pe

Executive Referral Service
141 South Avenue
Fanwood, NJ 07023
201-322-2324

Fran Farber, Ltd.
185 Bridge Plaza North, P.O. Box 2156
Fort Lee, NJ 07024
201-585-9500
i

Forest Associates
8 Forest Avenue, Suite 200
Caldwell, NJ 07006
201-226-2407
c; e
NAPC

Walter Frederick Friedman and Co., Inc.
111 Northfield Avenue
West Orange, NJ 07052
201-325-3700
M; pe

G.A. Agency
108 North Union Avenue
Cranford, NJ 07016
201-272-2080
b; g
NAPC

W. N. Garbarini & Associates
961 Cherokee Court
Westfield, NJ 07090
201-232-2737

Gendason Cooper Associates
333 Sylvan Avenue
Englewood Cliffs, NJ 07632
201-871-1905
R

Gilmore Personnel Consultants, Inc.
589 Franklin Turnpike
Ridgewood, NJ 07450
201-447-2300
pp; r; S

Glynn, Brooks & Co.
2175 Lemoine Avenue
Fort Lee, NJ 07024
201-947-7307
e; g; M; m; T

Graduates Unlimited Personnel, Inc.
1600 Route 22
Union, NJ 07083
201-964-7474
a; f; o

GV Personnel
50 Lafayette Place
Kenilworth, NJ 07033
201-467-8414
g
NAPC

The Hartshorn Group
300 Lanidex Plaza
Parsippany, NJ 07054
201-884-0700
g
NAPC

Joseph Keyes Associates
354 State Street
Hackensack, NJ 07601
201-489-1881
a; c; M

Krow Associates, Inc.
1061 Bloomfield Avenue
West Caldwell, NJ 07006
201-575-7007
e; M; m
NAPC

Lacrosse Associates, Inc.
1600 Route 22
Union, NJ 07083
201-964-7744
g; M; m; pe; r

McCooe & Associates, Inc.
1250 East Ridewood Avenue
Ridgewood, NJ 07450
201-445-3161

Martin Personnel Associates
100 West Mount Pleasant Avenue
Livingston, NJ 07039
201-994-1900
NAPC

Newcrest
21 Hillcrest Road
West Caldwell, NJ 07006
201-226-2022
NAPC

F. M. O'Grady & Associates
22 Angus Lane
Warren, NJ 07060
201-647-6280

Pascal Associates, Inc.
P.O. Box 197
Rutherford, NJ 07070
201-939-3030
H; ph

Peeney Associates, Inc.
141 South Avenue
Fanwood, NJ 07023
201-322-2324
a; f; g; M; m; pe; ph

Personnel Recruiters
P.O. Box 150
Springfield, NJ 07081
201-467-3600
e

Phillips Associates
10 Depot Square
Englewood, NJ 07631
201-569-5033
a; f; g; pe

Phillips Majewski & Associates
1961 Morris Avenue
Union, NJ 07083
201-851-0044
i

Purcell Employment Systems
900 Route 9
Woodbridge, NJ 07095
201-636-5100
e
NAPC

Rainess Associates
1129 Bloomfield Avenue
West Caldwell, NJ 07006
201-575-0190
a; f; g; M

Ryan/Smith & Associates, Inc.
P.O. Box 253
Westfield, NJ 07091
201-232-5720
C; f; H; i; ph; pu; re
AESC

Sampson, Neill & Wilkins, Inc.
543 Valley Road
Upper Montclair, NJ 07043
201-783-9600
H; ph

Search Consultants
10 Forest Avenue, P.O. Box 402
Paramus, NJ 07652
201-843-5090
a; b
NAPC

Select Finders Corp.
1129 Bloomfield Avenue
West Caldwell, NJ 07006
201-575-0370
b; e
NAPC

The Stevenson Group, Inc.
720 Palisades Avenue
Englewood Cliffs, NJ 07632
201-568-1900

Systems Search II
90 Millburn Avenue
Millburn, NJ 07041
201-761-4400
b; T
NAPC

Tech Recruiters
51 Cragwood Road
South Plainfield, NJ 07080
201-753-4449
e

Viking Recruiting Consultants, Inc.
115 Spring Valley Road, Box 343
Montvale, NJ 07645
201-573-1430
g; m

Emanuel Weintraub Associates, Inc.
2050 Center Avenue
Fort Lee, NJ 07024
201-947-2404
a; f; g; M; m; o

Wermert & Associates, Inc.
P.O. Box B
Park Ridge, NJ 07656
201-391-7600

NEW MEXICO

Dunhill of Albuquerque
1717 Louisiana, N.E., #218
Albuquerque, NM 87110
505-262-1871
a; e
NAPC

Robert Half
Box 3320
Albuquerque, NM 87190
505-884-4557
a; f;

Snelling and Snelling
2701 San Pedro, N.E.
Albuquerque, NM 87110
505-881-9800
e; g
NAPC

NEW YORK

Abbington Associates
Box 340, 21 Barnes Lane
East Northport, NY 11731
516-368-8811
c; r; T

Abbott Smith Associates, Inc
South Road
Millbrook, NY 12545
914-677-5051
g; pe

Accountants & Auditors Agency
30 East 42nd Street
New York, NY 10017
212-687-5656
a
NAPC

Accounting Resources International
11 Broadway
New York, NY 10004
212-269-0556
a

Jerome Ackels Associates
98 Cutter Mill Road
Great Neck, NY 11021
516-487-4999
m; o

Norma Adler, Inc.
59 East 54th Street
New York, NY 10022
212-355-1020
A

Advocate Search, Ltd.
60 East 42nd Street, Suite 2801
New York, NY 10165
212-867-7100
l

Affirmative Action Associates
443 West 50th Street
New York, NY 10020
212-688-5177

The Ahrens Agency
45 John Street, Suite 405
New York, NY 10038
212-732-3600
b

J. R. Akin & Company
211 East 51st Street, Suite 10F
New York, NY 10022
212-838-7582
g

Alberta-Smyth Personnel Agency, Inc.
60 East 42 Street
New York, NY 10165
212-953-0011
a; b; f

Don Allan Associates, Inc.
521 Fifth Avenue
New York, NY 10017
212-697-9775
c; m; s; T
NAPC

A-L Legal Search, Inc.
355 Lexington Avenue
New York, NY 10017
212-878-9000
l

Allen Personnel Agency
160 Broadway
New York, NY 10038
212-571-1150
b; i; se
NAPC

Ethan Allen Personnel Agency
59 Academy Street
Poughkeepsie, NY 12601
914-471-9700
a; e
NAPC

Allstates Professional Placement Consultants
1202 Troy-Schenectady Road
Latham, NY 12110
518-783-5595
e

Alpha Vector Search, Inc.
432 Park Avenue South
New York, NY 10016
212-684-7960

Ames-O'Neill Associates, Inc.
330 Vanderbilt Motor Parkway
Hauppauge, NY 11788
516-582-4800
M; S

Analytic Recruiting, Inc.
1 East 42nd Street, Suite 1002
New York, NY 10017
212-687-9163
b; c; f; i; M; m; re; T; t

Apple Agency
170 Broadway
New York, NY 10038
212-608-1490
i

APS Legal Search
150 Broadway
New York, NY 10038
212-233-7770
l

Aronow Associates, Inc.
2 Penn Plaza, Suite 1500
New York, NY 10001
212-947-3777
a; f; g; m; T

Ashway Ltd. Agency
295 Madison Avenue
New York, NY 10017
212-679-3300
e; M; r; S

Automotive Personnel Consultants
33 Jessica Place
Roslyn Heights, NY 11577
516-621-0110

Bader Research Corp.
6 East 45th Street
New York, NY 10017
212-682-4750
l

The Bankers Register
150 Broadway
New York, NY 10038
212-349-6900
b
NAPC

The Bankers Register
500 Fifth Avenue, #330
New York, NY 10110
212-840-0800
b
NAPC

The Barclay Group
441 Lexington Avenue
New York, NY 10017
212-883-8822
l

Barrister Referrals, Ltd.
515 Madison Avenue
New York, NY 10022
212-421-2300
l

Battalia & Associates, Inc.
275 Madison Avenue, Suite 2315
New York, NY 10016
212-683-9440
c; f; M; ph; T
AESC
foreign affiliates: Glasgow, London, Madrid,
  Paris, Toronto

Martin H. Bauman Associates, Inc.
410 Park Avenue
New York, NY 10022
212-752-6580
hr

Marcia Beilin, Inc.
230 Park Avenue, Suite 1255
New York, NY 10169
212-370-4330
l

Daniel Benjamin, Inc.
30 East 40th Street
New York, NY 10016
212-696-1111
a; pe

Bentley & Evans, Inc.
1 Penn Plaza
New York, NY 10119
212-371-1212
g; l

Robert Bennett Associates
50 East 42nd Street
New York, NY 10017
212-949-2355
l

Leslie Berglass Associates, Inc.
645 Madison Avenue
New York, NY 10022
212-980-3305
g; M; m; pp; r

The Berkshire Group, Inc.
P.O. Box 5861, Grand Central Station
New York, NY 10163
212-628-0413
l

Zachary Bernard Agency, Ltd.
424 Madison Avenue
New York, NY 10017
212-751-5040
l

Paula Berns, Inc.
310 Madison Avenue
New York, NY 10017
212-687-7850
re

Howard I. Bernstein, Esq.
230 West 13th Street
New York, NY 10011
212-255-8383
l

BH Folios, Ltd.
770 Lexington Avenue
New York, NY 10021
212-308-6150
A

Billington, Fox & Ellis, Inc.
551 Madison Avenue
New York, NY 10022
212-980-5900

Bil-Lu Personnel Agency
60 East 42nd Street, #1035
New York, NY 10165
212-682-5740
g; hr
NAPC

Blendow, Crowley & Oliver, Inc.
211 East 51st Street
New York, NY 10022
212-838-7580
ph; S

Marc-Paul Bloome, Ltd.
250 West 57th Street
New York, NY 10107
212-245-2828
e; f; T

Botal Associates
7 Dey Street
New York, NY 10007
212-227-7370
b; T
NAPC

Bradstreet Management, Inc.
60 East 42nd Street
New York, NY 10165
212-370-9677
f; T

Roberta Brenner Associates, Inc.
635 Madison Avenue
New York, NY 10022
212-308-7075
A; m

Broadcast Personnel, Inc.
200 West 57th Street
New York, NY 10020
212-977-3580
g; T

Brooks/Gay & Associates, Inc.
50 Park Avenue
New York, NY 10016
212-686-8917
H; i

Brucks Personnel Corp
300 Main Street
East Rochester, NY 14445
716-248-9090
c; e; M

Burns Personnel, Inc.
1 East Avenue
Rochester, NY 14604
716-232-7470
a; c; e; f; ;M; r

E. A. Butler Associates, Inc.
11 Fort Amherst Road
Glens Falls, NY 12801
518-793-3300

E. A. Butler Associates, Inc.
1270 Avenue of the Americas
New York, NY 10020
212-315-3900

CAH Executive Search
950 Third Avenue
New York, NY 10022
212-755-3313
A

Canny, Bowen, Inc.
425 Park Avenue
New York, NY 10022
212-986-8653
g

The Cantor Group, Inc.
171 Madison Avenue
New York, NY 10016
212-481-0000
P

Career Builders, Inc.
400 Madison Avenue
New York, NY 10017
212-758-4070
A; e; m; P; T

Career Concepts
62 West 45th Street
New York, NY 10036
212-790-2600
f

Career Directions
280 Broadway
Newburgh, NY 12250
914-565-8860
a; e
NAPC

Career Guides, Inc.
60 East 42nd Street
New York, NY 10016
212-697-3358
NAPC

Career Management
370 Seventh Avenue
New York, NY 10001
212-695-4800
R

Carre, Orban & Partners, Inc.
230 Park Avenue, Suite 2717
New York, NY 10169
212-953-7722
g
foreign affiliates: Brussels, Dusseldorf,
  Geneva, London

Carter Stone & Co., Inc.
61 Broadway, Suite 2522
New York NY 10006
212-363-7979
b; g; i; pe

Catalyst Legal Resources, Inc.
200 Park Avenue, 44th floor
New York, NY 10166
212-682-2100
l
NAPC

David Chambers & Associates, Inc.
6 East 43rd Street
New York, NY 10017
212-986-8653
g

Chanko-Ward, Ltd.
2 West 45th Street
New York, NY 10036
212-869-4040
a; c; f

Charter Executive Associates, Inc.
2 Ann Street, 10th floor
New York, NY 10038
212-227-6711
l

Chernuchin Associates, Inc.
166 East 63rd Street
New York, NY 10022
212-319-1677

Toby Clark Associates, Inc.
155 East 55th Street
New York, NY 10022
212-752-5670
m; P

Claveloux, McCaffrey & Associates, Inc.
35 West 36th Street
New York, NY 10018
212-695-3089
a; e; f; M; m; r

Clayton Personnel
160 Broadway, Suite 1011
New York, NY 10038
212-732-6880
se

Closman & Associates, Inc.
2 Penn Plaza
New York, NY 10001
212-868-3439
f; g; o

CMA Technical Search, Inc.
16 East 42nd Street
New York, NY 10017
212-599-1020
c; M; t

Cochran, Cochran & Yale, Inc.
945 East Henrietta Road
Rochester, NY 14623
716-424-6060
a; c; e; f; M

Laura Colangelo Legal Search Consultants, Inc.
919 Third Avenue
New York, NY 10022
212-888-7895
l

W. Hoyt Colton Associates, Inc.
67 Wall Street, 20th floor
New York, NY 10005
212-509-1800
b; se

Columbia EDP Agency, Inc.
342 Madison Avenue, Suite 1423
New York, NY 10173
212-661-3434
c; o

The Comnet Group
300 Garden City Plaza
Garden City, NY 11530
516-248-5721
c; T

Com-tek Agency
295 Madison Avenue, Suite 725
New York, NY 10017
212-682-8282
e; T
NAPC

Continental Search Group
353 Lexington Avenue
New York, NY 10016
212-685-5113
M; R

COR Management Services Ltd.
420 Lexington Avenue
New York, NY 10170
212-599-2640
g; T
NAPC

David P. Cordell Associates
130 Water Street, Suite 8B
New York, NY 10005
212-374-1445

Cornwall
180 Broadway, 3rd floor
New York, NY 10038
212-349-2520
b

Corporate Careers, Inc.
188 East Post Road
White Plains, NY 10601
914-946-2003
a; g
NAPC

Corporate Counsel Search, Inc.
370 Lexington Avenue
New York, NY 10017
212-687-4320
l

Council Legal Search, Inc.
99 Hudson Street
New York, NY 10013
212-219-1800
l

Cowin Associates
1 Old Country Road
Carle Place, NY 11514
516-741-3020
M; S

Crandall Associates, Inc.
501 Fifth Avenue
New York, NY 10017
212-687-2550
m

Creative Search Affiliates
1385 York Avenue
New York, NY 10021
212-734-5323
f; m

Cris Associates, Inc.
274 Madison Avenue
New York, NY 10016
212-685-6663
f; g; m

Crispi, Wagner & Co., Inc.
420 Lexington Avenue
New York, NY 10170
212-687-2340
a; f; g

Frank Cuomo & Associates, Inc.
42 Oak Avenue
Tuckahoe, NY 10707
914-779-6505
e; g; s
NAPC

DAPEXS Consultants, Inc.
1 Park Place
Syracuse, NY 13202
315-474-2477
a; c; e
NAPC

Darson Personnel Associates, Inc.
122 East 42nd Street
New York, NY 10168
212-986-5730
a; f

Bert Davis
400 Madison Avenue
New York, NY 10017
212-838-4000
pp; P; pu
NAPC

DeLalla-Fried Associates
201 East 69th Street, Suite 4K
New York, NY 10021
212-879-9100
g; m

Dependable
41 East 42nd Street
New York, NY 10017
212-867-6565
a

Devine, Baldwin & Peters, Inc.
250 Park Avenue
New York, NY 10177
212-867-5235
g

Elaine P. Dine, Inc.
P.O. Box 5237, FDR Station
New York, NY 10022
212-335-6182
l

Donaldson & Wharton Associates
159 West 33rd Street
New York, NY 10001
212-695-0732
e; H; M
NAPC

Dunhill of Huntington
535 Broadhollow Road
Melville, NY 11747
516-293-0055
a; e; g; T
NAPC

Earley Kielty & Associates, Inc.
2 Penn Plaza
New York, NY 10121
212-736-5626
a; c; f; g; pe

Eastman & Beaudine, Inc.
437 Madison Avenue
New York, NY 10022
212-486-9655

Edwards & Shepard
1170 Broadway
New York, NY 10001
212-725-1280
ar

Earl F. Eisenbach & Associates, Inc.
211 East 51st Street, Suite 10F
New York, NY 10022
212-838-5820

David M. Ellner Associates
2 Penn Plaza
New York, NY 10121
212-279-0665
a; f; g; M; m

Engineering Employment Agency
217 Broadway
New York, NY 10017
212-267-5640
c; e

W. H. Eolis International, Inc.
P.O. Box 352, FDR Station
New York, NY 10170
212-684-2400
l

Eslinger Patent Placements
133 East 58th Street, Suite 410
New York, NY 10022
212-888-9300

Essex Legal Search
507 Fifth Avenue
New York, NY 10017
212-268-0818
l

ES VEE EDP
421 Seventh Avenue, Suite 1205
New York, NY 10001
212-947-7730
c

Executive Careers, Inc.
11 Hanover Square, 27th floor
New York, NY 10005
212-509-5600
c

Executive Image, Inc.
353 Lexington Avenue
New York, NY 10016
212-532-8565
a; f

Executive Placement Corporation
949-51 Sibley Tower Building
Rochester, NY 14604
716-454-1424
a; e; M; s
NAPC

Exxell
6 Maiden Lane
New York, NY 10038
212-227-7100
a; f

Richard Farber Associates, Inc.
60 Cutter Mill Road
Great Neck, NY 11021
516-466-3690
c; e; T

Farrell & Phin
845 Third Avenue
New York, NY 10022
212-838-5511

A. E. Feldman Associates
111 Great Neck Road
Great Neck, NY 11021
516-466-4708
g

Fells & Baroody, Inc.
2 Penn Plaza
New York, NY 10001
212-736-9404
c; f

Fenvessy & Schwab, Inc.
645 Madison Avenue
New York, NY 10022
212-758-6800

Fergus Associates, Inc.
350 Fifth Avenue, Suite 5818
New York, NY 10118
212-947-1775
l

Jerry Fields Associates, Inc.
515 Madison Avenue
New York, NY 10022
212-319-7600
A; m; P

Fine Personnel Agency
507 Fifth Avenue, Suite 1100
New York, NY 10017
212-557-3737
ar; C; f; re

The Fisher Organization
545 Fifth Avenue
New York, NY 10017
212-986-9666
a; A; b
NAPC

Fitzgerald and Ready
310 Madison Avenue
New York, NY 10017
212-661-0450
hr

Forum Personnel
342 Madison Avenue
New York, NY 10017
212-687-4050
b; f; i; m; T

Friends & Co.
743 Park Avenue, P.O. Box B
Huntington, NY 11743
516-673-4666
S

Gerald Frisch Associates, Inc.
500 Fifth Avenue, 41st floor
New York, NY 10110
212-944-7170

The Fry Group
18 East 41st Street
New York, NY 10017
212-532-8100
A; m; P
NAPC

Furman Group, Ltd.
237 Park Avenue, 21st floor
New York, NY 10017
212-551-3614
b; f

Garofolo, Curtiss & Company
28 Oakwood Drive
Glen Falls, NY 12801
518-793-1139
H; i; n
AESC

J. B. Gilbert Associates, Inc.
420 Lexington Avenue, Suite 2114
New York, NY 10170
212-661-2122

Giles Intermediaries, Inc.
55 John Street
New York, NY 10038
212-285-2315
i

Bob Gill Associates
505 Fifth Avenue
New York, NY 10017
212-867-8918
c

Global Search
1 Huntington Quadrangle
Melville, NY 11747
516-293-3555
a; b; i
NAPC

Audrey Golden Associates, Ltd.
51 East 42nd Street
New York, NY 10017
212-661-5123
l

The Goodrich & Sherwood Company
521 Fifth Avenue
New York, NY 10017
212-697-4131

Gould & McCoy, Inc.
551 Madison Avenue
New York, NY 10022
212-688-8671
g
AESC

Gray-Kimball Associates
660 Broadway
Massapequa, NY 11758
516-799-5400
e
NAPC

Green & Green
15 East 40th Street
New York, NY 10016
212-679-8040
e

Group IV Recruitment Consultants
19 West 44th Street
New York, NY 10036
212-840-1124
f; g; M; m; o

Stephen M. Haas Legal Placement, Inc.
60 East 42nd Street
New York, NY 10165
212-661-5555
l

Haley Associates, Inc.
375 Park Avenue
New York, NY 10152
212-421-7860

Robert Half of New York, Inc.
522 Fifth Avenue
New York, NY 10036
212-221-6500
a; b

Hanzel & Mariaschin, Inc.
420 Lexington Avenue
New York, NY 10170
212-972-1830
b

William Harris Associates
25 Ann Street
New York, NY 10038
212-349-3610
A; i; n; P

Haskell & Stern Associates, Inc.
529 Fifth Avenue
New York, NY 10017
212-687-7292
b; f; M; S
AESC
foreign affiliates: London, Paris

W. T. Hawes Company
150 Broadway, Suite 1309
New York, NY 10038
212-608-2070
b

Hazel Associates
305 Madison Avenue, Suite 2214
New York, NY 10017
212-490-1394
c; T

F. P. Healy & Company
230 Park Avenue
New York, NY 10169
212-661-0366
e; f; M; m; S

Jay Heino Associates, Ltd.
420 Lexington Avenue, Suite 2617
New York, NY 10017
212-557-5044
a

E. B. Hendrick Associates
Village Mall, Vine Street
Liverpool, NY 13088
315-451-0121
a; e; M
NAPC

D. J. Hertz and Associates, Ltd.
475 Fifth Avenue
New York, NY 10017
212-689-9640
a; A; ar; g
NAPC

Ruth Hirsch Career Builders, Inc.
400 Madison Avenue
New York, NY 10017
212-758-4070
ar; C; f; P

Hotelmen's Executive Recruitment
305 West End Avenue, #5B
New York, NY 10023
212-582-1400
hr

Houston Associates, Inc.
300 Wheeler Road, Suite 106
Hauppauge, NY 11788
516-234-7467
pe

The Howard Group
521 Fifth Avenue
New York, NY 10175
212-599-2233

Howard-Sloan Associates, Inc.
545 Fifth Avenue
New York, NY 10017
212-661-5250
a; A
NAPC

Howard-Sloan Legal Search, Inc.
545 Fifth Avenue
New York, NY 10017
212-661-5250
1

Huff Associates
29 Hunting Ridge Road
Chappaqua, NY 10514
914-238-8536

Human Resource Services, Inc.
230 Park Avenue, Suite 640
New York, NY 10169
212-949-1000
l

Hunt Personnel Ltd.
342 Madison Avenue
New York, NY 10017
212-687-9140
g; i
NAPC

Huss Viseltear & Associates
505 Park Avenue
New York, NY 10022
212-486-9270
A

Image
5254 Merrick Road
Massapequa, NY 11758
516-798-3993
e

IMC Consulting Group, Ltd.
14 East 60th Street
New York, NY 10022
212-838-9535

Inside Management Associates
143 East 35th Street
New York, NY 10016
212-683-7200
foreign affiliate: Paris

Insight
11 East 44th Street, Suite 1502
New York, NY 10017
212-697-6655
c

Interlangue International, Inc.
41 East 42nd Street, Suite 1607
New York, NY 10017
212-949-0170
b

Internal Data Sciences
350 Fifth Avenue
New York, NY 10118
212-947-6444
c; o; T

International Management Advisors, Inc.
767 Third Avenue
New York, NY 10017
212-758-7770
g
AESC

Interquest Incorporated
747 Third Avenue
New York, NY 10017
212-319-0790
l

Charles Irish Co., Inc.
420 Lexington Avenue
New York, NY 10170
212-490-0040
g; M
AESC

Johnson, Smith and Knisely
475 Fifth Avenue
New York, NY 10017
212-686-9760
f; g; hr; m; pe

Judd-Falk Inc.
124 East 37th Street
New York, NY 10016
212-686-1500
A; f; m

JY Enterprises
299 Broadway, #1700
New York, NY 10007
212-743-6997
a; b; e; g
NAPC

Kahlert Associates, Inc.
P.O. Box 95, Grand Central Station
New York, NY 10163
914-337-6939

Kanarek & Shaw
310 East 53rd Street
New York, NY 10022
212-371-0967
l

Kanon
8 West 40th Street, Room 1410
New York, NY 10018
212-391-2610
b; f; g; se

Martin Kartin & Company
211 East 70th Street
New York, NY 10021
212-628-7676
c; f; M; m; r; S

Richard Kaye Personnel Agency, Inc.
551 Fifth Avenue
New York, NY 10017
212-661-0777
c; e; S

Kearney: Executive Search Group
875 Third Avenue
New York, NY 10022
212-751-7040

The Keating Division
   (Div. Nordeman Grimm)
717 Fifth Avenue
New York, NY 10022
212-758-2300
pe

Kenfield Research Associates, Inc.
24 East 38th Street
New York, NY 10016
212-686-9477
a; f; g; M; m; pe

Kenmore Executive Personnel, Inc.
555 Fifth Avenue
New York, NY 10017
212-599-6161
e; f; o; pe

Kenzer Corp.
777 Third Avenue
New York, NY 10017
212-563-4400
R

Barbara Kerner Consultants
122 East 42nd Street, Suite 3500
New York, NY 10017
212-682-1100
l

Kingsley Quinn, Ltd.
575 Madison Avenue, Suite 1006
New York, NY 10022
212-605-0388
H; m; pe; ph

Kinsale Managers
68 West Main Street
Oyster Bay, NY 11771
516-922-9450
g; i
NAPC

Kling Agency
180 Broadway, 5th floor
New York, NY 10038
212-964-3640
b; i

Bernard J. Klug
225 East 36th Street
New York, NY 10016
212-532-5026
l

KMS Associates
286 Clinton Avenue, UPO Box 3492
Kingston, NY 12401
914-339-3559
e; g; M
NAPC

Kozlin-Brooks Associates
9070 Main Street
Clarence, NY 14031
716-634-5955
NAPC

Lamalie Associates, Inc.
101 Park Avenue
New York, NY 10178
212-953-7900
g
AESC

Lancaster
10 John Street
New York, NY 10038
212-277-6430
se

Langer Associates, Inc.
188 East Post Road
White Plains, NY 10601
914-684-0505
g

Lawrence L. Lapham Associates
230 Park Avenue, Suite 923
New York, NY 10169
212-599-0644
g
AESC

Louise Lashaw
122 East 42nd Street, Suite 1012
New York, NY 10168
212-986-4666
l

LeMar Personnel Consultants
60 East 42nd Street
New York, NY 10165
212-922-1590
A

M. A. Liggett, Inc.
101 Executive Boulevard, P.O. Box 410
Elmsford, NY 10523
914-347-5590
e
NAPC

Linker Personnel Systems, Ltd.
507 Fifth Avenue
New York, NY 10017
212-661-9740
a; T.
NAPC

The R. J. Lipton Company
400 Madison Avenue, Suite 1106
New York, NY 10017
212-838-2212
l

Logic
170 Broadway, Suite 1708
New York, NY 10038
212-277-8000
a

London Scott Associates
1741 Route 9, P.O. Box 209
Clifton Park, NY 12065
518-383-2302
b; e; T
NAPC

Franklin Lorsch Associates, Inc.
41 East 42nd Street, Room 2312
New York, NY 10017
212-986-4411
a; f

Arthur J. Loveley Associates
60 East 42nd Street, Lincoln Building
New York, NY 10165
212-682-8110
a; f; g; M; m

Romano McAvoy Associates, Inc.
180 East Main Street
Smithtown, NY 11787
516-265-7878
a; c; f; M; m; pe

Edwin McDonald Associates
314 Madison Avenue
New York, NY 10017
212-490-2850
b; f; g

William K. McLaughlin Associates
Box 3808
Rochester, NY 14610
716-442-3094
l

McWilliams Personnel, Inc.
29 John Street
New York, NY 10038
212-619-0200
a; b; se

Management Scientists, Inc.
150 East 39th Street
New York, NY 10016
212-532-7710
c; T

Marbrook
295 Madison Avenue, Room 804
New York, NY 10017
212-689-1100
a; ar; b; c; o; p; pe; T

Mar-El Employment Agency
3000 Hempstead Turnpike
Levittown, NY 11756
516-579-7777
a; b; e; i
NAPC

Margolin
275 Madison Avenue
New York, NY 10016
212-679-3930
e; s

Marley Group Ltd.
261 East 18th Street
New York, NY 10003
212-420-9000
l

Marshall-Alan Associates
1466 Broadway
New York, NY 10038
212-382-2440
f

Marshall Consultants, Inc.
360 East 65th Street
New York, NY 10021
212-628-8400
P

Meehan Associates
Box 25081
Rochester, NY 14625
716-381-0770
b; f
NAPC

Martin H. Meisel Associates, Inc.
515 East 87th Street
New York, NY 10028
212-369-4300
hr; pe

Meridian Personnel Associates, Inc.
25 West 43rd Street, Suite 700
New York, NY 10036
212-354-9300
l

Metro Vantage Associates, Inc.
122 East 42nd Street, Suite 209
New York, NY 10168
212-490-1910
l

**Alan Metz Legal & Executive Search
Consultants**
242 East 72nd Street
New York, NY 10021
212-744-0830
l

Michaelson Associates
200 East 71st Street
New York, NY 10021
212-988-2487
l

Ruth Miles Associates, Inc.
6 East 45th Street
New York, NY 10017
212-687-3587
l

MKI Recruiting Associates
171 East Post Road, Suite 200
White Plains, NY 10601
914-682-0818
a; f; g; M; m

Mogul Consultants, Inc.
380 North Broadway
Jericho, NY 11753
516-822-4363
T

William Moore Associates, Inc.
41 East 42nd Street
New York, NY 10017
212-986-5805
l

Morgan Research
521 Fifth Avenue
New York, NY 10175
212-557-7977
b; f; i; re; se

The Morland Group
48 Burd Street
Nyack, NY 10960
914-353-2200
a

Morris Madden & Rice, Inc.
551 Fifth Avenue, Suite 222
New York, NY 10176
212-687-8055
f; m; pe; s

MPI
516 Fifth Avenue, Suite 1404
New York, NY 10017
212-840-7800
b

MPS, Executive Placement, Inc.
11 John Street
New York, NY 10038
212-571-0960
i

MSL International Consultants, Ltd.
Dag Hammarskjold Plaza, 18th floor
New York, NY 10017
212-644-5656

Robert Murphy Associates
230 Park Avenue
New York, NY 10169
212-661-0460

Jerome H. Nagel Associates
1 Hanson Place
Brooklyn, NY 11243
718-789-7400

N.E. Power and Electronics Personnel
R.D. #1, Atomic Project Road
Ballston Spa, NY 12020
518-885-1501
e; T
NAPC

Newell Associates, Inc.
502 Park Avenue
New York, NY 10022
212-758-4337
b; f

New York Legal Search, Inc.
101 Park Avenue, 44th floor
New York, NY 10178
212-599-4242
l

R. A. Nicholson
70 Each 40th Street
New York, NY 10016
212-889-2015
b

Nicholson & Associates, Inc.
230 Park Avenue
New York, NY 10169
212-686-7044
b; c; R; se

Nordeman Grim, Inc.—MBA Resources
717 Fifth Avenue
New York, NY 10022
212-935-1000
g

Robert E. Nurse Associates, Inc.
P.O. Box 1188
White Plains, NY 10530
914-684-0178
a; f; m; pe

Robert Oliver & Associates, Inc.
50 Broad Street
New York, NY 10004
212-747-1770

Oliver Associates, Inc.
734 Walt Whitman Road, Suite 405
Melville, NY 11747
516-549-4343
c; e; M; m

Oliver & Rosner Associates
598 Madison Avenue
New York, NY 10022
212-688-1850
c; e; f; g; m; pe; r; S

Omni
275 Madison Avenue
New York, NY 10016
212-683-7800
c; T

O'Neill Executive Search
Box 135
Buffalo, NY 14223
716-877-8051
a; f; M; m; pe; r

C. M. Oppenheim & Associates, Inc.
1212 Avenue of the Americas
New York, NY 10036
212-944-0060
g; M; m; pe

The Oram Group, Inc.
275 Madison Avenue
New York, NY 10016
212-889-2244
n

Ornstein Communications Associates, Inc.
5 Tulip Lane
New Rochelle, NY 10804
914-235-6877

Orso Associates International
420 Lexington Avenue
New York, NY 10170
212-687-8510
foreign affiliate: Geneva

PA Executive Search Group
780 Third Avenue
New York, NY 10017
212-759-0532
pe
foreign affiliates: Adelaide, Brisbane,
  Canberra, Melbourne

Carol Palmer Associates, Ltd.
237 Park Avenue, 21st floor
New York, NY 10017
212-551-3561
m

Parker Clark Associates
545 Fifth Avenue
New York, NY 10017
212-697-6996
a

Walter Parnes Management Co.
250 West 57th Street, Suite 1527
New York, NY 10019
212-333-3011
l

Robert Parrella Associates
666 Fifth Avenue
New York, NY 10103
212-541-4188
m; P

Bruce Payne Consultants, Inc.
666 Fifth Avenue
New York, NY 10019
212-581-5500

Al Perkell
18 East 41st Street, Room 900
New York, NY 10017
212-696-1330
R

The P & L Group
366 North Broadway
Jericho, NY 11753
516-938-7337
c; p

PRH Management
820 Second Avenue
New York, NY 10017
212-986-1313
a

E. J. Pritz & Associates
Box 246
Greenvale, NY 11548
516-626-3377
ph; R

The Psi-Com Group, Ltd.
250 West 57th Street
New York, NY 10019
212-245-7633
l

Quantum
124 East 40th Street, Suite 204
New York, NY 10016
212-286-0111
c; S

Queens Employment Service
29-27 41st Avenue
Long Island City, NY 11101
718-784-1010
e; M
NAPC

E. J. Rhodes Personnel Consultants
580 Fifth Avenue
New York, NY 10036
212-575-5990
a; b; g; R
NAPC

The Robert Group
130 East 67th Street
New York, NY 10021
212-737-8944
l

Alan Roberts & Associates, Inc.
101 Park Avenue
New York, NY 10178
212-490-1300
l

Rohn Rogers Associates
1140 Avenue of the Americas, 2nd floor
New York, NY 10036
212-921-1319
c

Mark Rosen
1 East 42nd Street, Suite 1036
New York, NY 10017
212-599-7900
re

John Rosen Associates
200 Park Avenue, Suite 303 East
New York, NY 10166
212-661-8009
b

Roth Young Associates
43 West 42nd Street
New York, NY 10036
212-869-0300
R

R.S.V.P. Agency
170 Broadway, Room 406
New York, NY 10038
212-964-5252
b

R.V.M. Associates, Inc.
701 Westchester Avenue, Suite 308 West
White Plains, NY 10604
914-328-7500
b; f; r

Salem Associates
60 East 42nd Street
New York, NY 10017
212-687-5380
b

Sales Recruiters International
984 North Broadway
Yonkers, NY 10701
914-423-8900
g; m; s
NAPC

George Saqqal & Company
501 Fifth Avenue, Suite 1411
New York, NY 10017
212-599-0844

Allan Sarn Associates, Inc.
420 Lexington Avenue, Suite 2559
New York, NY 10017
212-687-0600
pe

Saxon Morse Associates
P.O. Box 177, Northside Plaza
Pomona, NY 10970
914-362-1300
a; c; f; m

Scott, Rogers Associates
20 Squadron Boulevard
New City, NY 10956
914-638-4000
a; c; f; m

RitaSue Siegel Agency Inc.
60 West 55th Street
New York, NY 10019
212-586-4750
ar; m; pp; r; s

Daniel A. Silverstein Associates
162 East 64th Street
New York, NY 10021
212-759-4953
foreign affiliate: London

Silverstein Herman Company
708 Third Avenue
New York, NY 10017
212-687-3275
A

Skott/Edwards Consultants, Inc.
230 Park Avenue
New York, NY 10169
212-697-7640
g

Smith Hanley Associates, Inc.
60 East 42nd Street, Suite 1424
New York, NY 10165
212-687-9696
a; f; m

Smith's Fifth Avenue
17 East 45th Street
New York, NY 10017
212-682-5300
A; m

Source EDP
2 Corporate Park Drive, Room 409
White Plains, NY 10604
914-694-4400
c

Spencer Sanders Associates
500 Fifth Avenue
New York, NY 10175
212-944-7770
pp

Spencer Stuart & Associates
55 East 52nd Street, Suite 3100
New York, NY 10055
212-407-0200
g

Staat Personnel Agency, Inc.
233 Broadway
New York, NY 10279
212-967-2733
i

William Stack Associates, Inc.
230 Park Avenue, Suite 648
New York, NY 10017
212-490-0490

Paul Stafford Associates, Ltd.
45 Rochefeller Plaza
New York, NY 10111
212-765-7700
g
AESC

Staub, Warmbold & Associates, Inc.
655 Third Avenue
New York, NY 10017
212-599-4100

L. W. Stern Associates, Inc.
95 Madison Avenue, #1408
New York, NY 10016
212-725-1100
a; c; f; g; hr; m

Stonehill Management Consultants, Inc.
521 Fifth Avenue
New York, NY 10175
212-490-1776
a; c; f; m

Stone Management
104 East 40th Street
New York, NY 10016
212-599-0755
f

Streuli Personnel Agency
150 Broadway
New York, NY 10038
212-732-0158
b
NAPC

John S. Studwell Associates, Inc.
30 East 42nd Street
New York, NY 10017
212-867-5350

Joe Sullivan & Associates, Inc.
340 West 57th Street
New York, NY 10019
212-765-3330

Systech Organization
666 Fifth Avenue, 21st floor
New York, NY 10019
212-581-5790
b; c; g
NAPC

Taft
521 Fifth Avenue, 14th floor
New York, NY 10017
212-697-0100
a

Tallman Cohen Associates
200 Park Avenue, Suite 303 East
New York, NY 10166
212-972-1544

Tasa Inc.
875 Third Avenue, Suite 1501
New York, NY 10022
212-486-1490
g
AESC
foreign affiliates: Barcelona, Hong Kong,
Querétaro

F. L. Taylor & Co., Inc.
300 East 34th Street
New York, NY 10016
212-679-4674
a; f; g; o; R

Tecmark Associates, Inc.
450 Seventh Avenue
New York, NY 10123
212-947-6027
c; g; M; m; r

Thorndike Deland Associates
1440 Broadway
New York, NY 10018
212-840-8100

Traynor Associates, Ltd.
328 East Main Street
Rochester, NY 14604
716-325-6610
a; c; f; g

Trimbec
425 Electronic Parkway
Liverpool, NY 13088
315-451-4200
e
NAPC

TR Recruiters
139 Fulton Street
New York, NY 10038
212-732-3222
i

Wm. Van Nostrand & Associates
Box 621
Bronxville, NY 10708
914-337-4320
g

Van Reypen Enterprises, Ltd.
3100 Monroe Avenue, Professional Building
Rochester, NY 14618
716-586-8014

Vantage Careers, Inc.
180 East Post Road
White Plains, NY 10601
914-761-1120
a; c; f; pe
NAPC

Vinicombe, Nitka & Associates, Inc.
200 Garden City Plaza, Suite 124
Garden City, NY 11530
516-248-2120
g; pe

Viro Executive Search, Inc.
151 West 40th Street
New York, NY 10018
212-921-1616
R

Vision
2 West 45th Street, Suite 1508
New York, NY 10018
212-944-1818
S

V.V.R. Data Systems Ltd.
370 Lexington Avenue
New York, NY 10017
212-679-1403
c

Wachtel & Associates, Ltd.
200 East 42nd Street
New York, NY 10017
212-883-9577
a; f; g; m; pe

Judy Wald Agency, Inc.
110 East 59th Street
New York, NY 10022
212-421-6750
A

Don Waldron & Associates
450 Seventh Avenue, #1200
New York, NY 10123
212-532-5610
H; s
NAPC

Walz Associates
150 East 58th Street
New York, NY 10155
212-223-1182
l

Hank Ward Associates, Ltd.
8 Stanley Circle, Guptill Park
Latham, NY 12110
518-783-5145
g; s
NAPC

Ward Howell International, Inc.
99 Park Avenue
New York, NY 10016
212-697-3730
foreign affiliates: Amsterdam, Brussels,
 Dusseldorf, Sydney
g

Wareham Associates
184 East 75th Street
New York, NY 10021
212-988-5615

Hilton N. Wasserman & Associates, Inc.
200 Park Avenue
New York, NY 10166
212-661-8840

Webster Positions, Inc.
76 North Broadway
Hicksville, NY 11801
516-433-5656
c; e; M; r; S; T
NAPC

Wehinger Service, Inc.
150 Broadway, Suite 1306
New York, NY 10038
212-267-4540
b; g; i; se

Wells International
630 Third Avenue
New York, NY 10017
212-697-6120
l

Werbin Associates Executive Search, Inc.
521 Fifth Avenue, Suite 1749
New York, NY 10175
212-953-0909
c; e; m; o

Werner Management Consultants, Inc.
111 West 40th Street
New York, NY 10018
212-730-1280
g; M; m; o
foreign affiliate: Brussels

E. T. Wharton Associates
159 West 33rd Street
New York, NY 10001
212-695-0732
e; g; pp
NAPC

Whitehead Mann Limited
126 East 56th Street
New York, NY 10022
212-751-8989
foreign affiliate: London

J. W. Willard Associates, Inc.
100 East Washington Street, P.O. Box 1300
Syracuse, NY 13201
315-422-5111
a; f; m; pe

William H. Willis, Inc.
445 Park Avenue
New York, NY 10022
212-752-3456
f; H; S
AESC

Woodbury Personnel
375 North Broadway
Jericho, NY 11753
516-938-7910
a; b; g; i
NAPC

Charles Zabriskie Associates, Inc.
919 Third Avenue
New York, NY 10022
212-980-0700

Zachary & Sanders, Inc.
1 Penn Plaza, Suite 4507
New York, NY 10119
212-947-8877
m; pp; pu

NORTH CAROLINA

Action Personnel Services
1515 Mockingbird Lane, #100
Charlotte, NC 28209
704-527-9710
ar; M
NAPC

Beall Associates—Greensboro
P.O. Box 8915
Greensboro, NC 27419
919-299-5346
e; M
NAPC

Bell Professional Placement
Fullam Road, Box 198-A, Route 1
Arden, NC 28704
704-684-7302

The Borton-Wallace Co.
1209 1 Pack Square
Asheville, NC 28801
704-252-5831
M; S

Coleman Lew & Associates, Inc.
326 West 10th Street
Charlotte, NC 28202
704-377-0362
R

Dunhill of Greensboro
P.O. Box 9189
Greensboro, NC 27408
919-282-2400
g

Dunhill of Greenville
223 West 10th Street, Suite 101
Greenville, NC 27834
919-758-2107
b; e
NAPC

Dunhill of Hickory, N.C.
42 Third Street, NW, Suite 1
Hickory, NC 28601
704-322-7420
g
NAPC

Phil Ellis Associates
P.O. Box 58117
Raleigh, NC 27658
919-876-0945
e; g; H; T
NAPC

Executive Search
P.O. Box 220689
Charlotte, NC 28222
704-364-8315
b; e
NAPC

Graham & Associates Employee Consultants
2100-M West Cornwallis Drive
Greensboro, NC 27408
919-288-9330
a; b; e; M; m
NAPC

The Halyburton Company
Box 220812
Charlotte, NC 28222
704-372-0394
g

Hatchett & Cunningham Associates, Inc.
603 Hawthorne Lane
Charlotte, NC 28204
704-333-1215
NAPC

Nathaniel Hill & Associates, Inc.
4513 Creedmoor Road, Suite 503
Raleigh, NC 27612
919-787-6919
g

Charles Irish Co., Inc.
134 Mine Lake Court
Raleigh, NC 27609
919-847-3999
M; S
AESC

Locke & Associates
3145 NCNB Plaza
Charlotte, NC 28280
704-372-6600
C; e; f; M
AESC

Jon McRae & Associates, Inc.
2260 First Union Plaza
Charlotte, NC 28282
704-372-9151
f

Management South
1 Independence Center, Suite 1820
Charlotte, NC 28246
704-377-2497
g; s; S

Harold A. Miller Associates
Fearrington Post, Box 53
Pittsboro, NC 27312
919-542-5115
AESC

National Career Centers—USA
P.O. Box 447, 1830 Owen Drive, Suite L
Fayetteville, NC 28302
919-483-0413
e; g; M; m; s; T
NAPC

National Recruiters
1025 Dresser Court
Raleigh, NC 27609
919-872-2400
e; g
NAPC

Patton/Perry Associates
Tryon Center
Charlotte, NC 28284
704-376-4292
f; i; M; re; t

Professional Personnel Associates
4400 Morris Park Drive, Suite M
Charlotte, NC 28212
704-545-8904
e; M
NAPC

Robinson & McAulay
3100 NCNB Plaza
Charlotte, NC 28280
704-376-0059
AESC

Sanford Rose Associates—Charlotte
7401 Carmel Executive Park, #210
Charlotte, NC 28211
704-541-0093
e
NAPC

SHS International—Charlotte
310 Northwestern Bank Building
Charlotte, NC 28202
704-377-3414
s
NAPC

Sockwell & Hendrix
1 Tryon Center
Charlotte, NC 28284
704-372-1865
b; c; f; re

S.P. Associates
700 Kenilworth Avenue, Box 31335
Charlotte, NC 28231
704-372-7250
M; ph; pp

STO Fox Personnel Consultants
1834 Banking Street, P.O. Box 29269
Greensboro, NC 27429
919-378-9894
e
NAPC

Triangle Personnel Systems
1025 Dresser Court
Raleigh, NC 27609
919-872-1300
g
NAPC

VIP Personnel
3101 Guess Road, Suite C
Durham, NC 27705
919-471-6404
a; b
NAPC

VIP Personnel of Raleigh
104 Wind Chime Court, P.O. Box 19846
Raleigh, NC 27619
919-848-3800
e; M
NAPC

Wilson Personnel, Inc.
134 Montford Avenue
Asheville, NC 28801
704-258-3900
e

OHIO

The Adams Consulting Group
691 South Fifth Street
Columbus, OH 43206
614-431-1906
b; M; s; S
NAPC

Aim Executive Recruiting & Search
26250 Euclid Avenue, #805
Cleveland, OH 44132
216-261-6080
e; g; M
NAPC

Aim Executive Recruiting & Search
5151 Monroe Street, #120
Toledo, OH 43623
419-885-5044
a; e; g
NAPC

AMCR
50 Baker Boulevard, Suite 2
Akron, OH 44313
216-869-0777
e; T
NAPC

The Angus Group, Inc.
2337 Victory Parkway
Cincinnati, OH 45206
513-961-5575

Artgo, Inc.
1804 East Ohio Building
Cleveland, OH 44114
216-621-2535
g

Baldwin Associates
P.O. Box 9292
Cincinnati, OH 45209
513-281-0400
e
NAPC

Bason Associates, Inc.
401 Crescent Avenue
Cincinnati, OH 45215
513-761-9881
c; e; g

BCL Corporation
14701 Detroit
Cleveland, OH 44107
216-228-8787
a; f; g; m; pe

Bowden & Company, Inc.
5000 Rockside Road
Cleveland, OH 44131
216-447-1800
b; H; i; l; M; pp; R; S
AESC

Career Directions Services
160 Laurel Boulevard
Munroe Falls, OH 44626
216-867-8064
g
NAPC

CBS Personnel Services
One East Fourth Street, #1300
Cincinnati, OH 45202
513-651-1111
e; H; i; M; R
NAPC

CBS Personnel Services
1 First National Plaza, #1910
Dayton, OH 45402
513-222-2525
e; H; i; M; R; T
NAPC

Centennial Personnel
2211 Carew Tower
Cincinnati, OH 45202
513-381-4411
e; g
NAPC

Chemical Scientific Services
P.O. Box 27135
Columbus, OH 43227
614-863-5611
e; S
NAPC

Christopher, Drew & Associates, Inc.
28001 Chagrin Boulevard, Suite 311
Cleveland, OH 44122
216-831-7722
a; f; g; M; m; r

Clemo, Evans & Co., Inc.
33 River Street
Chagrin Falls, OH 44022
216-247-2030
foreign affiliate: London

Collis Associates, Inc.
6026 Winstead Road
Worthington, OH 43085
614-846-0171

Corporate Search
3540 Secor Road, #300
Toledo, OH 43606
419-535-1941
e
NAPC

Counsel Search Co.
124 North Summit Street, Suite 305
Toledo, OH 43604
419-242-8696
l

Cretney & Associates
6151 Wilson Mills Road
Cleveland, OH 44143
216-473-2700
a; f; M; m; pe; s

William N. Davis & Associates, Inc.
2401 Cleveland Road West
Huron, OH 44839
419-433-7600

DEI Executive Services
P.O. Box 9233
Cincinnati, OH 45209
513-321-9174
e; g; H; M
NAPC

Deveny & Associates
3864 Kettering Boulevard
Dayton, OH 45439
513-298-4955
e
NAPC

L. A. Elder & Associates
1700 East 13th Street, Suite 22P
Cleveland, OH 44114
216-241-4544

Laurence A. Elder & Associates, Inc.
1370 Ontario Street
Cleveland, OH 44113
216-241-4544
l

R. J. Evans & Associates, Inc.
26949 Chagrin Boulevard, Suite 300
Beachwood, OH 44122
216-464-5100
b; c; e; S

Fleming Associates
525 Metro Place North, Suite 100
Dublin, OH 43017
614-764-1587
a; f; M
AESC

Flowers and Associates
420 Holland Road, Box 538
Maumee, OH 43537
419-893-4816
e; M
NAPC

General Employment Enterprises, Inc.
88 East Broad Street, Suite 880
Columbus, OH 43229
614-228-5192
e

Granger & Associates, Inc.
8205 Weller Road, Suite 222
Cincinnati, OH 45242
513-489-6780
M; m; s

Grover & Associates
7870 Olentangy River Road
Worthington, OH 43085
614-885-8917
M

Hahn & Associates, Inc.
111 West First Street, Suite 510
Dayton, OH 45402
513-223-8130
a; e; f; g; m; pe
NAPC

Robert Half of Cincinnati
1 East Fourth Street
Cincinnati, OH 45202
513-621-7711
NAPC

Robert Half of Dayton
1 First National Plaza
Dayton, OH 45402
513-224-0600
a; b; e
NAPC

J. D. Hersey & Associates
3040 Riverside Drive, Suite 106
Columbus, OH 43221
614-766-5555
hr; m; re; r

Hogan Associates
26250 Euclid Avenue, Suite 811
Cleveland, OH 44132
216-289-1553
b; f

Richard Johns & Associates
23300 Chagrin Boulevard
Cleveland, OH 44122
216-464-2912
NAPC

Johnson Personnel
4557 Everhard Road, N.W.
Canton, OH 44718
216-494-8650
e; M
NAPC

KBK Management Associates
4800 Market Street
Youngstown, OH 44512
216-788-6508
e; M
NAPC

Kearney: Executive Search Group
1801 East Ninth Street
Cleveland, OH 44114
216-241-6880

Melvin Kent & Associates
88 East Broad Street
Columbus, OH 43215
614-228-1133
a; f; g; m; o

Lamalie Associates, Inc.
1900 East Ninth Street
Cleveland, OH 44114
216-694-3000
g
AESC

Management Recruiters International, Inc.
1015 Euclid Avenue
Cleveland, OH 44115
216-696-1122

Management Recruiters of Columbus
1395 Dublin-Granville Road, Room 430
Columbus, OH 43229
614-436-3200
c

Marvel Consultants
3690 Orange Place
Cleveland, OH 44122
216-292-2855
e

Million & Associates, Inc.
Carew Tower, Suite 1818
Cincinnati, OH 45202
513-579-8770

Monte Denbo Associates
644 Linn, #219
Cincinnati, OH 45203
513-241-4700
e
NAPC

C. B. Mueller Co.
550 East Fourth Street
Cincinnati, OH 45202
513-651-4700

National Recruiting Service
Box 75
Fairfield, OH 45014
513-894-8888
s; S

Perry Newcomb & Associates
7373 Beechmont Avenue
Cincinnati, OH 45230
513-232-2220
b; e; M; m; s

Professional Specialists
27801 Euclid Avenue
Euclid, OH 44132
216-289-9400
M; s
NAPC

Project-Career Inc.
4500 Rockside Road, Suite 130
Independence, OH 44131
216-447-1144
c

Psychological Assessments & Positions
650 South Detroit Avenue
Toledo, OH 43609
419-385-1781
g
NAPC

R.A.N. Associates, Inc.
140 Public Square, Park Building, Suite 804
Cleveland, OH 44114
216-696-6699

Renhil Group, Inc.
P.O. Box 527
Perrysburg, OH 43551
419-874-2203
M; T
NAPC

Romac & Associates of Columbus
150 East Broad Street
Columbus, OH 43215
614-221-7077
a; b; c

Roth Young of Columbus
6600 Busch Boulevard, #230
Columbus, OH 43229
614-846-2140
hr; R
NAPC

Sales Consultants International
1015 Euclid Avenue
Cleveland, OH 44115
216-696-1122
s

Sanford Rose Associates
25 East Boardman Street
Youngstown, OH 44503
216-744-4361
a; c; e; g
NAPC

Search Unlimited
3601 Green Road, Suite 312
Akron, OH 44122
216-831-7242
g
NAPC

Selective Search
4480 Refugee Road, #302
Columbus, OH 43232
614-863-0575
g
NAPC

S. K. Stewart & Associates
Executive Buidling, P.O. Box 40110
Cincinnati, OH 45240
513-771-2250
H; S
AESC

Teiper Personnel Service
4334 West Central Avenue #222
Toledo, OH 43615
419-531-5591
e; g
NAPC

The Thomas Group
5341 Acevedo Court
Columbus, OH 43220
614-457-2688
g
NAPC

Michael Thomas, Inc.
65 East Wilson Bridge
Worthington, OH 43085
614-846-0926
c

R. H. Warner Consulting
6124 Sunbury Road
Westerville, OH 43081
614-890-8405
e; g; M
NAPC

Western Reserve Associates
843 Ghent Square, Suite 5, Box 2510
Bath, OH 44210
216-666-0600
a; f; g; M; m; r

W. L. Wysong Associates
12700 Lake Avenue, Suite 1310
Lakewood, OH 44140
216-221-4550

The Zammataro Company
P.O. Box 339, 45 Milford Gardens
Hudson, OH 44236
216-656-1055
M

OKLAHOMA

M. Stephen Barrett & Associates
7633 East 63rd Place, Suite 240
Tulsa, OK 74133
918-250-7537
l

Gene Davis & Associates
P.O. Box 20325
Oklahoma City, OK 73156
405-495-7660
a; e; g; H; m; T
NAPC

Bob Delbridge & Associates
2233 West Lindsey Street
Norman, OK 73069
405-329-5463
l

Dunhill Personnel of N.E. Tulsa
10159 East 11th Street
Tulsa, OK 74128
918-832-8857
e; b
NAPC

J. Gifford, Inc.
5310 East 31st Street, Suite 514
Tulsa, OK 74135
918-665-2626
a; b; c; e; f
NAPC

International Search Corp.
3303 South Yale Avenue, #210
Tulsa, OK 74135
918-494-7936
e
NAPC

Lamont-Bruckner, Inc.
4629 South Harvard, Suite 104
Tulsa, OK 74135
918-745-0555
C; re

Lloyd Richards Personnel Service
507 South Main, Suite 502
Tulsa, OK 74103
918-582-5251
b; e; g; H; l; R; s; S; T

Management Search, Inc.
6161 North May Avenue, Suite 200-T
Oklahoma City, OK 73112
405-842-3173

Thomas E. Sowell
10960 South Houston
Jenks, OK 74037
918-299-4378
e; c; S

John Wylie Associates, Inc.
1727 East 71st Street
Tulsa, OK 74136
918-496-2100
a; C; f; g; M; pe

OREGON

Auguston & Associates
500 N.E. Multnomah, #670
Portland, OR 97232
503-239-6565
m; s
NAPC

Beck, Gerstenfeld & Associates
1367 North Pacific Highway
Woodburn, OR 97071
503-982-6410
e; g; M; m; S
NAPC

David Crowe Associates
P.O. Box 7292
Bend, OR 97708
503-389-2681
NAPC

Headhunters National
1750 S.W. Skyline Boulevard
Portland, OR 97221
503-297-1451
e; g
NAPC

Murphy Symonds and Stowell
1001 S.W. Fifth Avenue, #1110
Portland, OR 97204
503-242-2300
e; S
NAPC

O'Crowley & O'Toole Executive Search
14320 S.W. 100th
Portland, OR 97223
503-620-9757
b; i; l; re

R.M. Associates
7110 S.W. Fir Loop
Portland, OR 97223
503-620-5205
H; hr; M; m; s

Search Northwest & Affiliates
620 S.W. Fifth Avenue, #925
Portland, OR 97204
503-222-6461
e; S
NAPC

Wayne Executive Search
8305 S.E. Monterey, Suite 200
Portland, OR 97266
503-684-0066
e; s
NAPC

PENNSYLVANIA

Accounting Personnel Associates
239 Fourth Avenue, Suite 914
Pittsburgh, PA 15222
412-261-1015
a; g
NAPC

Alexander-Edward Associates, Inc.
1218 Chestnut Street, Suite 511
Philadelphia, PA 19107
215-923-2102
c; e; m; o; s

Allegheny County Bar Association
920 City-County Building
Pittsburgh, PA 15219
412-261-0518
l

Amansco Inc.
Amansco Building, 103 Smithfield Street
Pittsburgh, PA 15222
412-765-3710

Ames Personnel Service
3 Penn Center Plaza, Suite 623
Philadelphia, PA 19102
215-569-3737

The Andre Group, Inc.
Valley Forge Towers, Suite 108
King of Prussia, PA 19406
215-783-5100
a; f; g; M; m; pe

Atomic Personnel, Inc.
1518 Walnut Street
Philadelphia, PA 19102
215-735-4908
c; e; M; S; T
NAPC

Robert Becker & Co.
4088 Alpha Drive/Alpha Building
Allison Park, PA 15101
412-486-5553
b; g; M; m; pe

Becker Personnel Services
1 Bala Cynwyd Plaza
Bala Cynwyd, PA 19004
215-667-3010
a; i
NAPC

Belcher Personnel Consultants
5 Sentry Parkway East
Blue Bell, PA 19422
215-828-7700
e

Benham & Co., Inc.
P.O. Drawer A
Thorndale, PA 19372
215-383-1177
M; m

C. Berke & Associates
301 South Main Street, The Atrium
Doylestown, PA 18901
215-345-5600
e; M; m; r

E. J. Bettinger Co.
42 South 15th Street
Philadelphia, PA 19102
215-564-0700
a; f; M; m; o; pe

Bonner Gladney Associates
340 Forest Hills
Devon, PA 19333
215-688-0900
c; e; M; T
NAPC

The Bradbeer Co.
179 Hughes Road
Gulph Mills, PA 19406
215-293-1010
A; m

K. Robert Brian
1760 Market Street
Philadelphia, PA 19103
215-561-6550
a; b; c; i; M; pe

Robert J. Bushee & Associates, Inc.
1370 Washington Pike
Bridgeville, PA 15017
412-257-2300
a; e; f; g
NAPC

Daniel Cades & Associates
904 The Penn Square Building
Philadelphia, PA 19107
215-844-1131
g; M; m; pe; T

Cantor & Co., Inc.
Suburban Station Building
Philadelphia, PA 19103
215-563-9646
f; g; o; pe

Career Consultants
2555 South Queen Street
York, PA 17402
717-741-4841
e
NAPC

CHASE, Inc.
950 County Line Road
Rosemont, PA 19010
215-525-6630
H; S

William J. Christopher Associates, Inc.
307 North Walnut Street
West Chester, PA 19380
215-696-4397
A; R

Robert Clifton Associates, Inc.
200 Fleet Street, Suite 5045
Pittsburgh, PA 15220
412-922-1900
S

CMA
P.O. Box 184
Narberth, PA 19072
215-664-1756
e
NAPC

Cole, Warren & Long, Inc.
2 Penn Center Plaza, Suite 1020
Philadelphia, PA 19102
215-563-0701
b; c; f; g; i; M; m; ph

Corporate Recruiters, Inc.
613 West Cheltenham Ave., Suite 100
Philadelphia, PA 19126
215-782-1200
a; f; g; M; m; r
NAPC

Corporate Staffing Group
Barn Office Center/2 Village Road
Horsham, PA 19044
215-659-7600
e; g; M; m; T
NAPC

Craft Kraybill Bender
1 Oliver Plaza
Pittsburgh, PA 15222
412-288-0825
l

The Data Base
19 Rockhill Road
Bala Cynwyd, PA 19004
215-667-6865
c

N. Dean Davic Associates
400 Penn Center Boulevard, Suite 645
Pittsburgh, PA 15235
412-824-8100
a; e; g; M
NAPC

Deakyne Associates
1700 Walnut Street
Philadelphia, PA 19103
215-735-8357
b
NAPC

Peter Depasquale Associates
454 Pine Street, Suite A
Williamsport, PA 17701
717-326-1736
NAPC

Diversified Search, Inc.
2 Girard Plaza
Philadelphia, PA 19102
215-732-6666

Drew International Corp.
2000 Valley Forge Towers, #130
King of Prussia, PA 19406
215-783-5900
e

Dunhill Personnel Service
1420 Walnut Street, #1207
Philadelphia, PA 19102
215-735-0505
f; i; M
NAPC

Carolyn Evans Associates
P.O. Box 566
Plymouth Meeting, PA 19462
215-828-7080
a; b
NAPC

Executive Careers, Inc.
15 East Ridge Pike
Conshohocken, PA 19428
215-825-9295
c; o

Executive Finders
414 Lawyers Building
Pittsburgh, PA 15219
412-391-4555
s; S

Executive Search Company
Second Avenue & Fayette Street
Conshohocken, PA 19428
215-825-6710
a; f; M; m; pe

Financial Search
Riverfront Center, Suite 630
Pittsburgh, PA 15222
412-288-0505
a; b
NAPC

Fortune Personnel Consultants
1528 Walnut Street, Suite 2008
Philadelphia, PA 19102
215-546-9490

Fox-Morris Associates, Inc.
123 South Broad Street, Suite 2401
Philadelphia, PA 19109
215-561-6300
b; e; f; l

Fulton, Longshore & Associates, Inc.
349 Lancaster Avenue
Haverford, PA 19041
215-649-4101
H; pe

Garofolo, Curtiss & Company
326 West Lancaster Avenue
Ardmore, PA 19003
215-896-5080
H; i; n
AESC

Robert Gee & Associates
300 Penn Center Boulevard
Pittsburgh, PA 15235
412-823-9060
s
NAPC

General Employment Enterprises, Inc.
8 Penn Center, Suite 333
Philadelphia, PA 19103
215-564-3101
e

General Placement Service
121 North Main Street
Greensburg, PA 15601
412-836-2300
b; g; i

Graphic Search Associates, Inc.
P.O. Box 373
Newton Square, PA 19073
215-359-1234
pp

Growth Placement Associates, Inc.
Box 38, Creek Road, U.S. Route 282
Downingtown, PA 19335
215-269-5791
ar; e; H

Robert Half of Philadelphia, Inc.
Maschellmac Office Complex, First Avenue
King of Prussia, PA 19406
215-337-7300
f

Robert Half of Philadelphia, Inc.
2000 Market Street, Suite 706
Philadelphia, PA 19103
215-568-4580
f

Robert Half of Philadelphia, Inc.
5 Neshaminy Interplex, Suite 201
Trevose, PA 19047
215-244-1870
f

Robert Harkins Associates
1433 West Main Street, Box 236
Ephrata, PA 17522
717-733-9664
e; M
NAPC

T. G. Harper & Co., Inc.
900 Lafayette Building
Philadelphia, PA 19106
215-922-1000
f; i; re

Heberling Personnel
P.O. Box 2332
Harrisburg, PA 17105
717-763-8222
a; e; f; M; p; S
NAPC

J. L. Hoglund Co., Inc.
1425 Freeport Road
Natrona Heights, PA 15065
412-224-2004
c; e; g

Horizon Personnel
P.O. Box 3003
York, PA 17402
717-755-0955
e; M
NAPC

Hospitality Personnel, Inc.
Davis & Oakwood Roads
Valley Forge, PA 19481
215-783-5200
a; f; g; H; hr; pe

Insearch
1218 Chestnut Street, Suite 407
Philadelphia, PA 19107
215-928-9977
i

Insurance Personnel Recruiters
CP Mills Building, Seventh & Ranstead
Philadelphia, PA 19106
215-629-1703
i

D. Jackson and Associates
20 Briarcrest Square
Hershey, PA 17033
717-533-3213
b; R; s
NAPC

Nancy Jackson, Inc.
Wyoming Avenue & Spruce Street, 4th floor
Scranton, PA 18503
717-346-8711
a; b; e; m; r
NAPC

Kenneth James Associates
207 Buck Road
Holland, PA 18966
215-322-5080
b; i
NAPC

Jefferson-Ross Associates, Inc.
2 Penn Center Plaza
Philadelphia, PA 19102
215-564-5322

J.M. & Company
Box 285
Wayne, PA 19087
215-964-0200
g; m; r

Kelly & Thomas Associates, Inc.
225 East City Lane Avenue, Suite 101
Bala Cynwyd, PA 19004
215-667-3570
c; e

Keltech Executive Search
P.O. Box 123, 610 Crum Creek Road
Wallingford, PA 19086
215-874-4477
H

Ketchum, Inc. Executive Recruiting Service
1 Chatham Center
Pittsburgh, PA 15219
412-281-1481
n

Kiley-Owen Associates, Inc.
1218 Chestnut Street, Suite 510
Philadelphia, PA 19107
215-923-0740
c; g; M; m; pe

Kogen Personnel
202 Fisher Building
Johnstown, PA 15901
814-536-7571
a; b
NAPC

D. A. Kreuter Associates
1700 Walnut Street, Suite 1121
Philadelphia, PA 19103
215-546-1369
a; c; f; i; l; n

LaMonte Owens & Co., Inc.
Box 5894
Philadelphia, PA 19128
215-248-0500

Jack B. Larsen & Associates
334 West Eighth Street
Erie, PA 16502
814-459-3725
b

Lee Calhoon & Co., Inc.
Birchrun Road, Box 201
Birchrunville, PA 19421
215-469-9000
a; f; g; H; m; pe

Linda Lee Search Consultants
1518 Walnut Street, Suite 1304
Philadelphia, PA 19102
215-723-1100
i

Legal Placements, Inc.
1700 Walnut Street
Philadelphia, PA 19103
215-735-1190
l

George P. Lyon Associates
Broad & Mechanic Streets
Doylestown, PA 18901
215-345-5161
b; f; i; M; re; R

McNichol Associates
Box 534
Philadelphia, PA 19105
215-922-4142
ar; c; C; e

Main Line Personnel Services, Inc.
111 President Boulevard, P.O. Drawer 526
Bala Cynwyd, PA 19004
215-667-1820
c; C; e; M

George R. Martin Executive Search
Box 673
Doylestown, PA 18901
215-348-8146
ph; pp

Masland Management Services
239 West Highland Avenue
Philadelphia, PA 19118
215-247-5300
g; H; M; m; pe

MBH Associates, Inc.
1616 Walnut Street
Suite 711
Philadelphia, PA 19103
215-735-7060
e

Midland Consultants—Pittsburgh
100 West Mall
Carnegie, PA 15106
412-344-4244
g; m
NAPC

Ann B. Moran Associates, Inc.
805 East Willow Grove Avenue
Suite 2C
Philadelphia, PA 19118
215-233-4060

National Career Services
P.O. Box 2833
Harrisburg, PA 17105
717-652-1200
e; M
NAPC

O'Shea System of Employment
12 South 12th Street
Suite 1113
Philadelphia, PA 19107
215-925-7272
a; b; m

Pappas Coates & Del Vecchio
7 Wynnewood Road
Wynnewood, PA 19096
215-642-6900

Personnel Resources Organization
1315 Walnut Street
Suite 1718
Philadelphia, PA 19107
215-735-7500
l

Philadelphia Search Group, Inc.
1422 Chestnut Street
Suite 800
Philadelphia, PA 19102
215-864-9046
m; s

Phoenix Personnel Services
P.O. Box 1733
Harrisburg, PA 17105
717-763-7871
a; b; e; i
NAPC

Pratt Placement Service
1547 Pratt Street, Suite 300
Philadelphia, PA 19124
215-537-1212
e
NAPC

Probe Technology
570 West DeKalb Pike, Suite 215
King of Prussia, PA 19406
215-337-8544
e; g; M; r
NAPC

Professional Recruiters
7 Bala Avenue
Philadelphia, PA 19004
215-667-9355

Provident Personnel Consultants
P.O. Box 72
Prospect Park, PA 19076
215-586-5888
a; e
NAPC

Quinlivan & Company
137 East Market Street
York, PA 17401
717-846-7188
a; e
NAPC

Romac & Associates
1700 Market Street, Suite 2702
Philadelphia, PA 19103
215-568-6810
b

Roman & Associates
100 Residential Boulevard
Bala Cynwyd, PA 19004
215-667-7351
a; b; c; s

Romeo Associates
900 East Eighth Avenue, Suite 300
King of Prussia, PA 19406
215-337-1560

Sanmar Staffing Consultants
1211 Chestnut Street, #200
Philadelphia, PA 19107
215-563-9399
e
NAPC

Schneider, Hill & Spangler, Inc.
1346 Chestnut Street, Suite 710
Philadelphia, PA 19107
215-732-9560
s

Science Center
550 Pinetown Road
Fort Washington, PA 19034
215-643-3700
e
NAPC

SCL Executive Search
1600 Market Street, Suite 1412
Philadelphia, PA 19103
215-988-1700
a

Sinclair & Potts Associates, Inc.
120 Hardwick Drive
Pittsburgh, PA 15235
412-823-6615
a; f; M; pe

David Solol Personnel Consultant
P.O. Box 342
Kutztown, PA 19530
215-683-5500
e; M
NAPC

Soltis Management Services
876 Brower Road
Radnor, PA 19087
215-687-4200
a; f; M; pe; T

Speciality Consultants, Inc.
Gateway Towers, Suite 2710
Pittsburgh, PA 15222
412-355-8200
c; C; re

Sturm Burrows & Company
1420 Walnut Street
Philadelphia, PA 19102
215-546-4111
a; e; g
NAPC

Successmove, Inc.
P.O. Box 11
Blue Bell, PA 19422
215-542-0720
M; m; o; r

Systems Personnel
115 West State Street
Media, PA 19063
215-565-8880
g; T
NAPC

Technical Placement, Inc.
500 Valley Forge Plaza
King of Prussia, PA 19406
215-337-4030
e

Tomsett Consulting Associates, Inc.
402 Frick Building
Pittsburgh, PA 15219
412-885-9200

K. W. Tunnell Co., Inc.
1150 First Avenue, Valley Forge Plaza
King of Prussia, PA 19406
215-337-0820
M

Harry F. Twomey Associates
1601 Walnut Street, Suite 1415
Philadelphia, PA 19102
215-563-6484
M; m; pe; r

United Consultants
1508 East Market Street
York, PA 17403
717-846-2009
a; e; g; M
NAPC

Gordon Wahls Company
610 East Baltimore Pike, Box 905
Media, PA 19063
215-565-0800
g

Gordon Wahls Company
797 Harrison Road
Villanova, PA 19085
215-565-0800
g; M; pp; pu; s; S
NAPC

Albert J. Walsh & Associates
The Commons West, Suite 21
Newtown, PA 18940
215-968-0707
g; M; o; r

Whittlesey & Associates
300 South High Street
West Chester, PA 19380
215-436-6500
m; s

Worlco Computer
1600 Market Street
Philadelphia, PA 19103
215-636-1630

PUERTO RICO

Careers/Inc.
1919 Banco Popular Center
Hato Rey, PR 00918
809-764-2298
NAPC

J. V. DeMoss & Associates
Banco Popular Center
Hato Rey, PR 00918
809-763-5176

Management Recruiters of Puerto Rico, Inc.
416 Ponce de Leon Avenue, Suite 614
Hato Rey, PR 00918
809-753-9015
e

RHODE ISLAND

Bay Search Group
112 Union Street, #510
Providence, RI 02903
401-751-2870
c; f; g; m; T
NAPC

Becker Associates
126 Congdon Avenue
North Kingstown, RI 02852
401-737-9054
e; M
NAPC

ERA Placements
509 Armistice Boulevard
Pawtucket, RI 02861
401-724-3871
g; i; m
NAPC

Fortune of Providence
10 Dorrance Street
Providence, RI 02903
401-351-0200
a; e; M
NAPC

Greene Personnel Consultants
809-811 Fleet National Bank Building
Providence, RI 02903
401-272-4472
A; m; R
NAPC

Robert Half
900 Turks Head Building
Providence, RI 02903
401-274-8700
a; c; f

New England Consultants
156 Centerville Road, P.O. Box 6756
Warwick, RI 02887
401-732-4650
e; M
NAPC

Peterson Personnel Recruiters
500 Jefferson Boulevard
Warwick, RI 02886
401-732-3405
e; M
NAPC

Positions, Inc.
10 Orms Way
Providence, RI 02904
401-273-7600
a; b; f; g; i; p

Retail Recruiters
245 Waterman Street, Suite 303
Providence, RI 02906
401-421-9200
g; R
NAPC

Schattle Personnel Consultants, Inc.
2845 Post Road
Warwick, RI 02886
401-739-0500
b; c; e; f; S

Storti Associates, Inc.
4060 Post Road
Warwick, RI 02886
401-885-3100

Varone Personnel
23 Broad Street, Box 797
Pawtucket, RI 02860
401-725-4400
i; T
NAPC

Wellesley, Ltd.
1 Jackson Walkway, Suite 21
Providence, RI 02903
401-273-5435
b; g; se
NAPC

SOUTH CAROLINA

M. L. Alber Associates
1900 Broad River Road
Columbia, SC 29210
803-798-5480
e; m
NAPC

Atlantic Professional Recruiters
517 North Limeston Street
Gaffney, SC 29340
803-487-5141
a; g
NAPC

Beall Associates and Greenville
P.O. Box 4177
Greenville, SC 29608
803-232-8139
e; M
NAPC

Excel Personnel
20 West Antrim Drive
Greenville, SC 29607
803-233-2546
a; e
NAPC

Finley & Co.
33 Villa Road, Suite 400
Greenville, SC 29615
803-233-1675
A; g; m; s

Thomas Glover Associates
200 East Main Street
North Charleston, SC 29301
803-585-9890
e
NAPC

Harvey Personnel
205 North Pine Street, P.O. Box 1931
North Charleston, SC 29304
803-582-5616
a; e; g; H
NAPC

Keshlear Associates
3402 Fernandina Road
Aiken, SC 29210
803-772-9670
a; b; hr; i; s
NAPC

McCulloch and Company
P.O. Box 10211
Greenville, SC 29603
803-232-9921
e; T
NAPC

Nationwide Recruiters
3710 Landmark Drive, #111
Columbia, SC 29204
803-738-1790
H
NAPC

Personnel, Inc.
2999 Pine Street
Spartanburg, SC 29302
803-573-7427
a; c; i; M; m; s
NAPC

Walter Phillips Associates
P.O. Box 6613
Greenville, SC 29606
803-297-0000
g
NAPC

Phillips Resource Group
108 Edinburgh Court
Greenville, SC 29606
803-271-6350
a; f; M; m; pp; r
NAPC

Piedmont Personnel Consultants
317 Piedmont East Building
Greenville, SC 29615
803-233-4103
e; g
NAPC

Power Services
2162 Credit Union Lane, #504
North Charleston, SC 29406
803-572-3000
e; M
NAPC

Snelling & Snelling
600 Columbia Avenue
Lexington, SC 29072
803-359-7644 ·
e; s
NAPC

Southern Recruiters & Consultants
215 Park Avenue, S.E., P.O. Box 2745
Aiken, SC 29802
803-648-7834
e
NAPC

R. M. Whiteside Company
P.O. Box 2136
Hilton Head Island, SC 29925
803-681-5204
l

TENNESSEE

Austin-Allen Co.
1035 Oakwood Road
Memphis, TN 38119
901-761-4900
a; f; M; o; pe

Executive Personnel Consultants
606 South Mendenhall
Memphis, TN 38117
901-761-4560
b; c; e; f; M; m; s; S

Fleming Associates
6260 Poplar Avenue, P.O. Box 17521
Memphis, TN 38111
901-767-2161
a; f; M

The Hamilton/Ryker Company
P.O. Box 589
Martin, TN 38237
901-587-3161
e; M
NAPC

Randall Howard & Associates, Inc.
5353 Flowering Peach Drive
Memphis, TN 38115
901-365-2700
a; c; f
NAPC

Horizon Personnel
120 Gilbert Drive
Franklin, TN 37064
615-790-7902
e; M
NAPC

Jean's Personnel
5100 Poplar Avenue, Suite 2731
Memphis, TN 38137
901-682-3700
a; m

Quarles & Associates
2670 Union Avenue, #1206
Memphis, TN 38112
901-324-1200
b; g

Rasmussen & Associates
P.O. Box 5429
Kingsport, TN 37663
615-239-5125
e
NAPC

Allan Schoenberger & Associates
2129 Germantown Road South, Suite 212
Memphis, TN 38138
901-755-0441
m; s
NAPC

Southwestern Placement
P.O. Box 820
Memphis, TN 37202
615-790-4136
g; s

TEXAS

Accounting & Financial Recruiters
3000 Post Oak Boulevard, #1610
Houston, TX 77056
713-965-9975
a; f

Accounting Resources International
2212 Arlington Downs, Suite 203
Arlington, TX 76011
817-649-5272
a

Accounting Resources International
3131 Turtle Creek, Suite 222
Dallas, TX 75219
214-788-0044
a

Accounting Resources International
17629 El Camino Real, Suite 401
Houston, TX 77058
713-486-7037
a

Ackerman Johnson Career Consultants, Inc.
2525 North Loop West, Suite 130
Houston, TX 77008
713-863-0090
s

Dina Alessio & Associates
1 Northpark East, Suite 330
Dallas, TX 75231
214-373-7688
c

Charles P. Aquavella & Associates
3736 Princess Lane
Dallas, TX 75229
214-351-6500
C; re

ASC & Co.
1360 Post Oak Boulevard, Suite 800
Houston, TX 77056
713-965-0487
a; b; f; l; S

AY/ERC
2121 San Jacinto Street, Suite 700
Dallas, TX 75221
214-969-8768
g
AESC

Babich & Associates
6060 North Central Expressway, #544
Dallas, TX 75206
214-361-5735
a; e; s
NAPC

Babich & Associates
1 Summit Avenue, 602 Mallick Tower
Fort Worth, TX 76102
817-336-7261
e; s
NAPC

R. B. Bentsen Company
6102 East Mockingbird Lane, Suite 104
Dallas, TX 75214
214-821-3909
l

Bott & Associates, Inc., Engineering
10800 Richmond Avenue, Suite 216
Houston, TX 77042
713-782-9814
e

Brennan & Associates, Inc.
4020 McEwan Road, Suite 105
Dallas, TX 75234
214-980-0779
g; M; m; r

Bundy-Stewart Associates, Inc.
12800 Hillcrest, Suite 123
Dallas, TX 75230
214-458-0626
a; g
NAPC

Caldwell & Associates, Inc.
1201 Elm Street, Suite 2929
Dallas, TX 75270
214-698-9991
l

The Caldwell Partners International
2 Houston Center, Suite 610
Houston, TX 77010
713-757-1958
e; g; S
foreign affiliate: Canada

Cambridge Consulting Group
2400 Augusta, Suite 240
Houston, TX 77057
713-780-0001
g

William T. Campbell & Associates, Inc.
916 Esperson Building
Houston, TX 77002
713-224-0974

Career Resource Associates, Inc.
P.O. Box 8038
Houston, TX 77288
713-757-0847
m; pe

Andrew B. Carr & Associates
P.O. Box 5631
San Angelo, TX 76902
915-942-9109
e; g; S

Carrie & Co. Placement
1309 Main Street, Suite 1302
Dallas, TX 75202
214-741-4196
l

T. Don Clark
1701 River Run, Suite 307
Fort Worth, TX 76107
817-334-0400
b

T. Don Clark
3400 Bissonnet, Suite 270
Houston, TX 77005
713-661-2256
b

COMPRO Search, Inc.
3930 Kirby, Suite 205
Houston, TX 77098
713-529-4494
c

Continental Personnel
9494 S.W. Freeway, Suite 350
Houston, TX 77074
713-777-3821

Damon & Associates, Inc.
7515 Greenville Avenue, Suite 900
Dallas, TX 75231
214-696-6990
m; s

Data Search International
11111 Katy Freeway, #370
Houston, TX 77079
713-461-5041
c

John Davidson & Associates
3198 Royal Lane, Suite 100
Dallas, TX 75229
214-352-7800
a; g; R
NAPC

Davies Associates International, Ltd.
P.O. Box 218337
Houston, TX 77218
713-496-9551
a; f; g; M; s

Dunhill of Austin
1106 Clayton Lane, Suite 280W
Austin, TX 78723
512-458-5271
a; g
NAPC

Dunhill Personnel—Corpus Christi
5155 Flynn Parkway, #204
Corpus Christi, TX 78411
512-854-1424
a; e
NAPC

Eastman & Beaudine, Inc.
5400 LBJ Freeway, Suite 944
Dallas, TX 75240
214-661-5520

EDP Computer Services, Inc.
4600 Post Oak Place, Suite 204
Houston, TX 77027
713-739-8210
c

EMJAY Computer Careers
1824 Portsmouth
Houston, TX 77098
713-529-5000
c

The Energists
10260 Westheimer, #110
Houston, TX 77042
713-781-6881

Ensminger, Inc.
1800 West Loop South, Suite 1580
Houston, TX 77027
713-960-9604
l

Esquire, Ltd. Legal Executive Search
1100 Richmond, Suite 6
Houston, TX 77006
713-521-3951
l

ExecuSource International
4120 Rio Bravo, Suite 106
El Paso, TX 79902
915-542-4708
M; S

Fingers Personnel Office
4001 Gulf Freeway
Houston, TX 77001
713-221-4590
c

First Recruiting Group
872 Bettina, 330
Houston, TX 77024
713-932-1110
M; m; s

First Word Placement Service
147055 Preston
Dallas, TX 75240
214-880-0231
a; f; i
foreign affiliate: Geneva

Fleming Associates
9575 Katy Freeway, Suite 225
Houston, TX 77024
713-465-3791
a; f; M

Fox & Fleischer
1131 Rockingham Drive, Suite 110
Richardson, TX 75080
214-680-8700
a; f; pe

General Employment Enterprises, Inc.
8350 North Central
Dallas, TX 75206
214-987-0762
c

Graham & Associates, Inc.
13601 Preston Road, Suite 444E
Dallas, TX 75240
214-980-1998
c; m; S; T

Robert Half Personnel
2 Northpark
Dallas, TX 75231
214-363-3300
a; c

Haskell & Stern Associates, Inc.
1215 Country Club Lane, Suite 105
Fort Worth, TX 76112
817-332-6771
a; b; f; g; i; M; m; pe; re
AESC

Hayman & Company
2101 Skyway Tower, Southland Center
Dallas, TX 75201
214-742-3776
a; f; g; M; o; pe

Jack Holloway & Associates
1 Allen Center, Suite 1000
Houston, TX 77002
713-757-1791
l

Howard Associates
6350 LBJ Freeway
Dallas, TX 75240
214-233-9012
b

Jack Hurst & Associates, Inc.
First City Bank Center, Suite 706
Richardson, TX 75080
214-231-5075
c; f; M

Hyde Danforth & Co.
1145 Empire Central Place, Suite 200
Dallas, TX 75247
214-691-5966

Insurance Recruiters, Inc.
6060 North Central, #470
Dallas, TX 75206
214-361-9323
i

Intersearch Inc.
2537 South Gessner, Suite 203
Houston, TX 77063
713-977-0500
c

Interview Legal Search
2525 North Loop West, Suite 304
Houston, TX 77008
713-864-9898
l

J. L. Jordan Associates
14114 Dallas Parkway, Suite 250
Dallas, TX 75240
214-385-8251
C; M

Kenneth C. Kern Personnel Services
4444 Richmond Avenue
Houston, TX 77027
713-621-8010
e

Ketchum, Inc., Executive Recruiting Service
914 1 Main Place
Dallas, TX 75250
214-741-4591
n

King Computer Search
9221 LBJ Street, #208
Dallas, TX 75238
214-238-1021
c; T

Lamalie Associates, Inc.
1201 Elm Street
Dallas, TX 75270
214-747-1994
AESC

Largent Parks & Partners, Inc.
13601 Preston Road, Suite 402 East
Dallas, TX 75240
214-980-0047
a; f; i; re

Lineback Associates
5720 LBJ Freeway, Suite 101
Dallas, TX 75240
214-458-8100
a; c; e; f; pe

Lineback Associates
3535 Briarpark, Suite 105
Houston, TX 77042
713-789-2399
a; c; e; f; pe

Robert Lowell Associates, Inc.
12201 Merit Drive, Suite 680
Dallas, TX 75251
214-233-2270

Lucas Associates, Inc.
2525 North Loop West, Suite 306
Houston, TX 77008
713-880-2932
e

Patricia McDonald Legal Service Consultants, Inc.
717 North Harwood Street
Dallas, TX 75210
214-373-8173
l

Patricia McDonald Legal Search Consultants
2100 United Bank Plaza
Houston, TX 77002
713-789-0548
l

McHan Personnel
P.O. Box 27701–120
Houston, TX 77027
713-439-0177
c

McKeen Melancon & Company
4560 Belt Line Road, Suite 330
Dallas, TX 75234
214-231-9962

Pete Massarini & Associates, Employment Consultants
2630 Fountainview, Suite 400
Houston, TX 77057
713-977-0789
c; e

Bennett Munson, Inc.
4820 East University
Odessa, TX 79762
915-332-6823
NAPC

Arthur Newman Associates, Inc.
4615 S.W. Freeway, Suite 715
Houston, TX 77027
713-439-0080
M; S

The Niedhart Group, Inc.
P.O. Box 855175
Richardson, TX 75085
214-783-1905

Nobel, Albach & Associates
Box 18107
Dallas, TX 75218
214-321-0170
l

Omnisearch
9330 LBJ Parkway
Suite 300
Dallas, TX 75243
214-231-2585
c; e

Paul & Turner, Inc.
7616 LBJ Freeway
Suite 707
Dallas, TX 75251
214-386-9991

Perry-White & Associates, Inc.
8131 LBJ Freeway
Suite 650
Dallas, TX 75240
214-231-1800
e; S

Perry-White & Associates, Inc.
7324 S.W. Freeway
Suite 290
Houston, TX 77074
713-270-6800
e; S

PM Legal Search Consultants
717 North Harwood Street
Dallas, TX 75201
214-377-8173
l

PM Legal Search Consultants
5959 Westheimer
Suite 225
Houston, TX 77057
713-789-0548
l

Prescott Legal Search
801 Wesleyan Tower 24 Greenway Plaza
Houston, TX 77046
713-439-0911
l

Professional Career Placements
P.O. Box 170486
Arlington, TX 76003
817-572-3170
e; M; p
NAPC

Proquest Corporation
P.O. Box 680685
Houston, TX 77268
713-537-2244
c

Purcell Group Management Consultants
2401 Fountainview, Suite 416
Houston, TX 77057
713-266-8501
e; g; s; S

Railey & Associates
5702 Westerham Place
Houston, TX 77069
713-444-4346
l

Paul R. Ray & Co., Inc.
1208 Ridglea Bank Building
Fort Worth, TX 76116
817-731-4111

ROMAC Personnel Consultants
600 Travis, Suite 3751
Houston, TX 77002
713-227-7700
a; e; f

Roth Young
2525 North Loop West, Suite 323
Houston, TX 77008
713-868-1631
A; R

Ryan & Associates
27100 Lana Lane
Conroe, TX 77385
713-367-2714
a

Sadovsky Perry & Associates
3500 Oaklawn Avenue, Suite 400
Dallas, TX 75219
214-521-6860

Robert Sage & Associates
1212 North Elm Street, Suite F
Denton, TX 76201
817-382-1568
c

Ron Schmidt Personnel Service
9801 Westheimer, #302
Houston, TX 77042
713-880-0767
i

Scientific Placement, Inc.
Box 19949
Houston, TX 77224
713-496-6100
e; S
NAPC

Robert Shields & Associates
P.O. Box 580056
Houston, TX 77258
713-488-7961

John R. Stephens & Associates
711 Polk Street, Suite 1100
Houston, TX 77002
713-651-0067
g; M; m; o; r
NAPC

Summit Search Specialists
14825 St. Mary's
Houston, TX 77079
713-497-5840
i

Sumrall Personnel Consultants
4020 McEwen, Suite 123
Dallas, TX 75234
214-387-4801
a; e; T

J. Robert Thompson Co., Inc.
2200 West Loop South, Suite 800
Houston, TX 77027
713-627-1940
a; b; c; e; f; M; r

Vance Employment Service
Barfield Building, Suite 917
Amarillo, TX 79101
806-372-3456
g
NAPC

Denis P. Walsh & Associates, Inc.
2190 North Loop West, Suite 308
Houston, TX 77018
713-957-8480
c; C; e

Ward Howell International, Inc.
1601 Elm Street, Thanksgiving Tower
Dallas, TX 75201
214-749-0099

Watkins & Associates
7322 S.W. Freeway, Suite 620
Houston, TX 77074
713-777-5261
a; c; i

Wells International
11 Greenway Plaza, Suite 1904
Houston, TX 77046
713-840-7700
l

R. L. Wolff & Associates
2630 Fountainview
Houston, TX 77057
713-266-9921
c

Youngs & Co.
12750 Merit Drive, Suite 222
Dallas, TX 75251
214-458-2222

UTAH

Professional Recruiters of Salt Lake
220 East 3900 South
Salt Lake City, UT 84107
801-268-9940
a

STM Associates
39 Exchange Place
Salt Lake City, UT 84111
801-531-6500
c; e; f; M; S

VIRGINIA

Ardelle Associates
5101-1 Backlick Road
Annandale, VA 22003
703-642-9050
a

Brault & Associates, Ltd.
11703 Bowman Green Drive
Reston, VA 22090
703-471-0920
S

The Corporate Connection, Ltd.
4905 Radford Avenue
Richmond, VA 23230
804-359-2544
a; f; g; M; r
NAPC

Hyde & Seek
6 Newland Court
Sterling, VA 22170
703-450-2333
c

Key Financial Personnel
1655 North Fort Myer Drive, Suite 700
Rosslyn, VA 22209
703-528-1010
a

The McCormick Group, Inc.
1911 Fort Myer Drive
Arlington, VA 22209
703-841-1700
l

Management Search, Inc.
3273 Victor Circle
Annandale, VA 22003
703-556-0606
a; c; e; f

MD Resources, Inc.
12774 Flat Meadow Lane
Herndon, VA 22071
703-476-5529
g; H

The NRI Group
8133 Leesburg Pike, 220
Vienna, VA 22180
703-442-0320
a; f; g; o

Professional Search
4900 Leesburg Parkway
Alexandria, VA 22312
703-671-0010
b; c

Don Richard
7929 Jones Branch Drive, #400
McLean, VA 22102
703-379-4445
a

Romac
1600 Wilson Boulevard, Suite 805
Arlington, VA 22209
703-525-5160
b

Melissa S. Sacks Legal Search Firm
354 Woodburn Road, Suite 33
Annandale, VA 22003
703-560-3083
l

Source Finance
2070 Chain Bridge Road, Suite 375
Tysons Corner, VA 22180
703-448-6000
f

Staffing Consultants
5350 Shawnee Road
Alexandria, VA 22312
703-642-3232
c

Staffing Consultants
8027 Leesburg Pike
Vienna, VA 22180
703-790-1284
e

Wayne Associates, Inc.
2628 Barrett Street
Virginia Beach, VA 23452
804-340-0555
e; m
NAPC

WASHINGTON

Anderson-Gest & Associates
1621 114th Avenue, S.E.
Bellevue, WA 98004
206-455-1411
g; M; r

Career Specialists, Inc.
1200 112th Street, N.E.
Bellevue, WA 98004
206-455-0582
a; f; g; M; m; o

Carroll/Church Associates, Inc.
11058 Main Street, N.E., Suite 110
Bellevue, WA 98004
206-453-1313
c; m

The Executive Suite
600 Stewart Street, Suite 321
Seattle, WA 98101
206-622-7242
s

Houser, Martin, Morris & Associates
1940 116th Avenue, N.E.
Bellevue, WA 98004
206-453-2700
b

Marshall Consultants/West
Box 1749
Seattle, WA 98111
206-392-8660
g; m; pe; P

Harry J. Prior & Associates, Inc.
799 112th Avenue, N.E., Suite 300
Bellevue, WA 98004
206-455-1774

John J. Sudlow & Co.
1111 Third Avenue, Suite 700
Seattle, WA 98101
206-382-0563
a; f; g; M; m; pe

WISCONSIN

A Ability Consultants
202 North Midvale Boulevard
Madison, WI 53705
608-231-2421

Blum & Co.
33231 Linden Circle
Nashotah, WI 53058
414-547-1200
g

The Brand Company, Inc.
12740 North River Road
Mequon, WI 53092
414-242-6203
AESC

E. A. Butler Associates, Inc.
2040 West Wisconsin Avenue
Milwaukee, WI 53223
414-933-6255

Conley Associates, Inc.
810 Cardinal Lane
Hartland, WI 53029
414-367-7330

John Conway Associates
2040 West Wisconsin Avenue
Milwaukee, WI 53233
414-933-3355
g; H; pe

Executive Recruiters, Inc.
933 North Mayfair Road
Milwaukee, WI 53226
414-475-1990
a; c; f; M; m

H.S. Placements
Box 12295
Green Bay, WI 54302
414-494-9586
b; g; m; s

Jonas & Associates, Inc.
3333 North Mayfair Road, Suite 313
Milwaukee, WI 53222
414-257-3620

Robert E. Larson & Associates, Inc.
6101 Milwaukee Avenue, Larson Building
Milwaukee, WI 53213
414-259-0000

Maglio & Kendro, Inc.
450 North Sunnyslope Road
Brookfield, WI 53005
414-784-6020

Management Recruiters
444 South Adams Street
Green Bay, WI 54301
414-437-4353
f

Market Search, Inc.
216 North Green Bay Road
Thiensville, WI 53092
414-242-9103
m
NAPC

Medical Search Consultants, Inc.
3333 North Mayfair Road, Suite 313
Milwaukee, WI 53222
414-257-3620

P. J. Murphy & Associates, Inc.
735 North Water Street
Milwaukee, WI 53202
414-277-9777

Schwarzkopf Consultants, Inc.
15285 Watertown Plank Road
Elm Grove, WI 53122
414-784-4200
AESC

Siler & Associates, Inc.
5261 North Port Washington Road
Milwaukee, WI 53217
414-962-9400
AESC

Stanislaw & Associates, Inc.
P.O. Box 589, 210 Regency Court
Brookfield, WI 53005
414-785-9767
f; g; M; s

Lawrence A. Stich
3124 South Taylor Street
Milwaukee, WI 53207
414-483-6171
M

**TEMCO—The Executive Management
  Consulting Organization**
P.O. Box 303
Oconomowoc, WI 53066
414-367-4240

Frank X. Walsh & Co., Inc.
5325 West Burleigh Street
Milwaukee, WI 53210
414-444-2874

Wargo & Co., Inc.
260 Regency Court
Waukesha, WI 53186
414-785-1211
S; H

CANADA

Beech & Partners Ltd.
80 Bloor Street West, Suite 1502
Toronto, Ont., Canada
416-922-6336
g

The Caldwell Partners International
700 Fourth Avenue, S.W., Suite 1260
Calgary, Alta., Canada T2P3J4
403-265-8780
g
AESC

The Caldwell Partners International
1115 Sherbrooke Street, Suite 2201
Montreal, P.Q., Canada
514-849-5357
g
AESC

The Caldwell Partners International
50 Prince Arthur Avenue, Suite 103
Toronto, Ont., Canada
416-920-7702
g
AESC

The Caldwell Partners International
999 West Hastings Street, Suite 750
Vancouver, BC, Canada V6C2W2
604-669-3550
g
AESC

Rourke, Bourbonnais Associates, Ltd.
1808 Sherbrooke West
Montreal, P.Q., H3H 1E5, Canada
514-937-9525
g

Herman Smith International, Inc.
P.O. Box 255, Toronto Dominion Center
Toronto, Ont., Canada M5R 1B4
416-862-8830
g

Chapter Six

COMPANIES LISTED BY SPECIALIZATION

ACCOUNTING

Accountants & Auditors Agency
New York, NY 10017

Accountants Unlimited Personnel Services
Los Angeles, CA 90010

Accounting & Financial Recruiters
Houston, TX 77056

Accounting Management Resources
Santa Ana, CA 92705

Accounting Personnel Associates
Pittsburgh, PA 15222

Accounting Personnel Minnesota
Minneapolis, MN 55416

Accounting Resources International
Laguna Niguel, CA 92677

Accounting Resources International
Englewood, CO 80111

Accounting Resources International
New York, NY 10004

Accounting Resources International
Arlington, TX 76011

Accounting Resources International
Dallas, TX 75219

Accounting Resources International
Houston, TX 77058

ACI
Orlando, FL 32803

Jeffrey C. Adams & Co., Inc.
San Francisco, CA 94104

Advantage Personnel Agency
Miami, FL 33155

Aim Executive Recruiting & Search
Toledo, OH 43623

Alan & Associates Employee Search
Shreveport, LA 71104

Alaska Executive Search, Inc.
Anchorage, AK 99501

Alberta-Smyth Personnel Agency, Inc.
Union, NJ 07083

Alberta-Smyth Personnel Agency, Inc.
New York, NY 10165

Ethan Allen Personnel Agency
Poughkeepsie, NY 12601

Amity Consultants, Inc.
Fairfield, CT 06430

The Andre Group, Inc.
King of Prussia, PA 19406

Ardelle Associates
Annandale, VA 22003

Aristocrat Personnel Services
Santa Ana, CA 91423

Armstrong & Associates
Los Alamitos, CA 90720

Aronow Associates, Inc.
New York, NY 10001

Arthur Personnel
Caldwell, NJ 07006

ASC & Co.
Houston, TX 77027

E. J. Ashton & Associates, Ltd.
Arlington Heights, IL 60004

Atlantic Professional Recruiters
Gaffney, SC 29340

Auden Associates, Inc.
Middletown, CT 06457

Austin-Allen Co.
Memphis, TN 38119

Availability of Hartford
Hartford, CT 06103

Babich & Associates
Dallas, TX 75206

Bailey Employment Service
Waterbury, CT 06702

Baker Scott & Company
Parsippany, NJ 07054

James Bangert Associates, Inc.
Wayzata, MN 55391

Nathan Barry Associates, Inc.
Boston, MA 02109

The Bartlett Agency
Lewiston, ME 04240

The Baxter Group
Rancho Palos Verdes, CA 90274

BCL Corporation
Cleveland, OH 44107

Becker Personnel Services
Bala Cynwyd, PA 19004

Rick Beedle Associates, Inc.
North Hollywood, CA 91607

John Bell & Associates, Inc.
Chicago, IL 60611

Belle Oaks of America
Kansas City, MO 64106

Daniel Benjamin Inc.
New York, NY 10016

Benson McBride & Associates Agency, Inc.
Beverly Hills, CA 90212

Benton, Schneider & Associates, Inc.
Naperville, IL 60540

E. J. Bettinger Co.
Philadelphia, PA 19102

BFH Associates
Sharon, MA 02067

Blaine & Associates, Inc.
Encino, CA 91436

R. L. Booton & Associates
St. Louis, MO 63141

Bossler/Brown & Associates
Topeka, KA 66612

William H. Brawley Associates
New Canaan, CT 06840

K. Robert Brian
Philadelphia, PA 19103

Bryant Associates, Inc.
Chicago, IL 60611

Bundy-Stewart Associates, Inc.
Dallas, TX 75230

Burns Personnel Inc.
Rochester, NY 14604

Robert J. Bushee & Associates, Inc.
Bridgeville, PA 15017

Buzhardt Associates
Jackson, MI 39211

Career Directions
Newburgh, NY 12250

Career Specialists, Inc.
Bellevue, WA 98004

Chanko-Ward, Ltd.
New York, NY 10036

William J. Christopher Associates, Inc.
West Chester, PA 19380

Christopher, Drew & Associates, Inc.
Cleveland, OH 44122

Circare
Miami, FL 33138

City & National Employment
Waterloo, IA 50704

Clark Associates, Inc.
Atlanta, GA 30345

Claveloux, McCaffrey & Associates, Inc.
New York, NY 10018

Cochran, Cochran & Yale, Inc.
Rochester, NY 14623

Coker, Tyler & Co.
Atlanta, GA 30341

The Concord Group, Ltd.
Barrington, IL 60010

Consultant Group—Langlois & Associates, Inc.
Needham, MA 02194

Coopers & Lybrand
Los Angeles, CA 90017

Corporate Advisors Inc.
Miami, FL 33137

Corporate Career Consultants
San Francisco, CA 94111

Corporate Careers
White Plains, NY 10601

The Corporate Connection, Ltd.
Richmond, VA 23230

Corporate Consultants
New Orleans, LA 70112

Corporate Recruiters, Inc.
Philadelphia, PA 19126

Corporate Resource Group
Fairfield, CT 06430

Corporate Resource Group
Hartford, CT 06106

Corporate Service Group, Ltd.
San Francisco, CA 94102

Craighead Associates, Inc.
Stamford, CT 06901

Craig's Criterion
Contoocook, NH 03229

Creative Career Corporation
New Orleans, LA 70130

Cretney & Associates
Cleveland, OH 44143

Crispi, Wagner & Co., Inc.
New York, NY 10170

Crown, Michaels & Associates, Inc.
Los Angeles, CA 90067

Cruit Executive Search
Birmingham, AL 35259

Daly & Co., Inc.
Boston, MA 02116

DAPEXS Consultants
Syracuse, NY 13202

Darson Personnel Associates, Inc.
New York, NY 10168

N. Dean Davic Associates
Pittsburgh, PA 15235

David-Kris Associates
Westport, CT 06881

John Davidson & Associates
Dallas, TX 75229

Robert H. Davidson Associates
Norwood, MA 02062

Davies Associates International, Ltd.
Houston, TX 77218

Gene Davis & Associates
Oklahoma City, OK 73156

Davis Company
St. Louis, MO 63102

The Dean Group
Maplewood, NJ 07040

William S. DeFuniak, Inc.
Hinsdale, IL 60521

Delta Resource Group, Ltd.
Marietta, GA 30067

Jerry Demaso & Associates
Metairie, LA 70002

Dependable
New York, NY 10017

R. M. Donaldson Personnel
Cranford, NJ 07016

Dorison & Company
Coral Gables, FL 33134

Dunhill Personnel—Little Rock
Little Rock, AR 72212

Dunhill of Greater Jackson
Jacksonville, FL 39206

Dunhill of Albuquerque
Albuquerque, NM 87110

Dunhill of Huntington
Melville, NY 11747

Dunhill of Austin
Austin, TX 78723

Dunhill Personnel—Corpus Christi
Corpus Christi, TX 78411

Earley Kielty & Associates, Inc.
New York, NY 10121

E.D.P. World, Inc.
San Francisco, CA 94111

Edwards & Sowers, Inc.
Chicago, IL 60611

Eggers Personnel & Consulting
Omaha, NB 68144

The Elliott Company, Inc.
Woburn, MA 01801

David M. Ellner Associates
New York, NY 10121

Emerson Professionals
Burlington, MA 01803

The Engineers Index
Boston, MA 02110

Estar Execu/Search, Ltd.
Palatine, IL 60067

Evans Associates, Inc.
San Francisco, CA 94104

Carolyn Evans Associates
Plymouth Meeting, PA 19462

Kenneth Evans & Associates
New Orleans, LA 70130

Excel Personnel
Greenville, SC 29607

Executive Image, Inc.
New York, NY 10016

Executive Locators of America
Metairie, LA 70004

Executive Placement Corporation
Rochester, NY 14604

Executive Recruiters
Little Rock, AR 72211

Executive Recruiters, Inc.
Milwaukee, WI 53226

Executive Register, Inc.
Danbury, CT 06810

Executive Resources, Ltd.
Des Moines, IA 50321

Executive Search, Inc.
Anchorage, AK 99501

Executive Search
Stamford, CT 06901

Executive Search Company
Conshohocken, PA 19428

Exxell
New York, NY 10038

Fairfield Whitney
Stratford, CT 06497

Fanning Personnel of Boston
Boston, MA 02116

Financial Search
Pittsburgh, PA 15222

First Word Placement Service
Dallax, TX 75240

The Fisher Organization
New York, NY 10017

A. G. Fishkin & Associates, Inc.
Rockville, MD 20852

Fleming Associates
Atlanta, GA 30339

Fleming Associates
Columbus, IN 47202

Fleming Associates
Metairie, LA 70002

Fleming Associates
Dublin, OH 43017

Fleming Associates
Memphis, TN 38111

Fleming Associates
Houston, TX 77024

Flinn Consultants, Inc.
Highland Park, IL 60035

Ford & Ford
Dedham, MA 02026

Fortune of Providence
Providence, RI 02903

Fortune Personnel Consultants
Stamford, CT 06901

Fortune Personnel Consultants—Boston
Boston, MA 01803

Foster & Associates, Inc.
San Francisco, CA 94105

The Foster McKay Group
Tampa, FL 33614

Fox & Fleischer
Richardson, TX 75080

Fox Morris
Baltimore, MD 21204

Fox Personnel Consultants
Greensboro, NC 27429

Futures Personnel Services
Baltimore, MD 21204

Garrett Associates, Inc.
Atlanta, GA 30339

Edward Gaylord & Associates
Mill Valley, CA 94942

General Employment Enterprises, Inc.
Naperville, IL 60540

General Employment Enterprises
Palo Alto, CA 94303

J. Gifford, Inc.
Tulsa, OK 74135

Global Search
Melville, NY 11747

B. Goodwin, Ltd.
Fairfield, CT 06430

Gordon, Cook & Associates
Clayton, MO 63105

Graduates Unlimited Personnel, Inc.
Union, NJ 07083

Graham & Associates Employee Consultants
Greensboro, NC 27408

Griffith & Werner, Inc.
Hollywood, FL 33021

Hahn & Associates, Inc.
Dayton, OH 45402

Robert Half of Orange County
Newport Beach, CA 92660

Robert Half of Wilmington
Wilmington, DE 19810

Robert Half, Inc.
Chicago, IL 60601

Robert Half of Boston
Boston, MA 02110

Robert Half
Lexington, MA 02173

Robert Half
Worcester, MA 01608

Robert Half
Albuquerque, NM 87190

Robert Half of New York Inc.
New York, NY 10036

Robert Half of Dayton
Dayton, OH 45402

Robert Half
Providence, RI 02903

Robert Half Personnel
Dallas, TX 75231

Harvey Personnel
North Charleston, SC 29304

Haskell & Stern Associates, Inc.
Forth Worth, TX 76112

Hastings & Hastings
Miami, FL 33131

Hayden & Refo, Inc.
Boston, MA 02110

Hayman & Company
Dallas, TX 75201

Heberling Personnel
Harrisburgh, PA 17105

Jay Heino Associates, Ltd.
New York, NY 10017

E. B. Hendrick Associates
Liverpool, NY 13088

D. J. Hertz and Associates, Ltd.
New York, NY 10017

Higbee Associates, Inc.
Rowayton, CT 06853

Hipp Waters Professional Recruiting
Boston, MA 02109

Hipp Waters Professional Recruiters
Stamford, CT 06901

HiTech Consulting Group
Los Angeles, CA 90067

Holland & Associates
Towson, MD 21204

Hones and Company
Fort Myers, FL 33901

Hospitality Personnel, Inc.
Valley Forge, PA 19481

Houchins & Associates, Inc.
Atlanta, GA 30308

Howard-Sloan Associates, Inc.
New York, NY 10017

Robert Howe & Associates
Atlanta, GA 30341

Huxtable Associates, Inc.
Bridgeton, MO 63044

Nancy Jackson, Inc.
Scranton, PA 18503

Jean's Personnel
Memphis, TN 38137

A. G. Johnson & Co., Inc.
Irvine, CA 92715

JY Enterprises
New York, NY 10007

Karam Associates
Denver, CO 80224

Howard L. Karr & Associates, Inc.
San Mateo, CA 94402

Kenex Consultants
Aurora, CO 80014

Kenfield Research Associates, Inc.
New York, NY 10016

Melvin Kent & Associates
Columbus, OH 43215

Keshlear Associates
Aiken, SC 29210

Key Employment Services
West Des Moines, IA 50265

Key Financial Personnel
Rosslyn, VA 22209

Joseph Keyes Associates
Hackensack, NJ 07601

Kingston & Associates
Tucson, AZ 85710

Kinkead Associates
Hartford, CT 06103

James M. Kittleman & Associates, Inc.
Chicago, IL 60604

Kogen Personnel
Johnstown, PA 15901

D. A. Kreuter Associates
Philadelphia, PA 19103

Kunzer Associates, Ltd.
Chicago, IL 60604

Henry Labus Personnel
Detroit, MI 48226

Gilbert Lane Personnel
Hamden, CT 06517

Gilbert Lane Personnel Agency
Hartford, CT 06103

Gilbert Lane Associates
Atlanta, GA 30339

Largent Parks & Partners, Inc.
Dallas, TX 75240

Leahy & Company
Boston, MA 02110

Lee Calhoon & Co., Inc.
Birchrunville, PA 19421

Lineback Associates
Dallas, TX 75240

Lineback Associates
Houston, TX 77042

Linker Personnel Systems Ltd.
New York, NY 10017

Logic
New York, NY 10038

Franklin Lorsch Associates, Inc.
New York, NY 10017

Arthur J. Loveley Associates
New York, NY 10165

Arthur Lyle Associates, Inc.
Stamford, CT 06901

Lyman & Co.
Glendale, CA 91203

McCormack & Farrow
Long Beach, CA 90802

Ellie Mack Associates
Wilmington, DE 19810

McNitt Personnel Bureau
Minneapolis, MN 55402

McSherry & Associates
Chicago, IL 60601

McWilliams Personnel, Inc.
New York, NY 10038

Maetzold Associates, Inc.
Minnetonka, MN 55343

J. C. Malone Associates
Louisville, KY 40218

Management Recruiters
Washington, DC 20006

Management Search & Associates
Westport, CT 06880

Management Search, Inc.
Chicago, IL 60611

Management Search Inc.
Minneapolis, MN 55426

Management Search, Inc.
Annandale, VA 22003

Marbrook
New York, NY 10017

Mar-El Employment Agency
Levittown, NY 11756

Mason Concepts Agency, Inc.
Los Angeles, CA 90048

M. D. Mattes & Associates
Timonium, MD 21093

Medical Recruiters of America
Tampa, FL 33607

Metricor, Inc.
Oak Brook Terrace, IL 60181

Michaels, Patrick, O'Brien & Williams, Inc.
Columbia, MD 21044

MKI Recruiting Associates
White Plains, NY 10601

The Morland Group
Nyack, NY 10960

J. R. Morrison & Associates, Inc.
San Francisco, CA 94111

MRG Search & Placement
New Haven, CT 06510

Gary Nelson & Associates, Inc.
San Rafael, CA 94913

William H. Nenstiel & Associates, Inc.
Scottsdale, AZ 85251

Niermann Personnel Service
Morrow, GA 30260

Paul Norsell & Associates, Inc.
Anaheim, CA 92807

Paul Norsell & Associates, Inc.
Los Angeles, CA 90045

The NRI Group
Rockville, MD 20850

The NRI Group
Vienna, VA 22180

Robert E. Nurse Associates, Inc.
White Plains, NY 10530

O'Neill Executive Search
Buffalo, NY 14223

O'Shea System of Employment
Philadelphia, PA 19107

Paramount Personnel Service
Oakland, CA 94612

Parker Clark Associates
New York, NY 10017

Peeney Associates, Inc.
Fanwood, NJ 07023

Personnel, Inc.
Spartanburg, SC 29302

Peyser Associates, Inc.
Miami, FL 33125

Phillips Associates
Englewood, NJ 07631

Phillips Personnel Search
Denver, CO 80202

Phillips Resource Group
Greenville, SC 29606

Phoenix Personnel Services
Harrisburg, PA 17105

Pinkerton & Associates, Inc.
Chicago, IL 60611

The Placers, Inc.
Wilmington, DE 19806

Positions, Inc.
Providence, RI 02904

PRH Management
New York, NY 10017

Proctor & Davis
Santa Monica, CA 90403

Professional Personnel Consultants—Tampa
Tampa, FL 33607

Professional Personnel Consultants
Southfield, MI 48075

Professional Recruiters of Salt Lake
Salt Lake City, UT 84107

Provident Personnel Consultants
Prospect Park, PA 19076

Quinlivan & Company
York, PA 17401

Rainess Associates
West Caldwell, NJ 07006

Randall Howard & Associates, Inc.
Memphis, TN 38115

Redmond & Associates, Inc.
Danbury, CT 06810

E. J. Rhodes, Inc.
Framingham, MA 01701

E. J. Rhodes Personnel Consultants
New York, NY 10036

Don Richard
Washington, DC 20006

Don Richard
Bethesda, MD 20814

Don Richard
McLean, VA 22102

Ridenour & Associates
Chicago, IL 60601

Rita Personnel—West Massachusetts
Springfield, MA 01103

Roche Associates
Stamford, CT 06094

Rogers & Seymour Inc.
Portland, ME 04103

Romac & Associates, Inc.
Portland, ME 04112

Romac
Boston, MA 02110

Romac
Wellesley, MA 02181

Romac & Associates
Bala Cynwyd, PA 19004

Romac & Associates of Columbus
Columbus, OH 43215

ROMAC Personnel Consultants
Houston, TX 77002

Romano McAvoy Associates, Inc.
Smithtown, NY 11787

Louis Rudzinsky Associates, Inc.
Lexington, MA 02173

Charles Russ Associates, Inc.
Kansas City, MO 64114

Ryan &'Associates
Conroe, TX 77385

Sales & Management Search, Inc.
Chicago, IL 60606

Sanford Rose Associates
Youngstown, OH 44503

Saxon Morse Associates
Pomona, NY 10970

SCL Executive Search
Philadelphia, PA 19103

Scott, Rogers Associates
New City, NY 10956

Search Consultants
Paramus, NJ 07652

Search Source Inc.
Granite City, IL 62040

Siegel Shotland & Associates
Encino, CA 91436

Silver Employment Agency
Baltimore, MD 21217

Sinclair & Potts Associates, Inc.
Pittsburgh, PA 15235

Howard W. Smith Associates
Hartford, CT 06103

Smith Hanley Associates, Inc.
New York, NY 10165

Smyth Dawson Associates
Stamford, CT 06901

Soltis Management Services
Radnor, PA 19087

Source Finance
Century City, CA 90067

Source Finance
Los Angeles, CA 90017

Source Finance
Mountain View, CA 94043

Source Finance
Newport Beach, CA 92660

Source Finance
San Francisco, CA 94111

Source Finance
Van Nuys, CA 91406

Source Finance
Walnut Creek, CA 94596

Source Finance
Englewood, CO 80111

Source Finance
Atlanta, GA 30303

Southern Personnel Services
Palm Desert, CA 92260

L. W. Stern Associates, Inc.
New York, NY 10016

Stonehill Management Consultants, Inc.
New York, NY 10175

Streeter & Associates
Los Angeles, CA 90010

Sturm Burrows & Company
Philadelphia, PA 19102

John J. Sudlow & Co.
Chicago, IL 60611

John J. Sudlow & Co.
Seattle, WA 98101

Sumrall Personnel Consultants
Dallas, TX 75234

Synergistics Associates, Ltd.
Chicago, IL 60601

Taft
New York, NY 10017

F. L. Taylor & Co., Inc.
New York, NY 10016

Richard Theobald & Associates
San Mateo, CA 94404

J. Robert Thompson Co., Inc.
Houston, TX 77027

Toar Enterprises
Roswell, GA 30076

Traynor Associates, Ltd.
Rochester, NY 14604

United Consultants
York, PA 17403

VanMaldegiam Associates, Inc.
Chicago, IL 60606

Vantage Careers, Inc.
Stamford, CT 06904

Vantage Careers, Inc.
White Plains, NY 10601

VIP Personnel
Durham, NC 27705

Wachtel & Associates, Ltd.
New York, NY 10017

John H. Warner Associates, Inc.
Hartford, CT 06103

Warren & Associates
Geneseo, IL 61254

Watkins & Associates
Houston, TX 77074

Emanuel Weintraub Associates, Inc.
Fort Lee, NJ 07024

Western Personnel Associates, Inc.
Phoenix, AZ 85012

Western Reserve Associates
Bath, OH 44210

Thomas Whelan Associates
Washington, DC 20006

David J. White & Associates Inc.
Chicago, IL 60606

Whittaker & Associates, Inc.
Atlanta, GA 30339

E. N. Wilkins and Company, Inc.
Chicago, IL 60606

J. W. Willard Associates, Inc.
Syracuse, NY 13201

Duane I. Wilson Associates, Inc.
Birmingham, MI 48011

Winguth, Schweichler Associates, Inc.
San Francisco, CA 94111

Winter Wyman & Company
Bedford, MA 01730

Witt Associates, Inc.
Oak Brook, IL 60521

Woodbury Personnel
Jericho, NY 11753

Jim Woodson & Associates
Jackson, MS 39216

The Woodward Group
Chicago, IL 60601

Wunderlich & Associates, Inc.
Oak Brook, IL 60521

John Wylie Associates, Inc.
Tulsa, OK 74136

The Zivic Group
San Francisco, CA 94111

ADVERTISING

Norma Adler Inc.
New York, NY 10022

Benson & Associates Personnel & Management Consultants
Fort Lauderdale, FL 33309

BH Folios Ltd.
New York, NY 10021

Bialla & Associates, Inc.
Sausalito, CA 94965

The Bradbeer Co.
Gulph Mills, PA 19406

Roberta Brenner Associates, Inc.
New York, NY 10022

Brown-Bernardy, Inc.
Los Angeles, CA 90049

CAH Executive Search
New York, NY 10022

Career Builders, Inc.
New York, NY 10017

William J. Christopher Associates, Inc.
West Chester, PA 19380

Gwen Dycus, Inc.
Winter Park, FL 32790

Executive Locators of America
Metairie, LA 70004

Jerry Fields Associates, Inc.
New York, NY 10019

Finley & Co.
Greenville, SC 29615

The Fisher Organization
New York, NY 10017

The Fry Group
New York, NY 10017

Greene Personnel Consultants
Providence, RI 02903

Harreus & Strotz, Inc.
San Francisco, CA 94111

William Harris Associates
New York, NY 10086

Hastings & Hastings
Miami, FL 33131

D. J. Hertz and Associates, Ltd.
New York, NY 10017

Howard-Sloan Associates, Inc.
New York, NY 10017

Huss Viseltear & Associates
New York, NY 10022

Judd-Falk Inc.
New York, NY 10016

Jack Kennedy Associates, Inc.
Chicago, IL 60601

LeMar Personnel Consultants
New York, NY 10165

Lovewell & Associates, Inc.
Atlanta, GA 30361

McNitt Personnel Bureau
Minneapolis, MN 55402

Stephen W. Matson Associates, Inc.
Birmingham, MI 48011

National Hospitality Associates, Inc.
Tempe, AZ 85282

The Pamela Reeve Agency, Inc.
Los Angeles, CA 90069

Reichelt & Associates, Inc.
Los Angeles, CA 90024

Roth Young Personnel of Minneapolis
Edina, MN 55435

Roth Young
Houston, TX 77008

Charles Sharp & Associates
Los Angeles, CA 90024

Silverstein Herman Company
New York, NY 10017

Carolyn Smith Paschal International
Del Mar, CA 92014

Smith's Fifth Avenue
New York, NY 10017

Tesar-Reynes, Inc.
Chicago, IL 60601

Judy Wald Agency, Inc.
New York, NY 10022

Walker Recruitment
Minneapolis, MN 55416

Ward Liebelt Associates, Inc.
Greenwich, CT 06830

ARCHITECTURE

Action Personnel Services
Charlotte, NC 28209

Edwards & Shepard
New York, NY 10001

Executive Recruiters
Little Rock, AR 72211

Fine Personnel Agency
New York, NY 10017

Gold Card Recruiters
Camden, AR 71701

Growth Placement Associates, Inc.
Dowington, PA 19335

D. J. Hertz and Associates, Ltd.
New York, NY 10017

Ruth Hirsch Career Builders Inc.
New York, NY 10017

McNichol Associates
Philadelphia, PA 19105

Marbrook
New York, NY 10017

Miller-Hanna & Associates
Los Angeles, CA 90010

RitaSue Siegel Agency Inc.
New York, NY 10019

BANKING

Accounting Personnel Minnesota
Minneapolis, MN 55416

Accounting Resources International
Laguna Niguel, CA 92677

The Adams Consulting Group
Columbus, OH 43206

Advantage Personnel Agency
Miami, FL 33155

Agri-Business Services
St. Paul, MN 55113

The Ahrens Agency
New York, NY 10038

Alberta-Smyth Personnel Agency, Inc.
Union, NJ 07083

Alberta-Smyth Personnel Agency, Inc.
New York, NY 10165

Allen Personnel Agency
New York, NY 10038

Amity Consultants
Fairfield, CT 06430

Analytic Recruiting, Inc.
New York, NY 10017

Andcor Companies
Minneapolis, MN 55426

ASC & Co.
Houston, TX 77027

The Bankers Register
New York, NY 10038

The Bankers Register
New York, NY 10110

Barclays Recruiting Services, Inc.
Denver, CO 80222

Barger & Sargent, Inc.
Concord, NH 03301

The Baxter Group
Rancho Palos Verdes, CA 90274

Robert Becker & Co.
Allison Park, PA 15101

Benson & Associates Personnel &
  Management Consultants
Fort Lauderdale, FL 33309

Blake & Associates
Fort Lauderdale, FL 33316

Botal Associates
New York, NY 10007

Bowden & Company, Inc.
Cleveland, OH 44131

Brandjes Associates
Baltimore, MD 21202

K. Robert Brian
Philadelphia, PA 19103

Buxton & Associates
Denver, CO 80206

Careers Ltd.
Denver, CO 80203

Jaci Carroll Personnel Service
Waterbury, CT 06721

Richard Clark Associates
Fairfield, CT 06017

T. Don Clark
Fort Worth, TX 76107

T. Don Clark
Houston, TX 77005

Cole, Warren & Long, Inc.
Philadelphia, PA 19102

W. Hoyt Colton Associates, Inc.
New York, NY 10005

Coopers & Lybrand
Chicago, IL 60606

Cornwall
New York, NY 10038

Corporate Advisors Inc.
Miami, FL 33137

Corporate Consultants
New Orleans, LA 70112

Creative Career Corporation
New Orleans, LA 70130

Deakyne Associates
Philadelphia, PA 19103

Jerry Demaso & Associates
Metairie, LA 70002

Dorsey Love & Associates
Springfield, MO 65804

Driggers & Blackwell Personnel
Ruston, LA 71270

Dunhill of Fort Collins
Fort Collins, CO 80525

Dunhill of Greenville
Greenville, NC 27834

Dunhill Personnel of N.E. Tulsa
Tulsa, OK 74128

Eggers Personnel & Consulting
Omaha, NB 68144

Ells Personnel Systems
Minneapolis, MN 55402

Emco Personnel Service
Laguna Hills, CA 92635

Employment Opportunities
Danbury, CT 06810

Equinox Management Corp.
Norwalk, CT 06851

Carolyn Evans Associates
Plymouth Meeting, PA 19462

Kenneth Evans & Associates
New Orleans, LA 70130

R. J. Evans & Associates, Inc.
Beachwood, OH 44122

Executive Locators of America
Metairie, LA 70004

Executive Personnel Consultants
Memphis, TN 38117

Executive Resources, Ltd.
Des Moines, IA 50321

Executive Search
Charlotte, NC 28222

Fanning Personnel of Boston
Boston, MA 02116

Financial Search
Pittsburgh, PA 15222

The Fisher Organization
New York, NY 10017

Forum Personnel
New York, NY 10017

Fox-Morris Associates, Inc.
Philadelphia, PA 19109

A. O. Frost, Staffing Consultant
Springfield, MA 01101

Furman Group, Ltd.
New York, NY 10017

Futures Personnel Services
Baltimore, MD 21204

G.A. Agency
Cranford, NJ 07016

Geller Associates
Miami, FL 33131

General Placement Service
Greensburg, PA 15601

J. Gifford, Inc.
Tulsa, OK 74135

Global Search
Melville, NY 11747

**Graham & Associates Employee
  Consultants**
Greensboro, NC 27408

Great Southwestern Personnel Co.
Phoenix, AZ 85016

Robert Half of Wilmington
Wilmington, DE 19810

Robert Half of Boston
Boston, MA 02110

Robert Half of New York Inc.
New York, NY 10036

Robert Half of Dayton
Dayton, OH 45402

Hanzel & Mariaschin, Inc.
New York, NY 10170

Harris & U'Ren, Inc.
Phoenix, AZ 85003

Haskell & Stern Associates, Inc.
New York, NY 10017

Haskell & Stern Associates, Inc.
Forth Worth, TX 76112

W. T. Hawes, Company
New York, NY 10038

John Heckers & Associates
Aruada, CO 80002

Henrietta's Personnel Service
Miami, FL 33131

HiTech Consulting Group
Los Angeles, CA 90067

Hogan Associates
Cleveland, OH 44132

Holtzman & Associates
Washington, DC 20016

Houser, Martin, Morris & Associates
Bellevue, WA 98004

Howard Associates
Dallas, TX 75240

H.S. Placements
Green Bay, WI 54302

Interlangue International, Inc.
New York, NY 10017

D. Jackson and Associates
Hershey, PA 17033

Nancy Jackson, Inc.
Scranton, PA 18503

Kenneth James Associates
Holland, PA 18966

JNB Associates, Inc.
Boston, MA 02110

JY Enterprises
New York, NY 10007

Kanon
New York, NY 10018

Kennedy and Company
Chicago, IL 60606

Keshlear Associates
Aiken, SC 29210

Key Employment Services
West Des Moines, IA 50265

Kingston & Associates
Tucson, AZ 87510

Kling Agency
New York, NY 10038

Kogen Personnel
Johnstown, PA 15901

Henry Labus Personnel
Detroit, MI 48226

Gilbert Lane Personnel Service
Springfield, MA 01115

Jack B. Larsen & Associates
Erie, PA 16502

Mina Latham
Bal Harbour, FL 33154

Leon-Lawrence Personnel
Bridgeport, CT 06606

Leahy & Company
Boston, MA 02110

Alan Lewis Associates
Solana Beach, CA 92075

London Scott Associates
Clifton Park, NY 12065

Lyman & Co.
Glendale, CA 91203

George P. Lyon Associates
Doylestown, PA 18901

McCormack & Farrow
Long Beach, CA 90802

Edwin McDonald Associates
New York, NY 10017

McWilliams Personnel, Inc.
New York, NY 10038

J. C. Malone Associates
Louisville, KY 40218

Management Recruiters
Washington, DC 20006

Marbrook
New York, NY 10017

Mar-El Employment Agency
Levittown, NY 11756

Meehan Associates
Rochester, NY 14625

Morgan Research
New York, NY 10175

MPI
New York, NY 10017

Network Affiliates, Ltd.
Metairie, LA 70002

Perry Newcomb & Associates
Cincinnati, OH 45230

Newell Associates, Inc.
New York, NY 10022

Nicholson & Associates, Inc.
New York, NY 10169

R. A. Nicholson
New York, NY 10016

O'Crowley & O'Toole Executive Search
Portland, OR 97223

O'Shea System of Employment
Philadelphia, PA 19107

Paramount Personnel Service
Oakland, CA 94612

Personnel Search
Omaha, NB 68124

Phoenix Personnel Services
Harrisburg, PA 17105

The Placers, Inc.
Wilmington, DE 19306

Positions, Inc.
Providence, RI 02904

Professional Personnel Consultants
Southfield, MI 48075

Professional Personnel Consultants-Tampa
Tampa, FL 33607

Professional Placement Group
Boston, MA 02109

Professional Placement Services
Augusta, ME 04330

Professional Recruiters Inc.
Auburn, MA 01501

Professional Search
Alexandria, VA 22312

Quarles & Associates
Memphis, TN 38112

Regency Recruiters
Kansas City, MO 64106

E. J. Rhodes Personnel Consultants
New York, NY 10036

Lloyd Richards Personnel Service
Tulsa, OK 74103

Ken Richardson
Bethesda, MD 20817

Riley Recruiting Enterprises
Denver, CO 80218

Rogers & Seymour, Inc.
Portland, ME 04103

Romac & Associates
Bala Cynwyd, PA 19004

Romac & Associates
Portland, ME 04112

Romac
Boston, MA 02110

Romac
Wellesley, MA 02181

Romac & Associates of Columbus
Columbus, OH 43215

Romac & Associates
Philadelphia, PA 19103

Romac
Arlington, VA 22209

Ropes Associates, Inc.
Fort Lauderdale, FL 33394

John Rosen Associates
New York, NY 10166

R.S.V.P. Agency
New York, NY 10038

R.V.M. Associates, Inc.
White Plains, NY 10604

Salem Associates
New York, NY 10017

Schattle Personnel Consultants, Inc.
Warwick, RI 02886

Search Consultants
Paramus, NJ 07652

Select Finders Corp.
West Caldwell, NJ 07006

The September Group
Los Angeles, CA 90049

Sequent Personnel Services
Mountain View, CA 94041

Simon & Ryan, Inc.
San Francisco, CA 94104

Sockwell & Hendrix
Charlotte, NC 28284

Carter Stone & Co., Inc.
New York, NY 10006

Streuli Personnel Agency
New York, NY 10038

SysTech Organization
Baltimore, MD 21234

SysTech Organization
New York, NY 10019

Systems Search II
Millburn, NJ 07041

J. Robert Thompson Co., Inc.
Houston, TX 77027

VIP Personnel
Durham, NC 27705

Walters & Associates
Metairie, LA 70002

Warren & Associates
Geneseo, IL 61254

Waterford, Inc.
Atlanta, GA 30339

Wehinger Service Inc.
New York, NY 10038

Wellesley, Ltd.
Providence, RI 02903

Whitlow and Associates
Atlanta, GA 30326

Woodbury Personnel
Jericho, NY 11753

Yelverton & Company
San Francisco, CA 94111

COMPUTERS

Abbington Associates
East Northport, NY 11731

Administrative Resources
Elmhurst, IL 60126

Advancement Concepts
Norcross, GA 30093

The Advisory Group
Portola Valley, CA 94025

Alaska Executive Search, Inc.
Anchorage, AK 99501

Dina Alessio & Associates
Dallas, TX 75231

Alexander & Zier Associates
Trumbull, CT 06611

Alexander-Edward Associates, Inc.
Philadelphia, PA 19107

Don Allan Associates, Inc.
New York, NY 10017

Amity Consultants, Inc.
Fairfield, CT 06430

Analytic Recruiting, Inc.
New York, NY 10017

Armstrong & Associates
Los Alamitos, CA 90720

Associated Business Consultants, Inc.
Medford, NJ 08055

Atomic Personnel, Inc.
Philadelphia, PA 19102

James Bangert Associates, Inc.
Wayzata, MN 55391

Nathan Barry Associates, Inc.
Boston, MA 02109

Bason Associates, Inc.
Cincinnati, OH 45215

Battalia & Associates, Inc.
New York, NY 10016

Bay Search Group
Providence, RI 02903

Rick Beedle Associates, Inc.
North Hollywood, CA 91607

Belzano, Deane & Associates
Irvine, CA 92715

Benton, Schneider & Associates, Inc.
Naperville, IL 60540

Berman Associates
Atlanta, GA 30309

BFH Associates
Sharon, MA 02067

Blaine & Associates, Inc.
Encino, CA 91436

Bonner Gladney Associates
Devon, PA 19333

The Breen Group Inc.
Hamden, CT 06518

K. Robert Brian
Philadelphia, PA 19103

Brucks Personnel Corp
Rochester, NY 14618

Burns Personnel Inc.
Rochester, NY 14604

Business Personnel Associates
Glastonbury, CT 06033

Career Enterprises Agency
Long Beach, CA 90807

Carroll/Church Associates, Inc.
Bellevue, WA 98004

M. L. Carter & Associates
Atlanta, GA 30362

Chanko-Ward, Ltd.
New York, NY 10036

Richard Clark Associates
West Hartford, CT 06017

The Clayton Group, Inc.
Oakbrook Terrace, IL 60181

CMA Technical Search, Inc.
New York, NY 10017

Cochran, Cochran & Yale, Inc.
Rochester, NY 14623

Cole, Warren & Long, Inc.
Philadelphia, PA 19102

Columbia EDP Agency, Inc.
New York, NY 10173

The Comnet Group
Garden City, NY 11530

COMPRO Search, Inc.
Houston, TX 77098

Computer Network Resources
Atlanta, GA 30341

Computer People
Minneapolis, MN 55416

The Computer Resources Group, Inc.
San Francisco, CA 94111

The Computer Resources Group, Inc.
Walnut Creek, CA 94596

Computer Security Placement Service, Inc.
Northborough, MA 01532

The Concord Group, Ltd.
Barrington, IL 60010

Corporate Resource Group
Hartford, CT 06106

Corporate Resources, Inc.
Minneapolis, MN 55426

Corporate Search Group, Inc.
Homewood, IL 60430

Cross Country Consultants, Inc.
Baltimore, MD 21218

DAPEXS Consultants, Inc.
Syracuse, NY 13202

The Data Base
Bala Cynwyd, PA 19004

Data Finders, Inc.
Englewood Cliffs, NJ 07632

Data Management Resources
Stamford, CT 06901

Data Search International
Houston, TX 77079

William S. DeFuniak, Inc.
Hinsdale, IL 60521

Jerry Demaso & Associates
Metairie, LA 70002

Donegan Associates, Inc.
Yarmouthport, MA 02675

Dotson Benefield & Associates, Inc.
Atlanta, GA 30345

Drum/Companies, Inc.
Atlanta, GA 30346

Dynamic Search Systems, Inc.
Arlington Heights, IL 60004

Dyna-Search
Chicago, IL 60604

Earley Kielty & Associates, Inc.
New York, NY 10121

Eastern Executive Associates
Clifton, NJ 07012

R. E. Eckert & Associates, Inc.
Jacksonville, FL 32207

EDP Computer Services, Inc.
Houston, TX 77027

E.D.P. World, Inc.
San Francisco, CA 94111

Edwards & Sowers, Inc.
Chicago, IL 60611

EMJAY Computer Careers
Houston, TX 77098

Engineering Employment Agency
New York, NY 10017

The Engineers Index
Boston, MA 02110

Equinox Management Corp.
Norwalk, CT 06851

ES VEE EDP
New York, NY 10001

R. J. Evans & Associates, Inc.
Beachwood, OH 44122

Executive Careers, Inc.
New York, NY 10005

Executive Careers, Inc.
Conshohocken, PA 19428

Executive Personnel Consultants
Memphis, TN 38117

Executive Recruiters, Inc.
Milwaukee, WI 53226

Executive Recruiting Consultants, Inc.
Des Plaines, IL 60016

Executive Register, Inc.
Danbury, CT 06810

Exeter Associates, Inc.
Hampton, NH 03842

Fairfield Whitney
Stratford, CT 06497

Richard Farber Associates, Inc.
Great Neck, NY 11021

Fells & Baroody, Inc.
New York, NY 10001

Fingers Personnel Office
Houston, TX 77001

A. G. Fishkin & Associates, Inc.
Rockville, MD 20852

Forest Associates
Caldwell, NJ 07006

Fortune Personnel Consultants
Stamford, CT 06901

Foster & Associates, Inc.
San Francisco, CA 94105

Gabriel & Bowie Associates, Ltd.
Baltimore, MD 21228

General Employment Enterprises, Inc.
Los Angeles, CA 90010

General Employment Enterprises, Inc.
Naperville, IL 60540

General Employment Enterprises, Inc.
Dallas, TX

J. Gifford, Inc.
Tulsa, OK 74135

Bob Gill Associates
New York, NY 10017

Graham & Associates, Inc.
Dallas, TX 75240

Greene & Associates
Denver, CO 80222

The Gruen Co.
Oakland, CA 94618

Robert Half of Los Angeles Personnel Service
Los Angeles, CA 90010

Robert Half of Boston
Boston, MA 02110

Robert Half
Lexington, MA 02173

Robert Half
Worcester, MA 01608

Robert Half, Inc.
Chicago, IL 60601

Robert Half
Providence, RI 02903

Robert Half Personnel
Dallas, TX 75231

Hazel Associates
New York, NY 10017

W. Warner Hinman & Co.
Chicago, IL 60611

John Heckers & Associates
Aruada, CO 80002

HiTech Consulting Group
Los Angeles, CA 90067

J. L. Hoglund Co., Inc.
Natrona Heights, PA 15065

Horton Associates, Inc.
Helendale, CA 92342

Jack Hurst & Associates, Inc.
Richardson, TX 75080

Hyde & Seek
Sterling, VA 22170

Information Resources Group
Westlake Village, CA 91361

Input Search Agency
El Toro, CA 92630

Input Search Agency
Los Angeles, CA 90036

Insight
New York, NY 10017

Insurance Personnel Recruiters
Philadelphia, PA 19106

Internal Data Sciences
New York, NY 10118

International Personnel Consultants, Inc.
Hanover, NH 03755

International Staffing Consultants, Inc.
Newport Beach, CA 92660

Intersearch Inc.
Houston, TX 77063

Janus Consultants, Inc.
Washington, DC 20007

JDG Associates, Ltd.
Rockville, MD 20850

Paul Johnson Associates
Washington, DC 20036

Johnston & Associates
Naperville, IL 60565

Martin Kartin & Company
New York, NY 10021

Richard Kaye Personnel Agency, Inc.
New York, NY 10017

Kelly & Thomas Associates
Bala Cynwyd, PA 19004

Kenex Consultants
Aurora, CO 80014

Joseph Keyes Associates
Hackensaack, NJ 07601

Kiley-Owen Associates, Inc.
Philadelphia, PA 19107

King Computer Search
Dallas, TX 75238

Kinkead Associates
Hartford, CT 06103

Robert Kleven & Co., Inc.
Boston, MA 02109

Knorps Computer Consultants, Inc.
Winnetka, IL 60093

Knudson & Co.
Oak Brook, IL 60521

D. A. Kreuter Associates
Philadelphia, PA 19103

Kunzer Associates, Ltd.
Chicago, IL 60604

Arthur J. Langdon
Hartford, CT 06103

Lineback Associates
Dallas, TX 75240

Lineback Associates
Houston, TX 77042

McHan Personnel
Houston, TX 77027

McNichol Associates
Philadelphia, PA 19105

McSherry & Associates
Chicago, IL 60601

Main Line Personnel Services, Inc.
Bala Cynwyd, PA 19004

Management Decisions Agency
Sherman Oaks, CA 91423

Management Recruiters of Columbus
Columbus, OH 43229

Management Resources Executive Recruiters
Long Beach, CA 90803

Management Scientists, Inc.
New York, NY 10016

Management Search, Inc.
Chicago, IL 60611

Management Search Inc.
Minneapolis, MN 55426

Management Search, Inc.
Annandale, VA 22003

F. L. Mannix & Co., Inc.
Boston, MA 02109

Marbrook
New York, NY 10017

Mason Associates
Norwalk, CT 06851

Mason Concepts Agency, Inc.
Los Angeles, CA 90048

Pete Massarini & Associates, Employment Consultants
Houston, TX 77057

MBA Associates, Inc.
Boston, MA 02109

Metricor, Inc.
Oak Brook Terrace, IL 60181

Midgette Consultants, Inc.
Waterbury, CT 06702

Mini-Systems Associates
Marina Del Rey, CA 90291

Mini-Systems Associates
Newport Beach, CA 92658

Richard Mowell Associates, Inc.
Tallahassee, FL 32303

MPI Associates
Boulder, CO 80302

Multi Processing, Inc.
Lexington, MA 02173

Gary Nelson & Associates, Inc.
Cupertino, CA 95014

Gary Nelson & Associates, Inc.
San Rafael, CA 94913

Nicholson & Associates, Inc.
New York, NY 10169

Richard E. Nosky & Associates
Scottsdale, AZ 85251

The NRI Group
Washington, DC 20036

Oliver Associates, Inc.
Melville, NY 11747

Oliver & Rosner Associates
New York, NY 10022

Omni
New York, NY 10016

Omnisearch
Dallas, TX 75243

The P & L Group
Jericho, NY 11753

Paul-Tittle Associates, Inc.
Silver Springs, MD 20910

Pierce Associates, Inc.
San Francisco, CA 94111

Perry-White & Associates, Inc.
Los Angeles, CA 90010

Perry-White & Associates, Inc.
San Francisco, CA 94104

Perry-White & Associates, Inc.
Santa Clara, CA 95050

Personnel, Inc.
Spartanburg, SC 29302

Norman Powers Associates, Inc.
Saxonville, MA 01701

PPS Consultants
Phoenix, AZ 85004

Proctor & Davis
Santa Monica, CA 90403

Professional Computer Personnel
Waterbury, CT 06702

Professional Recruiters Inc.
Auburn, MA 01501

Professional Search
Alexandria, VA 22312

Project-Career Inc.
Independence, OH 44131

Proquest Corporation
Houston, TX 77268

Quantum
New York, NY 10016

The R & L Group
Arlington Heights, IL 60004

Randall Howard & Associates, Inc.
Memphis, TN 38115

E. J. Rhodes, Inc.
Framingham, MA 01701

Robertson, Spoerlein & Wengert
Chicago, IL 60606

Rogers & Seymour Inc.
Portland, ME 04103

Rohn Rogers Associates
New York, NY 10036

Romac & Associates
Bala Cynwyd, PA 19004

Romac & Associates, Inc.
Portland, ME 04112

Romac & Associates of Columbus
Columbus, OH 43215

Romano McAvoy Associates, Inc.
Smithtown, NY 11787

Ropes Associates, Inc.
Fort Lauderdale, FL 33394

Lowell N. Ross & Associates
Corte Madera, CA 94925

Ross MacAskills Associates, Inc.
Washington, DC 20036

Robert Sage & Associates
Denton, TX 76201

Sanford Rose Associates
Youngstown, OH 44503

Saxon Morse Associates
Pomona, NY 10970

Schattle Personnel Consultants, Inc.
Warwick, RI 02886

Scope Services, Inc.
St. Joseph, MI 49085

Scott, Rogers Associates
New City, NY 10956

Scully & Associates
Colorado Springs, CO 80918

Search West
Ontario, CA 91764

Slovin Personnel Associates
Worcester, MA 01609

Sockwell & Hendrix
Charlotte, NC 28284

The Software Alliance
Newton, MA 02164

Source EDP
White Plains, NY 10604

Thomas E. Sowell
Jenks, OK 74037

Speciality Consultants, Inc.
Pittsburgh, PA 15222

S.P.I. Personnel Consultants
Wellesley, MA 02181

Staffing Consultants
Alexandria, VA 22312

L. W. Stern Associates, Inc.
New York, NY 10016

STM Associates
Salt Lake, UT 84111

Stoneburner Associates, Inc.
Shawnee Mission, KS 66204

Stonehill Management Consultants, Inc.
New York, NY 10175

Streeter & Associates
Los Angeles, CA 90010

W. J. Stuart & Co.
Los Angeles, CA 90068

Synergistics Associates Ltd.
Chicago, IL 60601

SysTech Organization
Baltimore, MD 21234

SysTech Organization
New York, NY 10019

Systematics Agency
Los Angeles, CA 90025

Systems Careers
San Francisco, CA 94111

Tech Careers
Washington, DC 20037

Technical Recruiters
Washington, DC 20005

Technology Profiles, Inc.
Woburn, MA 01801

Tecmark Associates, Inc.
New York, NY 10123

Michael Thomas, Inc.
Worthington, OH 43085

J. Robert Thompson Co., Inc.
Houston, TX 77027

Torretto & Associates, Inc.
Sausalito, CA 94965

The Trattner Network
Citrus Heights, CA 95610

Traynor Associates, Ltd.
Rochester, NY 14604

Vantage Careers, Inc.
Stamford, CT 06904

Vantage Careers, Inc.
White Plains, NY 10601

C. J. Vincent Associates, Inc.
Columbia, MD 21044

V.V.R. Data Systems Ltd.
New York, NY 10017

Denis P. Walsh & Associates, Inc.
Houston, TX 77018

Watkins & Associates
Houston, TX 77074

Webster Positions, Inc.
Hicksville, NY 11801

Werbin Associates Executive Search, Inc.
New York, NY 10175

Wilkinson & Ives, Inc.
Orinda, CA 94563

R. L. Wolff & Associates
Houston, TX 77057

Dennis Wynn Associates, Inc.
St. Petersburg, FL 33704

Zackrison Associates, Inc.
West Hartford, CT 06110

Zackrison Associates, Inc.
Stamford, CT 06905

Zackrison Associates, Inc.
Fairfield, CT 06430

CONSTRUCTION

American Executive Management, Inc.
Salem, MA 01970

Charles P. Aquavella & Associates
Dallas, TX 75229

James Bangert Associates, Inc.
Wayzata, MN 55391

Barone Associates
Woodbridge, NJ 07095

J. W. Bell & Co.
Newport Beach, CA 92660

C/E Search Construction Engineering
Indian Wells, CA 92210

Fine Personnel Agency
New York, NY 10017

Foster & Associates, Inc.
San Francisco, CA 94105

Ruth Hirsch Career Builders, Inc.
New York, NY 10017

J. L. Jordan Associates
Dallas, TX 75240

Kuhnmuench & Cook Associates
Arcadia, CA 91006

Lamont-Bruckner, Inc.
Tulsa, OK 74135

Michael Latas & Associates, Inc.
St. Louis, MO 63132

Locke & Associates
Charlotte, NC 28280

Ross MacAskills Associates, Inc.
Washington, DC 20036

Main Line Personnel Services, Inc.
Bala Cynwyd, PA 19004

McNichol Associates
Philadelphia, PA 19105

Power & Co.
Boston, MA 02109

Ropes Associates, Inc.
Fort Lauderdale, FL 33394

Ryan/Smith & Associates, Inc.
Westfield, NJ 07091

Robert Sage & Associates
Denton, TX 76201

Specialized Search Associates
Greenwich, CT 06830

Specialty Consultants, Inc.
Pittsburgh, PA 15222

Torretto & Associates, Inc.
Sausalito, CA 94965

Denis P. Walsh & Associates, Inc.
Houston, TX 77018

John Wylie Associates, Inc.
Tulsa, OK 74136

ENGINEERING

Aaron Engineering Agency
Rochelle Park, NJ 07662

ACI
Orlando, FL 32803

ACME Agency
Clifton, NJ 07013

Advantage Personnel Agency
Miami, FL 33155

Agri-Business Services
St. Paul, MN 55113

Agri-Personnel
Atlanta, GA 30349

Aim Executive Recruiting & Search
Cleveland, OH 44132

Aim Executive Recruiting & Search
Toledo, OH 43623

Albany Personnel Service
Albany, GA 31701

M. L. Alber Associates
Columbia, SC 29210

Alexander-Edward Associates, Inc.
Philadelphia, PA 19107

Mark Allen Associates
Severna Park, MD 21146

Ethan Allen Personnel Agency
Poughkeepsie, NY 12601

**Allstates Professional Placement
 Consultants**
Latham, NY 12110

AMCR
Akron, OH 44313

AMD Associates
Silver Spring, MD 20906

American Executive Management, Inc.
Salem, MA 01970

Arista Corporation
Atlanta, GA 30338

Armstrong & Associates
Los Alamitos, CA 90720

Ashway Ltd. Agency
New York, NY 10017

Atlantic Personnel
Merritt Island, FL 32953

Atomic Personnel, Inc.
Philadelphia, PA 19102

Aubin International Inc.
Waltham, MA 02154

Auden Associates Inc.
Middletown, CT 06457

Availability of Hartford
Hartford, CT 06103

Babich & Associates
Dallas, TX 75206

Babich & Associates
Fort Worth, TX 76102

Bailey Employment Service
Waterbury, CT 06702

Baldwin Associates
Cincinnati, OH 45209

Banner Personnel Service
Chicago, IL 60602

Barone Associates
Woodbridge, NJ 07095

Barry & Co.
Los Angeles, CA 90017

The Bartlett Agency
Lewiston, ME 04240

Bason Associates, Inc.
Cincinnati, OH 45215

Beall Associates—Greensboro
Greensboro, NC 27419

Beall Associates of Greenville
Greenville, SC 29608

Beck, Gerstenfeld & Associates
Woodburn, OR 97071

Becker Associates
North Kingstown, RI 02852

Rick Beedle Associates, Inc.
North Hollywood, CA 91607

Belcher Personnel Consultants
Blue Bell, PA 19422

**Benson & Associates, Personnel &
 Management Consultants**
Fort Lauderdale, FL 33309

C. Berke & Associates
Doylestown, PA 18901

Berman Associates
Atlanta, GA 30309

BFH Associates
Sharon, MA 02067

Marc-Paul Bloome Ltd.
New York, NY 10107

Bonner Gladney Associates
Devon, PA 19333

Bott & Associates, Inc., Engineering
Houston, TX 77042

A. D. Boudreaux & Associates
New Orleans, LA 70126

R. L. Brown & Associates
Pompano Beach, FL 33062

Brucks Personnel Corp.
Rochester, NY 14618

Burns Personnel Inc.
Rochester, NY 14604

Robert J. Bushee & Associates, Inc.
Bridgeville, PA 15017

Business Personnel Associates
Glastonbury, CT 06033

The Caldwell Partners International
Houston, TX 77010

Career Builders, Inc.
New York, NY 10017

Career Consultants
Indianapolis, IN 46204

Career Consultants
York, PA 17403

Career Directions
Newburgh, NY 12250

Career Dynamics, Inc.
Melrose, MA 02176

Career Path
Ridgewood, NJ 07450

Career Specialists
Los Altos, CA 94022

Careers Ltd.
Denver, CO 80203

Careers Unlimited
Elkhart, IN 46516

Carpenter Consultants, Inc.
Chestnut Hill, MA 02167

Andrew B. Carr & Associates
San Angelo, TX 76902

Jaci Carroll Personnel Service
Waterbury, CT 06721

CBS Personnel Services
Cincinnati, OH 45202

CBS Personnel Services
Dayton, OH 45402

Centennial Personnel
Cincinnati, OH 45202

Chemical Scientific Services
Columbus, OH 43227

Chevigny Personnel Agency
Merrillville, IN 46410

City & National Employment
Waterloo, IA 50704

Claremont-Branan
Atlanta, GA 30341

Richard Clark Associates
Fairfield, CT 06017

Clark, Clark & Clark Associates
College Park, MD 20740

Darryl Clausing & Associates
Frankfort, IL 60423

Claveloux, McCaffrey & Associates, Inc.
New York, NY 10018

CMA
Narberth, PA 19072

Cochran, Cochran & Yale, Inc.
Rochester, NY 14623

Commonwealth Personnel
Rockville, MD 20852

Com-tek Agency
New York, NY 10017

Consultants, Inc.
North Brunswick, NJ 08902

Continental Search Associates
Birmingham, MI 48012

Corporate Consultants
New Orleans, LA 70112

Corporate Resource Group
Fairfield, CT 06430

Corporate Resource Group
Hartford, CT 06106

Corporate Search
Toledo, OH 43606

Corporate Search & Placement
Orange, CT 06477

Corporate Staffing Group
Horsham, PA 19044

Craig's Criterion
Contoocook, NH 03229

Cross Country Consultants, Inc.
Baltimore, MD 21218

Cruit Executive Search
Birmingham, AL 35259

Frank Cuomo & Associates
Tuckahoe, NY 10707

DAPEXS Consultants
Syracuse, NY 13202

Data Finders, Inc.
Englewood Cliffs, NJ 07632

N. Dean Davic Associates
Pittsburgh, PA 15235

Gene Davis & Associates
Oklahoma City, OK 73156

DEI Executive Services
Cincinnati, OH 45209

Monte Denbo Associates
Cincinnati, OH 45203

Paul DeRivera
Chicago, IL 60606

Deveny & Associates
Dayton, OH 45439

Dimmerling & Associates
Atlanta, GA 30339

Robert W. Dingman Co., Inc.
Westlake Village, CA 91360

Diversified Employment Services
New Haven, CT 06511

Donaldson & Wharton Associates
New York, NY 10001

Dotson Benefield & Associates, Inc.
Atlanta, GA 30345

Drew International Corp.
King of Prussia, PA 19406

Dunhill Personnel—Little Rock
Little Rock, AR 72212

Dunhill of Fort Collins
Fort Collins, CO 80525

Dunhill of Greater Jackson
Jacksonville, FL 39206

Dunhill of St. Petersburg
St. Petersburg, FL 33713

Dunhill of Cedar Rapids
Cedar Rapids, IA 52401

Dunhill of Albuquerque
Albuquerque, NM 87110

Dunhill of Huntington
Melville, NY 11747

Dunhill of Greenville
Greenville, NC 27834

Dunhill Personnel of Northeast Tulsa
Tulsa, OK 74128

Dunhill Personnel—Corpus Christi
Corpus Christi, TX 78411

Dyna-Search
Chicago, IL 60604

E.D.P. World, Inc.
San Francisco, CA 94111

Eggers Personnel & Consulting
Omaha, NB 68144

Electronics Systems Personnel Agency
Minneapolis, MN 55402

Phil Ellis Associates
Raleigh, NC 27658

Employment Opportunities
Danbury, CT 06810

Employment Specialists
Minneapolis, MN 55435

Engineering Employment Agency
New York, NY 10017

Engineering Search Associates
Madison, CT 06443

Employment Unlimited Agency
Baltimore, MD 21231

R. J. Evans & Associates, Inc.
Beachwood, OH 44122

Excel Personnel
Greenville, SC 29607

Executive Personnel Consultants
Memphis, TN 38117

Executive Placement Corporation
Rochester, NY 14604

Executive Recruiting Consultants, Inc.
Des Plaines, IL 60016

Executive Register, Inc.
Danbury, CT 06810

Executive Resource
St. Louis, MO 63132

Executive Search
Charlotte, NC 28222

Fairfield Whitney
Stratford, CT 06497

Richard Farber Associates, Inc.
Great Neck, NY 11021

Far Western Placement Services
Phoenix, AZ 85012

Flowers and Associates
Maumee, OH 43537

Ford and Ford
Dedham, MA 02026

Forest Associates
Caldwell, NJ 07006

Fortune of Providence
Providence, RI 02903

Fortune Personnel Consultants
Stamford, CT 06901

Fortune Personnel Consultants—Boston
Boston, MA 01803

Fortune Personnel Consultants
Nashua, NH 03062

Fox Morris
Baltimore, MD 21204

Fox-Morris Associates, Inc.
Philadelphia, PA 19109

A. O. Frost, Staffing Consultant
Springfield, MA 01101

Futures Personnel Services
Baltimore, MD 21204

Gather, Inc.
Chartley, MA 02712

General Employment Enterprises
Fremont, CA 94538

General Employment Enterprises
Palo Alto, CA 94303

General Employment Enterprises
Torrance, CA 90503

General Employment Enterprises
Woodland Hills, CA 91367

General Employment Enterprises
Chicago, IL 60606

General Employment Enterprises
Oak Brook, IL 60521

General Employment Enterprises, Inc.
Columbus, OH 43229

General Employment Enterprises, Inc.
Philadelphia, PA 19103

Genovese & Co. Management Consultants
Los Angeles, CA 90067

J. Gifford, Inc.
Tulsa, OK 74135

Glou International
Needham, MA 02192

Thomas Glover Associates
North Charleston, SC 29301

Glynn, Brooks & Co.
Fort Lee, NJ 07024

GMR, Inc.
Los Angeles, CA 90049

Gold Card Recruiters
Camden, AR 71701

Gordon, Cook & Associates
Clayton, MO 63105

Robert J. Grace Associates
Westwood, MA 02090

Graham & Associates Employee Consultants
Greensboro, NC 27408

Gray-Kimball Associates
Massapequa, NY 11758

Green & Green
New York, NY 10016

Growth Placement Associates, Inc.
Downingtown, PA 19335

The Gruen Co.
Oakland, CA 94618

Hahn & Associates
Dayton, OH 45402

Robert Half of Dayton
Dayton, OH 45402

The Hamilton/Ryker Company
Martin, TN 38237

Robert Harkins Associates
Ephrata, PA 17522

Harmon Anderson International
Westlake Village, CA 91362

Harris & U'Ren, Inc.
Phoenix, AZ 85003

Harvey Personnel
North Charleston, SC 29304

T. J. Hayes Associates
Assonet, MA 02702

Headhunters National
Portland, OR 97221

Health Industry Consultants, Inc.
Englewood, CO 80112

F. P. Healy & Company
New York, NY 10169

Heberling Personnel
Harrisburg, PA 17105

E. B. Hendrick Associates
Liverpool, NY 13088

Hipp Waters Professional Recruiters
Stamford, CT 06901

Hipp Waters Professional Recruiting
Boston, MA 02109

J. L. Hoglund Co., Inc.
Natroma Heights, PA 15065

Hones and Company
Fort Myers, FL 33901

Horizon Personnel
York, PA 17402

Horizon Personnel
Franklin, TN 37064

Human Resource Consultants Ltd.
Hartford, CT 06103

A. R. Hutton Agency
Yuma, AZ 85364

Hytex Engineering
Los Alamitos, CA 90720

Image
Massapequa, NY 11758

Indusearch
Newington, CT 06111

Intelcom Professional Services
Columbia, MD 21044

International ExecuSearch, Ltd.
Scottsdale, AZ 85254

International Personnel Consultants, Inc.
Hanover, NH 03755

International Search Corp.
Tulsa, OK 74135

International Staffing Consultants, Inc.
Newport Beach, CA 92260

Nancy Jackson, Inc.
Scranton, PA 18503

JAMAR Personnel Service
Rock Island, IL 61201

Job Finders/Jobs Temporary
Des Moines, IA 50312

Johnson & Genrich, Inc.
Chicago, IL 60630

Johnson Personnel
Canton, OH 44718

Jorgenson Associates
Englewood, CO 80111

JPM & Associates
Los Angeles, CA 92660

JPM Associates, DBA
San Clemente, CA 92672

JY Enterprises
New York, NY 10007

Richard Kaye Personnel Agency, Inc.
New York, NY 10017

KBK Management Associates
Youngstown, OH 44512

E. A. Keepy—National Recruiters
Davenport, IA 52805

Kelly & Thomas Associates, Inc.
Bala Cynwyd, PA 19004

Kendall and Davis Company
St. Louis, MO 63102

Kenex Consultants
Aurora, CO 80014

Kenmore Executive Personnel, Inc.
New York, NY 10017

James H. Kennedy
Fitzwilliam, NH 03447

Kenneth C. Kern Personnel Services
Houston, TX 77027

Key Employment Services
West Des Moines, IA 50265

KGC Associates
East Hartford, CT 06108

Kinkead Associates
Hartford, CT 06103

Lou Klein Associates
Bridgeport, CT 06606

Robert Kleven & Co., Inc.
Boston, MA 02109

KMS Associates
Kingston, NY 12401

Kors, Marlar, Savage & Associates
Annapolis, MD 21401

Krow Associates, Inc.
West Caldwell, NJ 07006

Kuebler Associates
Portland, ME 04101

Kuhnmuench & Cook Associates
Arcadia, CA 91006

Lane Employment Service
Worcester, MA 01608

Gilbert Lane Personnel
Hamden, CT 06517

Gilbert Lane Personnel Agency
Hartford, CT 06103

Gilbert Lane Associates
Atlanta, GA 30339

Gilbert Lane Personnel Service
Springfield, MA 01115

Arthur J. Langdon
Hartford, CT 06103

Larsen Personnel
Needham, MA 02192

Leon-Lawrence Personnel
Bridgeport, CT 06606

W. R. Lawry, Inc.
Simsbury, CT 06070

Mike Lawson Personnel
Louisville, KY 40217

M. A. Liggett, Inc.
Elmsford, NY 10523

Lineback Associates
Dallas, TX 75240

Lineback Associates
Houston, TX 77042

Locke & Associates
Charlotte, NC 28280

London Scott Associates
Clifton Park, NY 12065

Longs Personnel Service
Mobile, AL 36616

Lucas Associates Inc.
Houston, TX 77008

Ludot Personnel Services
Southfield, MI 48075

McCulloch and Company
Greenville, SC 29603

Ellie Mack Associates
Wilmington, DE 19810

McMahon & Associates
Stone Mountain, GA 30086

McNichol Associates
Philadelphia, PA 19105

Mahony Associates
Atlanta, GA 30328

Main Line Personnel Services, Inc.
Bala Cynwyd, PA 19004

J. C. Malone Associates
Louisville, KY 40218

Management Recruiters Midwest
Thousand Oaks, CA 91360

Management Recruiters—Hamden
Hamden, CT 06518

Management Recruiters of Puerto Rico, Inc.
Hato Rey, PR 00918

Management Resource Associates
Woburn, MA 01801

Management Search, Inc.
Chicago, IL 60611

Management Search, Inc.
Annandale, VA 22003

Mar-El Employment Agency
Levittown, NY 11756

Margolin
New York, NY 10016

Marshall Group
Los Angeles, CA 92660

Marvel Consultants
Cleveland, OH 44122

Pete Massarini & Associates, Employment
  Consultants
Houston, TX 77057

M. D. Mattes & Associates
Timonium, MD 21093

MBH Associates, Inc.
Philadelphia, PA 19103

Midcom Agency
Orange, CA 92665

Morgan & Associates
Springfield, MA 01115

MPI Associates
Boulder, CO 80302

Mullins & Associates
Barrington, IL 60010

Multi Technology Inc.
Framingham, MA 01701

Gordon Mulvey & Associates
Louisville, KY 40207

Murphy Symonds and Stowell
Portland, OR 97204

National Career Centers—USA
Fayetteville, NC 28302

National Career Services
Harrisburg, PA 17105

National Recruiters
Raleigh, NC 27609

Nationwide Business Service
Springfield, MA 01103

Gary Nelson & Associates, Inc.
Cupertino, CA 95014

N.E. Power and Electronics Personnel
Ballston Spa, NY 12020

Perry Newcomb & Associates
Cincinnati, OH 45230

New Dimensions
Woburn, MA 01801

New England Consultants
Warwick, RI 02887

Nicastro Associates
Westport, CT 06880

The NRI Group
Rockville, MD 20852

Oliver & Rosner Associates
New York, NY 10022

Oliver Associates, Inc.
Melville, NY 11747

Omnisearch
Dallas, TX 75243

Ott & Hansen, Inc.
Pasadena, CA 91101

Paramount Personnel Service
Oakland, CA 94612

Robert Pencarski & Company
Dedham, MA 02026

People Management Inc.
Simsbury, CT 06070

Perry-White & Associates, Inc.
Los Angeles, CA 90010

Perry-White & Associates, Inc.
San Francisco, CA 94104

Perry-White & Associates, Inc.
Santa Clara, CA 95050

Perry-White & Associates, Inc.
Waltham, MA 02154

Perry-White & Associates, Inc.
Dallas, TX 75240

Perry-White & Associates, Inc.
Houston, TX 77074

Personnel Center
Gainesville, FL 32602

Personnel Director Associates
Ann Arbor, MI 48104

Personnel Recruiters
Springfield, NJ 07081

Personnel Search
Omaha, NB 68124

Peterson Personnel Recruiters
Warwick, RI 02886

Phillips Personnel Search
Denver, CO 80202

Phoenix Personnel Services
Harrisburg, PA 17105

Piedmont Personnel Consultants
Greenville, SC 29615

Placement Experts
Huntsville, AL 35801

The Placers, Inc.
Wilmington, DE 19806

Polytechnical Consultants, Inc.
Chicago, IL 60659

Power Industry Personnel
Groton, CT 06340

Power Services
North Charleston, SC 29406

Norman Powers Associates, Inc.
Saxonville, MA 01701

PPS Consultants
Phoenix, AZ 85004

Pratt Placement Service
Philadelphia, PA 19124

Preferred Positions
Nashua, NH 03060

Probe Technology
King of Prussia, PA 19406

Proctor & Davis
Santa Monica, CA 90403

Professional Career Placements
Arlington, TX 76003

Professional Computer Personnel
Waterbury, CT 06702

Professional Executive Consultants
Northbrook, IL 60062

Professional Personnel Consultants—Tampa
Tampa, FL 33607

Professional Personnel Consultants
Southfield, MI 48075

Professional Personnel Associates
Charlotte, NC 28212

Professional Recruiters
Omaha, NB 68106

The Protech Group
Chicago, IL 60606

Provident Personnel Consultants
Prospect Park, PA 19076

Purcell Employment Systems
Los Angeles, CA 90010

Purcell Employment Systems
Woodbridge, NJ 07095

Purcell Group Management Consultants
Houston, TX 77057

Quality Control Recruiters
Bristol, CT 06010

Queens Employment Service
Long Island City, NY 11101

Quinlivan & Company
York, PA 17401

Quinn Associates, Ltd.
Stratford, CT 06497

Rasmussen & Associates
Kingsport, TN 37663

The Recruiter
Des Moines, IA 50311

The Recruiting Group
Laguna Hills, CA 92653

Research Technologies
Madison, CT 06443

Retail Recruiters, Spectra Professional Search
Fort Lauderdale, FL 33311

Reynolds Technical Services
Stratford, CT 06497

Lloyd Richards Personnel Service
Tulsa, OK 74103

Rita Personnel—West Massachusetts
Springfield, MA 01103

RJS Associates
Hartford, CT 06103

Robertson, Spoerlein & Wengert
Chicago, IL 60606

Rocky Mountain Recruiters
Denver, CO 80202

ROMAC Personnel Consultants
Houston, TX 77002

Richard R. Rosche
St. Louis, MO 63163

Lowell N. Ross & Associates
Corte Madera, CA 94925

Roth Young Personnel of Minneapolis
Edina, MN 55435

Russ Fallstad and Associates
Minneapolis, MN 55426

Sales Recruiters of Kansas City
Kansas City, MO 64106

Sanford Rose Associates of Hartford
Windsor, CT 06095

Sanford Rose Associates—Charlotte
Charlotte, NC 28211

Sanford Rose Associates
Youngstown, OH 44503

Sanmar Staffing Consultants
Philadelphia, PA 19107

Savannah Personnel Consultants
Savannah, GA 31406

Schattle Personnel Consultants, Inc.
Warwick, RI 02886

Science Center
Fort Washington, PA 19034

Scientific Placement Inc.
Houston, TX 77224

Scully & Associates
Colorado Springs, CO 80918

Search Northwest & Affiliates
Portland, OR 97204

Search Specialists, Inc.
Orland Park, IL 60462

Search Tech Associates
Calabasas, CA 91302

Select Finders Corp.
West Caldwell, NJ 07006

Sequent Personnel Services
Mountain View, CA 94041

Siegel & Bishop, Inc.
San Francisco, CA 94112

Snelling and Snelling
Albuquerque, NM 87110

Snelling & Snelling
Lexington, SC 29072

David Solol Personnel Consultant
Kutztown, PA 19530

Southern Recruiters & Consultants
Aiken, SC 29802

Thomas E. Sowell
Jenks, OK 74037

Spectra Professional Search
New Haven, CT 06511

Staffing Consultants
Vienna, VA 22180

STM Associates
Salt Lake, UT 84111

STO Fox Personnel Consultants
Greensboro, NC 27429

Stoneburner Associates, Inc.
Shawnee Mission, KS 66204

W. J. Stuart & Co.
Los Angeles, CA 90068

Sturm Burrows & Company
Philadelphia, PA 19102

Sumrall Personnel Consultants
Dallas, TX 75234

Sun Valley Personnel Agency
Walnut Creek, CA 94596

Roy Talman & Associates
Chicago, IL 60601

Target Search
Rockville, MD 20850

The Technical Group
Westport, CT 06880

Technical Placement, Inc.
King of Prussia, PA 19406

Technical Search Associates
Danbury, CT 06810

Technical Support Etc.
Marlboro, MA 01752

Tech Recruiters
South Plainfield, NJ 07080

Tech Search
Rockville, MD 20852

Teiper Personnel Service
Toledo, OH 43615

J. Robert Thompson Co., Inc.
Houston, TX 77027

The Trattner Network
Citrus Heights, CA 95610

M. D. Treadway & Company
Olive Branch, MS 38654

Trimbec
Liverpool, NY 13088

P. T. Unger Associates
Washington, DC 20036

Uni/Search of New Haven
Woodbridge, CT 06525

United Consultants
York, PA 17403

Varo & Lund Corp.
Los Angeles, CA 90028

Vezan-West & Co.
West Hartford, CT 06107

C. J. Vincent Associates, Inc.
Columbia, MD 21044

VIP Personnel of Raleigh
Raleigh, NC 27619

Vlcek & Company
Los Angeles, CA 92660

Wallach Associates
Rockville, MD 20850

Denis P. Walsh & Associates, Inc.
Houston, TX 77018

Sally Walters Placement Agency
San Francisco, CA 94104

R. H. Warner Consulting
Westerville, OH 43081

Wayne Associates, Inc.
Virginia Beach, VA 23452

Wayne Executive Search
Portland, OR 97266

Webster Positions, Inc.
Hicksville, NY 11801

Werbin Associates Executive Search, Inc.
New York, NY 10175

Western Executive Consultants
Las Vegas, NV 89108

Western Personnel Associates, Inc.
Phoenix, AZ 85012

E. T. Wharton Associates
New York, NY 10001

Whitlow and Associates
Atlanta, GA 30326

Whitman Stone Associates
Orange, CA 92668

Whittaker and Associates, Inc.
Atlanta, GA 30339

Wilson Personnel, Inc.
Asheville, NC 28801

Woodson Associates
Ashland, MA 01721

Jim Woodson & Associates
Jackson, MS 39216

Xagas & Associates
Geneva, IL 60134

XXCAL
Los Angeles, CA 90025

Zackrison Associates, Inc.
Fairfield, CT 06430

Zackrison Associates, Inc.
Stamford, CT 06905

Zackrison Associates, Inc.
West Hartford, CT 06110

The Zivic Group
San Francisco, CA 94111

FINANCE

Accounting & Financial Recruiters
Houston, TX 77056

Accounting Resources International
Laguna Niguel, CA 92677

Jeffrey C. Adams & Co., Inc.
San Francisco, CA 94104

Alberta-Smyth Personnel Agency, Inc.
Union, NJ 07083

Alberta-Smyth Personnel Agency, Inc.
New York, NY 10165

Analytic Recruiting, Inc.
New York, NY 10017

The Andre Group, Inc.
King of Prussia, PA 19406

Armstrong & Associates
Los Alamitos, CA 90720

Aronow Associates, Inc.
New York, NY 10001

Arthur Personnel
Caldwell, NJ 07006

ASC & Co.
Houston, TX 77056

E. J. Ashton & Associates, Ltd.
Arlington Heights, IL 60004

Ashworth Consultants
Boston, MA 02109

Austin-Allen Co.
Memphis, TN 38119

Availability Personnel Consultants
Bedford, NH 03102

James Bangert Associates, Inc.
Wayzata, MN 55391

Barclays Recruiting Services, Inc.
Denver, CO 80222

Nathan Barry Associates, Inc.
Boston, MA 02109

Battalia & Associates, Inc.
New York, NY 10016

The Baxter Group
Rancho Palos Verdes, CA 90274

Bay Search Group
Providence, RI 02903

BCL Corporation
Cleveland, OH 44107

Rick Beedle Associates, Inc.
North Hollywood, CA 91607

Richard Beers & Associates, Ltd.
Glenview, IL 60025

John Bell & Associates, Inc.
Chicago, IL 60611

Benton, Schneider & Associates
Naperville, IL 60540

E. J. Bettinger Co.
Philadelphia, PA 19102

Blaine & Associates, Inc.
Encino, CA 91436

Marc-Paul Bloome Ltd.
New York, NY 10017

R. L. Booton & Associates
St. Louis, MO 63141

Bradstreet Management, Inc.
New York, NY 10165

William H. Brawley Associates
New Canaan, CT 06840

The Breen Group Inc.
Hamden, CT 06518

Breitmayer Associates
Guilford, CT 06437

Bryant Associates, Inc.
Chicago, IL 60611

Burns Personnel Inc.
Rochester, NY 14604

Robert J. Bushee & Associates, Inc.
Bridgeville, PA 15017

Buzhardt Associates
Jackson, MS 39211

Cantor & Co., Inc.
Philadelphia, PA 19103

Career Concepts
New York, NY 10036

Career Specialists, Inc.
Bellevue, WA 98004

Chanko-Ward, Ltd.
New York, NY 10036

Christenson & Montgomery
Morristown, NJ 07960

Christopher, Drew & Associates, Inc.
Cleveland, OH 44122

Clark Associates, Inc.
Atlanta, Ga 30345

Claveloux, McCaffrey & Associates, Inc.
New York, NY 10018

Closman & Associates, Inc.
New York, NY 10001

Cochran, Cochran & Yale, Inc.
Rochester, NY 14623

Cole, Warren & Long, Inc.
Philadelphia, PA 19102

Conaway Personnel Associates, Inc.
Baltimore, MD 21202

The Concord Group, Ltd.
Barrington, IL 60010

Consultant Group-Langlois & Associates, Inc.
Needham, MA 02194

Coopers & Lybrand
Los Angeles, CA 90017

Corporate Advisors Inc.
Miami, FL 33137

Corporate Career Consultants
San Francisco, CA 94111

The Corporate Connection, Ltd.
Richmond, VA 23230

Corporate Recruiters, Inc.
Philadelphia, PA 19126

Corporate Service Group, Ltd.
San Francisco, CA 94102

Craighead Associates
Stamford, CT 06901

Creative Search Affiliates
New York, NY 10021

Cretney & Associates
Cleveland, OH 44143

Cris Associates, Inc.
New York, NY 10016

Crispi, Wagner & Co., Inc.
New York, NY 10170

Cross Country Consultants, Inc.
Baltimore, MD 21218

Crown, Michaels & Associates, Inc.
Los Angeles, CA 90067

Daly & Co., Inc.
Boston, MA 02116

Darson Personnel Associates, Inc.
New York, NY 10168

David-Kris Associates
Westport, CT 06881

Davies Associates International
Houston, TX 77218

Robert H. Davidson Associates
Norwood, MA 02062

The Dean Group
Maplewood, NJ 07040

William S. DeFuniak, Inc.
Hinsdale, IL 60521

Delta Resource Group, Ltd.
Marietta, GA 30067

Jerry Demaso & Associates
Metairie, LA 70002

Deven Associates, Inc.
Verona, NJ 07044

R. M. Donaldson Personnel
Cranford, NJ 07016

Dorison & Company
Coral Gables, FL 33134

Dotson Benefield & Associates, Inc.
Atlanta, GA 30345

Dumont Kiradjieff & Moriarty
Boston, MA 02109

Dunhill Personnel Service
Philadelphia, PA 19102

Earley Kielty & Associates, Inc.
New York, NY 10121

E.D.P. World, Inc.
San Francisco, CA 94111

Edwards & Sowers, Inc.
Chicago, IL 60611

The Elliott Company, Inc.
Woburn, MA 01801

David M. Ellner Associates
New York, NY 10121

Emerson Professionals
Burlington, MA 01803

The Engineers Index
Boston, MA 02110

Equinox Management Corp.
Norwalk, CT 06851

Estar Execu/Search, Ltd.
Palatine, IL 60067

Evans Associates, Inc.
San Francisco, CA 94104

Executive Image, Inc.
New York, NY 10016

Executive Personnel Consultants
Memphis, TN 38117

Executive Recruiters
Little Rock, AR 72211

Executive Recruiters, Inc.
Milwaukee, WI 53226

Executive Register, Inc.
Danbury, CT 06810

Executive Search
Stamford, CT 06901

Executive Search Company
Conshohocken, PA 19428

Exxell
New York, NY 10038

Fanning Personnel of Boston
Boston, MA 02116

Fells & Baroody, Inc.
New York, NY 10001

Fine Personnel Agency
New York, NY 10017

First Word Placement Service
Dallas, TX 75240

A. G. Fishkin & Associates, Inc.
Rockville, MD 20852

Fleming Associates
Miami, FL 33166

Fleming Associates
Sarasota, FL 33577

Fleming Associates
Atlanta, GA 30339

Fleming Associates
Columbus, IN 47202

Fleming Associates
Louisville, KY 40220

Fleming Associates
Metairie, LA 70002

Fleming Associates
Dublin, OH 43017

Fleming Associates
Memphis, TN 38111

Fleming Associates
Houston, TX 77024

Flinn Consultants, Inc.
Highland Park, IL 60035

Ford & Ford
Dedham, MA 02026

Forum Personnel
New York, NY 10017

Foster & Associates, Inc.
San Francisco, CA 94105

Fox & Fleischer
Richardson, TX 75080

Fox-Morris
Philadelphia, PA 19109

Edmund A. Frank & Associates
Westchester, IL 60153

Furman Group, Ltd.
New York, NY 10017

Garrett Associates, Inc.
Atlanta, GA 30339

Edward Gaylord & Associates
Mill Valley, CA 94942

J. Gifford, Inc.
Tulsa, OK 74135

B. Goodwin, Ltd.
Fairfield, CT 06430

Graduates Unlimited Personnel, Inc.
Union, NJ 07083

Paul C. Green & Associates, Ltd.
Green Valley, AZ 85614

Griffith & Werner, Inc.
Hollywood, FL 33021

Group IV Recruitment Consultants
New York, NY 10036

Hahn & Associates, Inc.
Dayton, OH 45402

Robert Half of Orange County
Newport Beach, CA 92660

Robert Half of Northern California
San Francisco, CA 94111

Robert Half, Inc.
Chicago, IL 60601

Robert Half
New Orleans, LA 70157

Robert Half of Boston
Boston, MA 02110

Robert Half
Lexington, MA 02173

Robert Half
Worcester, MA 01608

Robert Half
Albuquerque, NM 87190

Robert Half of Philadelphia, Inc.
King of Prussia, PA 19406

Robert Half of Philadelphia, Inc.
Philadelphia, PA 19103

Robert Half of Philadelphia, Inc.
Trevose, PA 19047

Robert Half
Providence, RI 02903

Harper Associates
Southfield, MI 48075

T. G. Harper & Co., Inc.
Philadelphia, PA 19106

Haskell & Stern Associates, Inc.
New York, NY 10017

Haskell & Stern Associates, Inc.
Fort Worth, TX 76112

Hayden & Refo, Inc.
Boston, MA 02110

Hayman & Company
Dallas, TX 75201

F. P. Healy & Company
New York, NY 10169

Heberling Personnel
Harrisburg, PA 17105

Higbee Associates, Inc.
Rowayton, CT 06853

Hipp Waters Professional Recruiting
Boston, MA 02109

Ruth Hirsch Career Builders, Inc.
New York, NY 10017

HiTech Consulting Group
Los Angeles, CA 90067

Hogan Associates
Cleveland, OH 44132

Holland & Associates
Towson, MD 21204

Hospitality Personnel, Inc.
Valley Forge, PA 19481

Randall Howard & Associates, Inc.
Memphis, TN 38115

Robert Howe & Associates
Atlanta, GA 30341

Jack Hurst & Associates, Inc.
Richardson, TX 75080

Huxtable Associates, Inc.
Bridgeton, MO 63044

JNB Associates, Inc.
Boston, MA 02110

A. G. Johnson & Co., Inc.
Irvine, CA 92715

Johnson, Smith and Knisely
New York, NY 10017

Judd-Falk Inc.
New York, NY 10016

Kanon
New York, NY 10018

Karam Associates
Denver, CO 80224

Howard L. Karr & Associates, Inc.
San Mateo, CA 94402

Martin Kartin & Company
New York, NY 10021

Melvin Kent & Associates
Columbus, OH 43215

Kenfield Research Associates, Inc.
New York, NY 10016

Kenmore Executive Personnel, Inc.
New York, NY 10017

KGC Associates
East Hartford, CT 06108

Kingston & Associates
Tucson, AZ 85710

James M. Kittleman & Associates, Inc.
Chicago, IL 60604

Kors, Marlar, Savage & Associates
Annapolis, MD 21401

D. A. Kreuter Associates
Philadelphia, PA 19103

Kunzer Associates, Ltd.
Chicago, IL 60604

Gilbert Lane Associates
Atlanta, GA 30339

Largent Parks & Partners, Inc.
Dallas, TX 75240

Michael Latas & Associates, Inc.
St. Louis, MO 63132

Mina Latham
Bal Harbour, FL 33154

Leahy & Company
Boston, MA 02110

Lee Calhoon & Co., Inc.
Birchrunville, PA 19421

Leonard Associates
Rocky Hill, CT 06067

Lineback Associates
Dallas, TX 75240

Lineback Associates
Houston, TX 77042

Locke & Associates
Charlotte, NC 28280

Franklin Lorsch Associates, Inc.
New York, NY 10017

Arthur J. Loveley Associates
New York, NY 10165

Arthur Lyle Associates, Inc.
Stamford, CT 06901

Lyman & Co.
Glendale, CA 91203

George P. Lyon Associates
Doylestown, PA 18901

McCormack & Farrow
Long Beach, CA 90802

Edwin McDonald Associates
New York, NY 10017

The Foster McKay Group
Tampa, FL 33614

Jon McRae & Associates, Inc.
Charlotte, NC 28282

McSherry & Associates
Chicago, IL 60601

Maetzold Associates, Inc.
Minnetonka, MN 55343

Management Recruiters
Green Bay, WI 54301

Management Search & Associates
Westport, CT 06880

Management Search, Inc.
Chicago, IL 60611

Management Search Inc.
Minneapolis, MN 55426

Management Search, Inc.
Annandale, VA 22003

Marshall-Alan Associates
New York, NY 10038

MBA Associates, Inc.
Boston, MA 02109

Medical Recruiters of America
Tampa, FL 33607

Meehan Associates
Rochester, NY 14625

Metricor, Inc.
Oak Brook Terrace, IL 60181

Michaels, Patrick, O'Brien & Williams, Inc.
Columbia, MD 21044

MKI Recruiting Associates
White Plains, NY 10601

Morgan Research
New York, NY 10175

Morris Madden & Rice, Inc.
New York, NY 10176

J. R. Morrison & Associates, Inc.
San Francisco, CA 94111

Richard Mowell Associates, Inc.
Tallahassee, FL 32303

MRG Search & Placement
New Haven, CT 06510

Gary Nelson & Associates, Inc.
Cupertino, CA 95014

Gary Nelson & Associates, Inc.
San Rafael, CA 94913

William H. Nenstiel & Associates, Inc.
Scottsdale, AZ 85251

Newell Associates, Inc.
New York, NY 10022

Ronald Norris & Associates
Skokie, IL 60076

Paul Norsell & Associates, Inc.
Anaheim, CA 92807

Paul Norsell & Associates, Inc.
Los Angeles, CA 90045

The NRI Group
Washington, DC 20036

The NRI Group
Rockville, MD 20850

The NRI Group
Rockville, MD 20852

The NRI Group
Vienna, VA 22180

Robert E. Nurse Associates, Inc.
White Plains, NY 10530

Oliver & Rosner Associates
New York, NY 10022

O'Neill Executive Search
Buffalo, NY 14223

Patton/Perry Associates
Charlotte, NC 28202

Peeney Associates, Inc.
Fanwood, NJ 07023

Peyser Associates, Inc.
Miami, FL 33125

Phillips Associates
Englewood, NJ 07631

Phillips Resource Group
Greenville, SC 29606

Pinkerton & Associates, Inc.
Chicago, IL 60611

The Placers, Inc.
Wilmington, DE 19806

Positions, Inc.
Providence, RI 02904

Proctor & Davis
Santa Monica, CA 90403

Professional Placement Group
Boston, MA 02109

Professional Recruiters Inc.
Auburn, MA 01501

Rainess Associates
West Caldwell, NJ 07006

Redmond & Associates, Inc.
Danbury, CT 06810

E. J. Rhodes, Inc.
Framingham, MA 01701

Ridgefield Search International
Ridgefield, CT 06877

Roche Associates
Stamford, CT 06094

Rogers & Sands Inc.
Burlington, MA 02108

Rogers & Seymour Inc.
Portland, ME 04103

Romac & Associates, Inc.
Portland, ME 04112

Romac
Boston, MA 02110

Romac
Wellesley, MA 02181

ROMAC Personnel Consultants
Houston, TX 77002

Romano McAvoy Associates, Inc.
Smithtown, NY 11787

Ross MacAskills Associates, Inc.
Washington, DC 20036

Louis Rudzinsky Associates, Inc.
Lexington, MA 02173

Charles Russ Associates, Inc.
Kansas City, MO 64114

R.V.M. Associates, Inc.
White Plains, NY 10604

Ryan/Smith & Associates, Inc.
Westfield, NJ 07091

Sales & Management Search, Inc.
Chicago, IL 60606

Saxon Morse Associates
Pomona, NY 10970

Schattle Personnel Consultants, Inc.
Warwick, RI 02886

Schuyler Associates, Ltd.
Atlanta, GA 30339

Scott, Rogers Associates
New City, NY 10956

Search Source Inc.
Granite City, IL 62040

Siegel Shotland & Associates
Encino, CA 91436

Simon & Ryan, Inc.
San Francisco, CA 94104

Sinclair & Potts Associates, Inc.
Pittsburgh, PA 15235

Carolyn Smith Paschal International
Del Mar, CA 92014

Howard W. Smith Associates
Hartford, CT 06103

Smith Hanley Associates, Inc.
New York, NY 10165

Smyth Dawson Associates
Stamford, CT 06901

Sockwell & Hendrix
Charlotte, NC 28284

Soltis Management Services
Radnor, PA 19087

Source Finance
Century City, CA 90067

Source Finance
Los Angeles, CA 90017

Source Finance
Mountain View, CA 94043

Source Finance
Newport Beach, CA 92660

Source Finance
San Francisco, CA 94111

Source Finance
Van Nuys, CA 91406

Source Finance
Walnut Creek, CA 94596

Source Finance
Englewood, CO 80111

Source Finance
Washington, DC 20006

Source Finance
Atlanta, GA 30303

Source Finance
Tysons Corner, VA 22180

S.P.I. Personnel Consultants
Wellesley, MA 02181

Stanislaw & Associates, Inc.
Brookfield, WI 53005

L. W. Stern Associates, Inc.
New York, NY 10016

STM Associates
Salt Lake, UT 84111

Stonehill Management Consultants, Inc.
New York, NY 10175

Stone Management
New York, NY 10016

Streeter & Associates
Los Angeles, CA 90010

John J. Sudlow & Co.
Chicago, IL 60611

John J. Sudlow & Co.
Seattle, WA 98101

Synergistics Associates Ltd.
Chicago, IL 60601

F. L. Taylor & Co., Inc.
New York, NY 10016

Richard Theobald & Associates
San Mateo, CA 94404

Thomas, Whelan Associates, Inc.
Washington, DC 20006

J. Robert Thompson, Co., Inc.
Houston, TX 77027

Torretto & Associates, Inc.
Sausalito, CA 94965

Traynor Associates, Ltd.
Rochester, NY 14604

Coker, Tyler & Co.
Atlanta, GA 30341

VanMaldegiam Associates, Inc.
Chicago, IL 60606

Vantage Careers, Inc.
Stamford, CT 06904

Vantage Careers, Inc.
White Plains, NY 10601

Wachtel & Associates, Ltd.
New York, NY 10017

John H. Warner Associates, Inc.
Hartford, CT 06103

Emanuel Weintraub Associates, Inc.
Fort Lee, NJ 07024

Western Personnel Associates, Inc.
Phoenix, AZ 85012

Western Reserve Associates
Bath, OH 44210

David J. White & Associates Inc.
Chicago, IL 60606

E. N. Wilkins & Company, Inc.
Chicago, IL 60606

Wilkinson & Ives, Inc.
La Canada, CA 91011

Wilkinson, & Ives, Inc.
Orinda, CA 94563

J. W. Willard Associates, Inc.
Syracuse, NY 13201

William H. Willis, Inc.
New York, NY 10022

Duane I. Wilson Associates, Inc.
Birmingham, MI 48011

Winguth, Schweichler Associates, Inc.
San Francisco, CA 94111

Winter Wyman & Company
Bedford, MA 01730

Witt Associates, Inc.
Oak Brook, IL 60521

The Woodward Group
Chicago, IL 60601

Wunderlich & Associates, Inc.
Oak Brook, IL 60521

John Wylie Associates, Inc.
Tulsa, OK 74136

Zackrison Associates, Inc.
Fairfield, CT 06430

Zackrison Associates, Inc.
Stamford, CT 06905

Zackrison Associates, Inc.
West Hartford, CT 06110

The Zivic Group
San Francisco, CA 94111

GENERAL MANAGEMENT

Abbott Smith Associates, Inc.
Millbrook, NY 12545

Accounting Personnel Associates
Pittsburgh, PA 15222

Advantage Executive Search
Atlanta, GA 30341

Advantage Personnel Agency
Miami, FL 33155

Agra Placements, Ltd.
Lincoln, IL 62656

Agra Placements, Ltd.
Peru, IN 46970

Agra Placements, Ltd.
West Des Moines, IA 50265

Agri-Associates
Davenport, IA 52803

Agri-Personnel
Atlanta, GA 30349

Aim Executive Recruiting & Search
Cleveland, OH 44132

Aim Executive Recruiting & Search
Toledo, OH 43623

J. R. Akin & Company
New York, NY 10022

Thomas R. Aldrich & Associates
Westford, MA 01886

Mark Allen Associates
Severna Park, MD 21146

Allied Search
Norcross, GA 30092

Allied Search
San Francisco, CA 94123

American Executive Search Services, Inc.
San Jose, CA 95135

American Executive Search Services, Inc.
Santa Clara, CA 95051

Andcor Companies
Minneapolis, MN 55426

Anderson-Gest & Associates
Bellevue, WA 98004

Anderson, Graham & Stewart
Marietta, GA 30061

The Andre Group, Inc.
King of Prussia, PA 19406

Armstrong & Associates
Los Alamitos, CA 90720

Aronow Associates, Inc.
New York, NY 10001

Artgo, Inc.
Cleveland, OH 44114

Arthur Personnel
Caldwell, NJ 07006

E. J. Ashton & Associates, Ltd.
Arlington Heights, IL 60004

Atlantic Professional Recruiters
Gaffney, SC 29340

Auden Associates, Inc.
Middletown, CT 06457

AY/ERC
Dallas, TX 75221

Baker Scott & Company
Parsippany, NJ 07054

Banner Personnel Service
Chicago, IL 60602

Nathan Barry Associates, Inc.
Boston, MA 02109

The Barry Companies
Wilmington, DE 19801

Barry & Co.
Los Angeles, CA 90017

Bason Associates, Inc.
Cincinnati, OH 45215

Bay Search Group
Providence, RI 02903

BCL Corporation
Cleveland, OH 44107

Beall International, Inc.
Atlanta, GA 30328

Beck, Gerstenfeld & Associates
Woodburn, OR 97071

Robert Becker & Co.
Allison Park, PA 15101

Beech & Partners Ltd.
Toronto, Ont., Canada

Richard Beers & Associates, Ltd.
Glenview, IL 60025

Gary S. Bell Associates, Inc.
Wyckoff, NJ 07481

Belle Oaks of America
Kansas City, MO 64106

Belzano, Deane & Associates
Irvine, CA 92715

Bentley & Evans, Inc.
New York, NY 10119

Benton, Schneider & Associates
Naperville, IL 60540

Leslie Berglass Associates, Inc.
New York, NY 10022

Billington, Fox & Ellis, Inc.
Chicago, IL 60606

Billington, Fox & Ellis, Inc.
San Francisco, CA 94104

Bil-Lu Personnel Agency
New York, NY 10165

Blackshaw & Olmstead
Atlanta, GA 30303

Blum & Co.
Nashotah, WI 53058

BMR Associates
Hollywood, FL 33020

J. L. Bohart & Co.
San Mateo, CA 94401

Bone Personnel
Fort Wayne, IN 46802

Bowker, Brown & Co.
Miami, FL 33129

Rick Brank & Associates
Lithonia, GA 30058

Breitmayer Associates
Guilford, CT 06437

Brennan & Associates, Inc.
Dallas, TX 75234

Broadcast Personnel, Inc.
New York, NY 10020

R. L. Brown & Associates
Pompano Beach, FL 33062

Dan Buckley & Associates, Inc.
Washington, DC 20036

Bundy-Stewart Associates
Dallas, TX 75230

G. A. Burns Associates, Inc.
Grand Rapids, MI 49503

Robert J. Bushee & Associates, Inc.
Bridgeville, PA 15017

Buxton & Associates
Denver, CO 80206

Buzhardt Associates
Jackson, MS 39211

Daniel Cades & Associates
Philadelphia, PA 19107

The Caldwell Partners International
Houston, TX 77010

The Caldwell Partners International
Calgary, Alta., Canada

The Caldwell Partners International
Vancouver, BC, Canada

The Caldwell Partners International
Toronto, Ont., Canada M5R 1B4

The Caldwell Partners International
Montreal, P.Q., Canada H3A 1H3

Cambridge Consulting Group
Houston, TX 77057

Canny, Bowen Inc.
New York, NY 10022

Cantor & Co., Inc.
Philadelphia, PA 19103

Career Center
Hackensack, NJ 07601

Career Consultants
Indianapolis, IN 46204

Career Directions Services
Munroe Falls, OH 44626

Career Dynamics, Inc.
Melrose, MA 02176

Career Path
Ridgewood, NJ 07450

Career Personnel Service
Montgomery, AL 36116

Career Specialists, Inc.
Bellevue, WA 98004

Careers Unlimited
Elkhart, IN 46516

Carpenter Consultants, Inc.
Chestnut Hill, MA 02167

Andrew B. Carr & Associates
San Angelo, TX 76902

Carre, Orban & Partners, Inc.
New York, NY 10169

CDH & Associates
Irvine, CA 92715

Centennial Personnel
Cincinnati, OH 45202

David Chambers & Associates, Inc.
New York, NY 10017

Christopher, Drew & Associates, Inc.
Cleveland, OH 44122

Citizens Employment Service
Fort Lee, NJ 07024

Clark, Clark & Clark Associates
College Park, MD 20740

Closman & Associates, Inc.
New York, NY 10001

Cole International
Berkeley, CA 94709

Cole, Warren & Long, Inc.
Philadelphia, PA 19102

Concept Corp.
Sausalito, CA 94966

The Concord Group, Ltd.
Barrington, IL 60010

Consultant Group—Langlois & Associates, Inc.
Needham, MA 02194

Continental Search Associates
Birmingham, MI 48012

John Conway Associates
Milwaukee, WI 53233

COR Management Services, Ltd.
New York, NY 10170

Corporate Advisors Inc.
Miami, FL 33137

Corporate Career Consultants
San Francisco, CA 94111

Corporate Careers Inc.
White Plains, NY 10601

The Corporate Connection, Ltd.
Richmond, VA 23230

Corporate Environment Ltd.
Crystal Lake, IL 60014

Corporate Recruiters Inc.
Philadelphia, PA 19126

Corporate Resource Group
Hartford, CT 06106

Corporate Search & Placement
Orange, CT 06477

Corporate Service Group, Ltd.
San Francisco, CA 94102

Corporate Staffing Group
Largo, FL 33541

Corporate Staffing Group
Horsham, PA 19044

Crippin, Inc.
Overland Park, KS 66210

Cris Associates, Inc.
New York, NY 10016

Crispi, Wagner & Co., Inc.
New York, NY 10170

Crown, Michaels & Associates, Inc.
Los Angeles, CA 90067

Frank Cuomo & Associates, Inc.
Tuckahoe, NY 10707

Data Management Resources
Stamford, CT 06901

N. Dean Davic Associates
Pittsburgh, PA 15235

John Davidson & Associates
Dallas, TX 75229

R. H. Davidson Associates
Norwood, MA 02062

Davies Associates International, Ltd.
Houston, TX 77218

Gene Davis & Associates
Oklahoma City, OK 73156

The Dean Group
Maplewood, NJ 07040

DEI Executive Services
Cincinnati, OH 45209

DeLalla-Fried Associates
New York, NY 10021

Delaney & Associates
Las Vegas, NV 89109

Devine, Baldwin & Peters, Inc.
New York, NY 10177

Ned E. Dickey and Associates
Rockford, IL 61110

Dimarchi & Associates
Denver, CO 80201

R. M. Donaldson Personnel
Cranford, NJ 07016

Dorison & Company
Coral Gables, FL 33134

Driggers & Blackwell Personnel
Ruston, LA 71270

J. H. Dugan & Co.
Chicago, IL 60611

Dunhill of St. Petersburg
St. Petersburg, FL 33713

Dunhill of Troy
Troy, MI 48084

Dunhill of Huntington
Melville, NY 11747

Dunhill of Greensboro
Greensboro, NC 27408

Dunhill of Hickory, N.C.
Hickory, NC 28601

Dunhill of Austin
Austin, TX 78723

Dunsmore & Associates, Ltd.
Guilford, CT 06437

Earley Kielty & Associates, Inc.
New York, NY 10121

Eggers Personnel & Consulting
Omaha, NB 68144

The Elliott Co, Inc.
Woburn, MA 01801

Phil Ellis Associates
Raleigh, NC 27658

David M. Ellner Associates
New York, NY 10121

Ells Personnel Systems
Minneapolis, MN 55402

Employment Opportunities
Danbury, CT 06810

Employment Unlimited Agency
Baltimore, MD 21231

ERA Placements
Pawtucket, RI 02861

Henry H. Eskay
West Orange, NJ 07052

Estar Execu/Search, Ltd.
Palatine, IL 60067

Evans Associates, Inc.
San Francisco, CA 94104

Executive Career Consultants
St. Louis, MO 63122

Executive Locators of America
Metairie, LA 70004

Fairchild, Gould & Associates
Rockford, IL 61105

A. E. Feldman Associates
Great Neck, NY 11021

Finley & Co.
Greenville, SC 29615

A. G. Fishkin & Associates, Inc.
Rockville, MD 20852

Flinn Consultants, Inc.
Highland Park, IL 60035

Ford Employment Agency
Glen Burnie, MD 21061

Foster & Associates, Inc.
San Francisco, CA 94105

Edmund A. Frank & Associates
Westchester, IL 60153

G. A. Agency
Cranford, NJ 07016

Gabriel & Bowie Associates, Ltd.
Baltimore, MD 21228

Garrett Associates, Inc.
Atlanta, GA 30339

Gather, Inc.
Chartley, MA 02712

Edward Gaylord & Associates
Mill Valley, CA 94942

General Employment Enterprises
Palo Alto, CA 94303

General Employment Enterprises
Woodland Hills, CA 91367

General Employment Enterprises
Chicago, IL 60606

General Placement Service
Greensburg, PA 15601

Genovese & Co. Management Consultants
Los Angeles, CA 90067

Glynn, Brooks & Co.
Fort Lee, NJ 07024

Gould & McCoy, Inc.
New York, NY 10022

Griffith & Werner, Inc.
Hollywood, FL 33021

Group IV Recruitment Consultants
New York, NY 10036

Robert T. Guard & Associates, Inc.
Honolulu, HI 96813

GV Personnel
Kenilworth, NJ 07033

Hahn & Associates, Inc.
Dayton, OH 45402

D. N. Hall & Associates
Chicago, IL 60646

The Halyburton Company
Charlotte, NC 28222

The Hartshorn Group
Parsippany, NJ 07054

Harvey Personnel
North Charleston, SC 29304

Haskell & Stern Associates, Inc.
Fort Worth, TX 76112

Hayden & Refo, Inc.
Boston, MA 02110

Hayman & Company
Dallas, TX 75201

Headhunters National
Portland, OR 97221

Health Industry Consultants, Inc.
Englewood, CO 80112

The Heidrick Partners, Inc.
Chicago, IL 60606

D. J. Hertz and Associates, Ltd.
New York, NY 10017

Herz, Stewart & Company
Stamford, CT 06905

Nathaniel Hill & Associates, Inc.
Raleigh, NC 27612

W. Warner Hinman & Co.
Chicago, IL 60611

Hire Counseling and Personnel Service
Fairfield, CT 06110

The Hite Company
Chicago, IL 60603

Hodge-Cronin and Associates, Inc.
Rosemont, IL 60018

J. L. Hoglund Co., Inc.
Natrona Heights, PA 15065

Horton Associates, Inc.
Helendale, CA 92342

Hospitality Personnel, Inc.
Valley Forge, PA 19481

Houchins & Associates, Inc.
Atlanta, GA 30308

H. S. Placements
Green Bay, WI 54307

Human Resources
Geneseo, IL 61254

Hunt Personnel Ltd.
New York, NY 10017

Huxtable Associates, Inc.
Bridgeton, MO 63044

Industry Consultants
Atlanta, GA 30338

Intelcom Professional Services
Columbia, MD 21044

International Management Advisors, Inc.
New York, NY 10017

Charles Irish Company, Inc.
New York, NY 10170

Robert J. Irmen Associates
Hinsdale, IL 60521

JM & Company
Wayne, PA 19087

Job Finders/Jobs Temporary
Des Moines, IA 50312

A. G. Johnson & Co., Inc.
Irvine, CA 92715

Johnson & Genrich, Inc.
Chicago, IL 60630

Johnson, Smith and Knisely
New York, NY 10017

JY Enterprises
New York, NY 10007

Kanon
New York, NY 10018

Karam Associates
Denver, CO 80224

Howard L. Karr & Associates, Inc.
San Mateo, CA 94402

Kenfield Research Associates, Inc.
New York, NY 10016

James H. Kennedy
Fitzwilliam, NH 03447

Melvin Kent & Associates
Columbus, OH 43215

Ketchum, Inc. Executive Recruiting Service
Chicago, IL 60601

Kiley-Owen Associates, Inc.
Philadelphia, PA 19107

Kinsale Managers
Oyster Bay, NY 11771

Robert Kleven & Co., Inc.
Lexington, MA 02173

KMS Associates
Kingston, NY 12401

Kuebler Associates
Portland, ME 04101

Kuehne & Co., Inc.
Chicago, IL 60602

Kuhnmuench & Cook Associates
Arcadia, CA 91006

Kunzer Associates, Ltd.
Chicago, IL 60604

Lacrosse Associates, Inc.
Union, NJ 07083

Lamalie Associates, Inc.
Tampa, FL 33618

Lamalie Associates, Inc.
Atlanta, GA 30026

Lamalie Associates, Inc.
New York, NY 10178

Lamalie Associates, Inc.
Cleveland, OH 44114

Langer Associates, Inc.
White Plains, NY 10601

Lawrence L. Lapham Associates
New York, NY 10169

Paul W. Larson Associates, Inc.
San Juan Capistrano, CA 92675

Lauer, Sbarbaro Associates, Inc.
Chicago, IL 60602

John Lawrence Agency of Los Angeles
Chatsworth, CA 91311

W. R. Lawry, Inc.
Simsbury, CT 06070

Lee Calhoon & Co., Inc.
Birchrunville, PA 19421

Alan Lewis Associates
Solana Beach, CA 92075

Littman Associates
Troy, MI 48084

Arthur J. Loveley Associates
New York, NY 10165

Ludot Personnel Services
Southfield, MI 48075

Lyman & Co.
Glendale, CA 91203

McCormack & Farrow
Long Beach, CA 90802

Edwin McDonald Associates
New York, NY 10017

MacFarlane & Co., Inc.
Atlanta, GA 30318

Went MacKenzie
Atlanta, GA 30360

McNitt Personnel Bureau
Minneapolis, MN 55402

McSherry & Associates
Chicago, IL 60601

Maetzold Associates, Inc.
Minnetonka, MN 55343

Mahony Associates
Atlanta, GA 30328

Management Search
Atlanta, GA 30346

Management Search Inc.
Minneapolis, MN 55426

Management South
Charlotte, NC 28246

Thomas Mangum Co.
Los Angeles, CA 90041

Markett Personnel
Miami, FL 33116

Marshall Consultants
Seattle, WA 98111

Edwin Martin & Associates
Chicago, IL 60606

Masland Management Services
Philadelphia, PA 19118

MD Resources, Inc.
Herndon, VA 22071

Medical Recruiters of America
Tampa, FL 33607

The Mendheim Co., Inc.
Chicago, IL 60659

Metricor, Inc.
Oak Brook Terrace, IL 60181

Midland Consultants—Pittsburgh
Carnegie, PA 15106

Bill Miller & Associates
San Diego, CA 92128

MKI Recruiting Associates
White Plains, NY 10601

Modern Employment Service
Chicago, IL 60602

J. R. Morrison & Associates, Inc.
San Francisco, CA 94111

Herbert H. Moss, Inc.
Palm Springs, CA 92262

Richard Mowell Associates, Inc.
Tallahassee, FL 32303

MSL International Consultants, Ltd.
San Francisco, CA 94111

MSL International Consultants, Ltd.
Atlanta, GA 30339

MSL International Consultants, Ltd.
Chicago, IL 60601

Gordon Mulvey & Associates
Louisville, KY 40207

Murphy Employment Service
Tampa, FL 33609

National Career Centers—USA
Fayetteville, NC 28302

National Hospitality Associates, Inc.
Tempe, AZ 85282

National Recruiters
Raleigh, NC 27609

National Recruiting Service
Dyer, IN 46311

Nation-Wide Recruiting, Inc.
Encino, CA 91316

William H. Nenstiel & Associates, Inc.
Scottsdale, AZ 85251

Network Affiliates, Ltd.
Metairie, LA 70002

Perry Newton Associates
Rockville, MD 20850

Nordeman Grim, Inc.—MBA Resources
New York, NY 10022

Paul Norsell & Associates, Inc.
Anaheim, CA 92807

Paul Norsell & Associates, Inc.
Los Angeles, CA 90045

North Employment Agency
Anchorage, AK 99501

NPF Associates, Ltd.
Coral Springs, FL 33065

The NRI Group
Vienna, VA 22180

Oliver & Rosner Associates
New York, NY 10022

OMNI Executive Search, Inc.
Atlanta, GA 30328

C. M. Oppenheim & Associates, Inc.
New York, NY 10036

Parker Page Associates
Atlanta, GA 30341

Harry D. Parkhurst & Associates, Inc.
Minneapolis, MN 55426

Peeney Associates, Inc.
Fanwood, NJ 07023

The Personnel Center
Champaign, IL 61820

Personnel Director Associates
Ann Arbor, MI 48104

Phillips Associates
Englewood, NJ 07631

Walter Phillips Associates
Greenville, SC 29606

Piedmont Personnel Consultants
Greenville, SC 29615

Pinkerton & Associates, Inc.
Chicago, IL 60611

Positions, Inc.
Providence, RI 02904

Prime Selection
Waltham, MA 02254

Probe Technology
King of Prussia, PA 19406

Professional Employment Registry
Bethel, CT 06801

Professional Executive Consultants
Northbrook, IL 60062

Professional Personnel Consultants—Tampa
Tampa, FL 33607

Professional Personnel Consultants
Southfield, MI 48075

Professional Placement Services
Augusta, ME 04330

The Protech Group
Chicago, IL 60606

Psychological Assess & Positions
Toledo, OH 43609

Purcell Employment Systems
Los Angeles, CA 90010

Purcell Group Management Consultants
Houston, TX 77057

Quarles & Associates
Memphis, TN 38112

QVSCC Employment Connection
Brooklyn, CT 06239

Rainess Associates
West Caldwell, NJ 07006

Rambert & Co., Inc.
Lake Bluff, IL 60044

The Recruiter
Des Moines, IA 50311

Redlands Employment Agency
Redlands, CA 92373

Research Technologies
Madison, CT 06443

Retail Recruiters
Providence, RI 02906

E. J. Rhodes, Inc.
Framingham, MA 01701

E. J. Rhodes Personnel Consultants
New York, NY 10036

Lloyd Richards Personnel Service
Tulsa, OK 74103

Ken Richardson
Bethesda, MD 20817

Rita Personnel—West Massachusetts
Springfield, MA 01103

Robertson, Spoerlein & Wengert
Chicago, IL 60606

Roche Associates
Stamford, CT 06094

Roth Young of Atlanta
Atlanta, GA 30359

Roth Young Personnel of Minneapolis
Edina, MN 55435

Rourke, Bourbonnais Associates, Ltd.
Montreal, P.Q., H3H 1E5, Canada

Louis Rudzinsky Associates, Inc.
Lexington, MA 02173

James Russell, Medical Search Consultants
Bloomington, IL 61701

St. Clair International
Menlo Park, CA 94025

Sales Consultants—Birmingham
Birmingham, AL 35223

Sales Consultants—New Haven
Rocky Hill, CT 06067

Sales Consultants of Hartford
Hartford, CT 06067

Sales Consultants of Wellesley
Wellesley, MA 02181

Sales & Management Search, Inc.
Chicago, IL 60606

Sales Recruiters International
Yonkers, NY 10701

Sanford Rose Associates
Youngstown, OH 44503

Savannah Personnel Consultants
Savannah, GA 31406

Search Unlimited
Akron, OH 44122

Security Jobs Corporation
Honolulu, HI 96813

Selective Search
Columbus, OH 43232

Leo J. Shea Associates, Inc.
Miami, FL 33129

Skott/Edwards Consultants, Inc.
New York, NY 10169

Herman Smith International Inc.
Toronto, Ont., Canada

Howard W. Smith Associates
Hartford, CT 06103

Smyth Dawson Associates
Stamford, CT 06901

Snelling and Snelling
Albuquerque, NM 87110

William Snyder Associates
Tucson, AZ 85710

Sollmar Incorporated
Tustin, CA 92681

Southwestern Placement
Memphis, TN 37202

Specialized Search Associates
Greenwich, CT 06830

Spencer Stuart & Associates
New York, NY 10055

Paul Stafford Associates, Ltd.
San Francisco, CA 94104

Paul Stafford Associates, Ltd.
Chicago, IL 60606

Paul Stafford Associates, Ltd.
New York, NY 10111

Stanislaw & Associates, Inc.
Brookfield, WI 53005

Status, Inc.
Atlanta, GA 30326

John R. Stephens & Associates
Houston, TX 77002

L. W. Stern Associates
New York, NY 10016

Carter Stone & Co., Inc.
New York, NY 10006

Stumbaugh Associates, Inc.
Atlanta, GA 30035

Sturm Burrows & Company
Philadelphia, PA 19102

John J. Sudlow & Co.
Chicago, IL 60611

John J. Sudlow & Co.
Seattle, WA 98101

Synergistics Associates Ltd.
Chicago, IL 60601

Systech Organization
Baltimore, MD 21234

Systech Organization
New York, NY 10019

Systems Network Assistance
Glenview, IL 60048

Systems Personnel
Media, PA 19063

Tanzi Executive Search
San Diego, CA 92101

Tanzi Executive Search
San Francisco, CA 94104

Target Search
Rockville, MD 20850

TASA Inc.
Coral Gables, FL 33134

TASA Inc.
New York, NY 10022

F. L. Taylor & Co., Inc.
New York, NY 10016

Tecmark Associates, Inc.
New York, NY 10123

Teiper Personnel Service
Toledo, OH 43615

Richard Theobald & Associates
San Mateo, CA 94404

The Thomas Group
Columbus, OH 43220

Tidewater Group, Inc.
Stamford, CT 06906

Toar Enterprises
Roswell, GA 30076

Traynor Associates, Ltd.
Rochester, NY 14604

Triangle Personnel Systems
Raleigh, NC 27609

Trotter, Mitchell, Larsen & Zilliacus
Los Angeles, CA 90014

Trotter, Mitchell, Larsen & Zilliacus
Santa Ana, CA 92704

United Consultants
York, PA 17403

Vance Employment Service
Amarillo, TX 79101

VanMaldegiam Associates, Inc.
Chicago, IL 60606

Vannah/Rowe, Inc.
Bethel, CT 06002

Wm. Van Nostrand & Associates
Bronxville, NY 10708

Varo & Lund Corp.
Los Angeles, CA 90028

Vezan-West & Co.
West Hartford, CT 06107

Viking Recruiting Consultants, Inc.
Montvale, NJ 07645

Vine Associates Inc.
North Hollywood, CA 91602

Vinicombe, Nitka & Associates, Inc.
Garden City, NY 11530

Wachtel & Associates, Ltd.
New York, NY 10017

Gordon Wahls Co.
Media, PA 19063

Gordon Wahls Company
Villanova, PA 19085

Walker Recruitment
Minneapolis, MN 55416

Albert J. Walsh & Associates
Newtown, PA 18940

Hank Ward Associates, Ltd.
Latham, NY 12110

Ward Howell International, Inc.
New York, NY 10016

John H. Warner Associates, Inc.
Hartford, CT 06103

R. H. Warner Consulting
Westerville, OH 43081

Wehinger Service
New York, NY 10038

Emanuel Weintraub Associates, Inc.
Fort Lee, NJ 07024

Wellesley, Ltd.
Providence, RI 02903

Werner Management Consultants, Inc.
New York, NY 10018

Western Executive Consultants
Las Vegas, NV 89108

Western Personnel Associates, Inc.
Phoenix, AZ 85012

Western Reserve Associates
Bath, OH 44210

E. T. Wharton Associates
New York, NY 10001

Wheeler Associates
San Francisco, CA 94102

Betty White Agency
Oxnard, CA 93030

E. N. Wilkins and Company, Inc.
Chicago, IL 60606

Wilkinson & Ives, Inc.
Orinda, CA 94563

Wills & Company
Chicago, IL 60601

Winchester Consultants Inc.
New Canaan, CT 06840

The Winchester Group
San Mateo, CA 94404

Winguth, Schweichler Associates, Inc.
San Francisco, CA 94111

Witt Associates, Inc.
Oak Brook, IL 60521

Woltz & Associates, Inc.
Wood Dale, IL 60191

Woodbury Personnel
Jericho, NY 11753

The Woodward Group
Chicago, IL 60601

John Wylie Associates, Inc.
Tulsa, OK 74136

Dennis Wynn Associates, Inc.
St. Petersburg, FL 33704

**Arthur Young Executive Resource
Consultants**
Los Angeles, CA 90071

**Arthur Young Executive Resource
Consultants**
San Francisco, CA 94104

**Arthur Young Executive Resource
Consultants**
Chicago, IL 60611

The Zivic Group
San Francisco, CA 94111

HEALTH CARE/HOSPITALS

Associated Business Consultants, Inc.
Medford, NJ 08055

Banner Personnel Service
Chicago, IL 60602

Nathan Barry Associates, Inc.
Boston, MA 02109

Gary S. Bell Associates, Inc.
Wyckoff, NJ 07481

Belzano, Deane & Associates
Irvine, CA 92715

Bowden & Company, Inc.
Cleveland, OH 44131

Bowman & Associates, Inc.
Atlanta, GA 30345

Brooks/Gay & Associates, Inc.
New York, NY 10016

R. L. Brown & Associates
Pompano Beach, FL 33062

G. A. Burns Associates, Inc.
Grand Rapids, MI 49503

Capitol Medical Placement Agency
Tallahassee, FL 32317

Career Personnel Service
Montgomery, AL 36116

M. L. Carter & Associates
Atlanta, GA 30362

CBS Personnel Services
Cincinnati, OH 45202

CBS Personnel Services
Dayton, OH 45402

Center for Health Care Personnel
Wethersfield, CT 06109

CHASE, Inc.
Rosemont, PA 19010

Chevigny Personnel Agency
Merrillville, IN 46410

Christenson & Montgomery
Morristown, NJ 07960

Clapp, Kleffer & Associates, Ltd.
Chicago, IL 60611

Coker, Tyler & Co.
Atlanta, GA 30341

Cole International
Berkeley, CA 94709

Concept Corp.
Sausalito, CA 94966

Consultant Group—Langlois Associates, Inc.
Needham, MA 02194

John Conway Associates
Milwaukee, WI 53233

Corporate Resource Group
Hartford, CT 06106

Gene Davis & Associates
Oklahoma City, OK 73156

The Dean Group
Maplewood, NJ 07040

DEI Executive Services
Cincinnati, OH 45209

Donaldson & Wharton Associates
New York, NY 10001

Druthers Agency
Marina Del Rey, CA 90291

Dunhill of Paramus
Paramus, NJ 07652

Phil Ellis Associates
Raleigh, NC 27658

Equinox Management Corp.
Norwalk, CT 06851

Harry E. Fear & Associates
Deerfield Beach, FL 33441

Fleming Associates
Miami, FL 33166

Fleming Associates
Louisville, KY 40220

Fleming Associates
Sarasota, FL 33577

Fulton, Longshore & Associates, Inc.
Haverford, PA 19041

Futures Personnel Services
Baltimore, MD 21204

Garofolo, Curtiss & Company
Washington, DC 20036

Garofolo, Curtiss & Company
Boston, MA 02110

Garofolo, Curtiss & Company
Glens Falls, NY 12801

Garofolo, Curtiss & Company
Ardmore, PA 19003

Garrett Associates, Inc.
Atlanta, GA 30339

Gather, Inc.
Chartley, MA 02712

Growth Placement Associates, Inc.
Dowingtown, PA 19335

Hans & Associates, Inc.
Phoenix, AZ 85017

Harper Associates
Southfield, MI 48075

Harvey Personnel
North Charleston, SC 29304

Health Care Executive Search
Lafayette, CA 94549

Health Industry Consultants, Inc.
Englewood Cliffs, CO 80112

Health Link Systems, Inc.
Woodland Hills, CA 91367

Hilton Research Associates
Woburn, MA 01801

Hospitality Personnel, Inc.
Valley Forge, PA 19481

Houchins & Associates, Inc.
Atlanta, GA 30308

Inaba Consultants
Irvine, CA 91403

Job Finders/Jobs Temporary
Des Moines, IA 50312

Kearney: Executive Search Group
Englewood, CO 80111

Keltech Executive Search
Wallingford, PA 19086

Kimball Shaw Associates, Inc.
Hingham, MA 02043

King & Associates, Inc.
Woodland Hills, CA 91364

Kingsley Quinn, Ltd.
New York, NY 10022

Kors, Marlar, Savage & Associates
Annapolis, MD 21401

Lamson, Griffiths Associates, Inc.
Palatine, IL 60067

Lee Calhoon & Co., Inc.
Birchrunville, PA 19421

Lynn Associates
Farmington, CT 06032

Ross MacAskills Associates, Inc.
Washington, DC 20036

Marshall Group
Los Angeles, CA 92660

Masland Management Services
Philadelphia, PA 19118

MD Resources, Inc.
Miami, FL 33173

MD Resources, Inc.
Herndon, VA 22071

Medical Recruiters of America
Tampa, FL 33607

Bill Miller & Associates
San Diego, CA 92128

Nationwide Recruiters
Columbia, SC 29204

Northern Consultants, Inc.
Hampden, ME 04444

Pascal Associates, Inc.
Rutherford, NJ 07070

Personnel Center
Gainesville, FL 32602

Personnel Pool of America
Fort Lauderdale, FL 33335

Pickett Professional Placement
Tallahassee, FL 32308

Pinsker and Shattuck, Inc.
San Francisco, CA 94104

Pinsker and Shattuck, Inc.
Saratoga, CA 95070

The Placers, Inc.
Wilmington, DE 19306

Professional Health Care Services
Fort Lauderdale, FL 33310

Quality Control Recruiters
Bristol, CT 06010

Retail Recruiters, Spectra Professional Search
Fort Lauderdale, FL 33311

Lloyd Richards Personnel Service
Tulsa, OK 74103

Rogers & Sands Inc.
Burlington, MA 02108

R. M. Associates
Portland, OR 97223

Roth Young Personnel of Minneapolis
Edina, MN 55435

Roth Young Personnel
St. Louis, MO 63105

Royal Recruiters
Fort Lauderdale, FL 33334

James Russell, Medical Search Consultant
Bloomington, IL 61701

Ryan/Smith & Associates, Inc.
Westfield, NJ 07091

Sales Consultants—Birmingham
Birmingham, AL 35223

Sampson, Neill & Wilkins, Inc.
Upper Montclair, NJ 07043

Sanford Rose Associates of Hartford
Windsor, CT 06095

Schuyler Associates, Ltd.
Atlanta, GA 30339

S. K. Stewart & Associates
Cincinnati, OH 45240

Torretto & Associates, Inc.
Sausalito, CA 94965

Don Waldron & Associates
New York, NY 10123

Wargo & Co., Inc.
Waukesha, WI 53186

E. N. Wilkins and Company, Inc.
Chicago, IL 60606

William H. Willis, Inc.
New York, NY 10022

Witt Associates, Inc.
Oak Brook, IL 60521

Wytmar & Company, Inc.
Chicago, IL 60606

Xagas & Associates
Geneva, IL 60134

Hotel and Restaurant

Allied Search
San Francisco, CA 94123

Atlantic Personnel
Merritt Island, FL 32953

Martin H. Bauman Associates, Inc.
New York, NY 10022

Bil-Lu Personnel Agency
New York, NY 10165

The Bradford Group, Inc.
Laguna Hills, CA 92653

R. L. Brown & Associates
Pompano Beach, FL 33062

Career Consultants
Indianapolis, IN 46204

The Concord Group, Ltd.
Barrington, IL 60010

Corporate Consultants
New Orleans, LA 70112

R. H. Davidson Associates
Norwood, MA 02062

Executive Recruiters
Bethesda, MD 20814

Fitzgerald and Ready
New York, NY 10017

S. Ronald Gaston & Associates
Littleton, CO 80161

Hans & Associates, Inc.
Phoenix, AZ 85017

Harper Associates
Southfield, MI 48075

J. D. Hersey & Associates
Columbus, OH 43221

Hospitality Personnel, Inc.
Valley Forge, PA 19481

**Hotelmen's Executive Personnel and
  Management Services**
New York, NY 10023

Main Hurdman
West Palm Beach, FL 33409

JAMAR Personnel Service
Rock Island, IL 61201

Johnson, Smith and Knisely
New York, NY 10017

Keshlear Associates
Aiken, SC 29210

Gary W. Little and Associates
Birmingham, AL 35244

McGuire Executive Search
Orlando, FL 32819

Martin H. Meisel Associates, Inc.
New York, NY 10028

National Hospitality Associates, Inc.
Tempe, AZ 85282

NRI Rockville
Rockville, MD 20852

Retail Recruiters
Rocky Hill, CT 06067

R.M. Associates
Portland, OR 97223

Ropes Associates, Inc.
Fort Lauderdale, FL 33394

Roth Young—Los Angeles
Fox Hills, CA 90230

Roth Young of Atlanta
Atlanta, GA 30359

Roth Young Personnel
St. Louis, MO 63105

Roth Young of Columbus
Columbus, OH 43229

Security Jobs Corporation
Honolulu, HI 96813

Southern Personnel Services
Palm Desert, CA 92260

Paul Stafford Associates, Ltd.
Washington, DC 20006

Paul Stafford Associates, Ltd.
Chicago, IL 60606

L. W. Stern Associates
New York, NY 10016

Whittaker and Associates
Atlanta, GA 30339

INSURANCE

Agra Placements, Ltd.
Peru, IN 46970

Alexander & Associates, Inc.
Elkhart, IN 46515

Allen Personnel Agency
New York, NY 10038

Amato & Associates, Inc.
San Francisco, CA 94104

Analytic Recruiting, Inc.
New York, NY 10017

Apple Agency
New York, NY 10038

Apple One Personnel Service
Glendale, CA 91203

Apple One Personnel Service
La Puente, CA 91744

Apple One Personnel Service
Los Angeles, CA 90010

Apple One Personnel Service
Los Angeles, CA 90024

Apple One Personnel Service
Torrance, CA 90504

Apple One Personnel Service
West Hollywood, CA 90069

E. J. Ashton & Associates, Ltd.
Arlington Heights, IL 60004

Ashworth Consultants
Boston, MA 02109

Availability Personnel Consultants
Bedford, NH 03102

Banner Personnel Service
Chicago, IL 60602

Barclays Recruiting Services, Inc.
Denver, CO 80222

Barger & Sargent, Inc.
Concord, NH 03301

Becker Personnel Services
Bala Cynwyd, PA 19004

The Best People
Stamford, CT 06905

Bone Personnel
Fort Wayne, IN 46802

Bowden & Company, Inc.
Cleveland, OH 44131

Brandon Associates
Fort Lee, NJ 07024

K. Robert Brian
Philadelphia, PA 19103

Brooks/Gay & Associates, Inc.
New York, NY 10016

Business Personnel Associates
Glastonbury, CT 06033

Career Consultants
Indianapolis, IN 46204

Careers Unlimited
Elkhart, IN 46516

CBS Personnel Services
Cincinnati, OH 45202

CBS Personnel Services
Dayton, OH 45402

Chevigny Personnel Agency
Merrillville, IN 46410

Circare
Miami, FL 33138

Citizens Employment Service
Fort Lee, NJ 07024

Richard Clark Associates
Fairfield, CT 06017

CMZ Recruiting
Lutherville, MD 21093

Cole, Warren & Long, Inc.
Philadelphia, PA 19103

Computer Network Resources
Atlanta, GA 30341

Jerry Demaso & Associates
Metairie, LA 70002

Deven Associates, Inc.
Verona, NJ 07044

Dumont Kiradjieff & Moriarty
Boston, MA 02109

Dunhill Personnel Service
Philadelphia, PA 19102

Don Ellis Personnel
Boston MA 02108

Employment Specialists
Minneapolis, MN 55435

ERA Placements
Pawtucket, RI 02861

Fanning Personnel of Boston
Boston, MA 02116

Fran Farber, Ltd.
Fort Lee, NJ 07024

First Word Placement Service
Dallas, TX 75240

Fleming Associates
Columbus, IN 47202

Forum Personnel
New York, NY 10017

Futures Personnel Services
Baltimore, MD 21204

Garofolo, Curtiss & Company
Washington, DC 20036

Garofolo, Curtiss & Company
Boston, MA 02110

Garofolo, Curtiss & Company
Glen Falls, NY 12801

Garofolo, Curtiss & Company
Ardmore, PA 19003

General Employment Enterprises
Oak Brook, IL 60521

General Placement Service
Greensburg, PA 15601

Giles Intermediaries, Inc.
New York, NY 10038

Global Search
Melville, NY 11747

Paul C. Green & Associates, Ltd.
Green Valley, AZ 85614

D. N. Hall & Associates
Chicago, IL 60646

T. G. Harper & Co., Inc.
Philadelphia, PA 19106

William Harris Associates
New York, NY 10038

Haskell & Stern Associates, Inc.
Fort Worth, TX 76112

D. J. Hertz and Associates, Ltd.
New York, NY 10017

Hunt Personnel Ltd.
New York, NY 10017

Insearch
Philadelphia, PA 19107

Insurance Personnel, Martin Grant Associates
Boston, MA 02110

Insurance Personnel Recruiters
Philadelphia, PA 19106

Insurance Personnel Resources
Atlanta, GA 30338

Insurance Placement
Los Angeles, CA 90048

Insurance Recruiters Inc.
Dallas, TX 75206

Insurance Recruitment Agency
Los Angeles, CA 90049

Kenneth James Associates
Holland, PA 18966

Barbara Jensen Employment
Edina, MN 55435

Kennedy and Company
Chicago, IL 60606

Keshlear Associates
Aiken, SC 29210

KGC Associates
East Hartford, CT 06108

Kinkead Associates
Hartford, CT 06103

Kinsale Managers
Oyster Bay, NY 11771

Kling Agency
New York, NY 10038

D. A. Kreuter Associates
Philadelphia, PA 19103

Gilbert Lane Personnel Agency
Hartford, CT 06103

Arthur J. Langdon
Hartford, CT 06103

Largent Parks & Partners, Inc.
Dallas, TX 75240

Michael Latas & Associates, Inc.
St. Louis, MO 63132

John Lawrence Agency of Los Angeles
Chatsworth, CA 91311

Mike Lawson Personnel
Louisville, KY 40217

Linda Lee Search Consultants
Philadelphia, PA 19102

Leonard Associates
Rocky Hill, CT 06067

Lynn Associates
Farmington, CT 06032

George P. Lyon Associates
Doylestown, PA 18901

McFadden Associates
Philadelphia, PA 19102

McMahon & Associates
Stone Mountain, GA 30086

Mar-El Employment Agency
Levittown, NY 11756

MBA Associates, Inc.
Boston, MA 02109

Morgan Research
New York, NY 10175

Richard Mowell Associates, Inc.
Tallahassee, FL 32303

MPS Executive Placement, Inc.
New York, NY 10038

National Recruiting Service
Dyer, IN 46311

Network Affiliates, Ltd.
Metairie, LA 70002

Niermann Personnel Service
Morrow, GA 30260

O'Crowley & O'Toole Executive Search
Portland, OR 97223

Parker Page Associates
Atlanta, GA 30341

Patton/Perry Associates
Charlotte, NC 28202

Personnel, Inc.
Spartanburg, SC 29302

Phillips Majewski & Associates
Union, NJ 07083

Phoenix Personnel Services
Harrisburg, PA 17105

Positions, Inc.
Providence, RI 02904

Pro, Inc.
La Jolla, CA 92037

Professional Placement Group
Boston, MA 02109

Ramming & Bennett, Inc.
Indianapolis, IN 46241

Rogers & Sands Inc.
Burlington, MA 02108

Ryan/Smith & Associates, Inc.
Westfield, NJ 07091

Robert Sage Recruiting
Elkhart, IN 46514

Robert Sage & Associates
Denton, TX 76201

St. Clair International
Menlo Park, CA 94025

Ron Schmidt Personnel Service
Houston, TX 77042

Leo J. Shea Associates, Inc.
Miami, FL 33129

S.P.I. Personnel Consultants
Wellesley, MA 02181

Carter Stone & Co., Inc.
New York, NY 10006

Staat Personnel Agency, Inc.
New York, NY 10279

Summit Search Specialists
Houston, TX 77079

TR Recruiters
New York, NY 10038

Peter Van Leer & Associates
Wayzata, MN 55391

Varone Personnel
Pawtucket, RI 02860

Watkins & Associates
Houston, TX 77074

Wehinger Service Inc. Agency
New York, NY 10038

Wilkinson & Ives, Inc.
Orinda, CA 94563

Woodbury Personnel
Jericho, NY 11753

Xagas & Associates
Geneva, IL 60134

Yorkshire Consulting Group, Inc.
Newton Upper Falls, MA 02164

LEGAL

Ackerman Associates, Inc.
Boston, MA 02109

Advocate Search, Ltd.
New York, NY 10165

A-L Legal Search, Inc.
New York, NY 10017

Allegheny County Bar Association
Pittsburgh, PA 15219

APS Legal Search
New York, NY 10038

ASC & Co.
Houston, TX 77056

Bader Research Corp.
New York, NY 10017

The Barclay Group
New York, NY 10017

M. Stephen Barrett & Associates
Tulsa, OK 74133

Barrister Referrals, Ltd.
New York, NY 10022

Ted Bavly Associates, Inc.
Newport Beach, CA 92660

Rick Beedle Associates, Inc.
North Hollywood, CA 91607

Marcia Beilin, Inc.
New York, NY 10169

Bellon & Hughes, Inc.
Atlanta, GA 30305

Bench Ltd.
Los Angeles, CA 90048

Robert Bennett Associates
New York, NY 10017

Bentley & Evans, Inc.
New York, NY 10119

R. B. Bentsen Company
Dallas, TX 75214

The Berkshire Group, Inc.
New York, NY 10163

Zachary Bernard Agency, Ltd.
New York, NY 10017

Howard I. Bernstein, Esq.
New York, NY 10011

Bostonian Personnel Co., Inc.
Boston, MA 02109

Bowden & Company, Inc.
Cleveland, OH 44131

BRJ Associates, Inc.
Mountainside, NJ 07092

Dan Buckley & Associates, Inc.
Washington, DC 20036

Caldwell & Associates, Inc.
Dallas, TX 75270

California Legal Search
San Diego, CA 92101

Neal Carden & Associates
Wheaton, IL 60187

Carrie & Co. Placement
Dallas, TX 75202

Catalyst Legal Resources, Inc.
New York, NY 10166

Charter Executive Associates, Inc.
New York, NY 10038

Laura Colangelo Legal Search Consultants
 Inc.
New York, NY 10022

Conaway Legal Search
Baltimore, MD 21202

Conaway Personnel Associates, Inc.
Baltimore, MD 21202

Mabel Cook & Associates
Northridge, CA 91323

Corporate Counsel Search, Inc.
New York, NY 10017

Council Legal Search, Inc.
New York, NY 10013

The Counselors Consultant
Washington, DC 20005

Counsel Search Co.
Toledo, OH 43604

Craft Kraybill Bender
Pittsburgh, PA 15222

Bob Delbridge & Associates
Norman, OK 73069

Elaine P. Dine, Inc.
New York, NY 10022

Dunhill—Legal
Washington, DC 20005

Laurence A. Elder & Associates, Inc.
Cleveland, OH 44113

Ensminger, Inc.
Houston, TX 77027

W. H. Eolis International, Inc.
New York, NY 10170

E.S.Q. Legal Search, Ltd.
Chicago, IL 60602

Esquire, Ltd., Legal Executive Search
Houston, TX 77006

Essex Legal Search
New York, NY 10017

Fanning Personnel
Hartford, CT 06103

George Fee Associates
Chicago, IL 60606

Fergus Associates, Inc.
New York, NY 10118

Jacquelyn Finn & Susan Schneider Associates, Inc.
Washington, DC 20006

Fox-Morris Associates, Inc.
San Francisco, CA 94111

Fox-Morris Associates, Inc.
Philadelphia, PA 19109

Gillard Associates
Dedham, MA 02026

Barry Goldberg & Associates, Inc.
Beverly Hills, CA 90210

Audrey Golden Associates Ltd.
New York, NY 10017

Linda Goldsman Ltd.
Washington, DC 20006

Gottschalk & Associates, Inc.
Menlo Park, CA 94025

Stephen M. Haas Legal Placement, Inc.
New York, NY 10165

K. M. Harrison Associates, Inc.
Greenwich, CT 06830

Keyth Hart & Associates, Inc.
Tucson, AZ 85710

Keyth Hart & Associates, Inc.
Northridge, CA 91324

Higbee Associates, Inc.
Rowayton, CT 06853

Holderman Partners, Ltd.
San Francisco, CA 94104

Jack Holloway & Associates
Houston, TX 77002

Howard-Sloan Legal Search, Inc.
New York, NY 10017

Human Resource Services, Inc.
New York, NY 10169

Interface Group, Ltd.
Washington, DC 20007

The Interface Group, Inc.
Washington, DC 20007

International Staffing Consultants, Inc.
Newport Beach, CA 92260

Interquest, Incorporated
Farmington, CT 06032

Interquest, Incorporated
New York, NY 10017

Interview Legal Search
Houston, TX 77008

Jacobson Associates
Chicago, IL 60625

J.D. Limited Enterprise
Palatine, IL 60074

J.D. Limited Enterprise
Sioux City, IA 51104

Paul Johnson Associates
Washington, DC 20036

Kanarek & Shaw
New York, NY 10022

Kass/Abell & Associates
Los Angeles, CA 90025

Keith Management Company, Inc.
Beverly Hills, CA 90210

Thomas E. Kenney
Washington, DC 20036

Barbara Kerner Consultants
New York, NY 10017

Bernard J. Klug
New York, NY 10016

D. A. Kreuter Associates
Philadelphia, PA 19103

Henry Labus Personnel, Inc.
Detroit, MI 48226

Louise Lashaw
New York, NY 10168

Lawsearch Inc.
Encino, CA 91436

Lee, Jackson & Bowe
Beverly Hills, CA 90212

Legal Headhunters, Inc.
Metairie, LA 70001

Legal Placements, Inc.
Philadelphia, PA 19103

The R. J. Lipton Company
New York, NY 10017

Lyman & Co.
Glendale, CA 91203

The McCormick Group, Inc.
Arlington, VA 22209

Patricia McDonald Legal Service Consultants, Inc.
Dallas, TX 75210

Patricia McDonald Legal Search Consultants
Houston, TX 77002

William K. McLaughlin Associates
Rochester, NY 14610

McMorrow Associates, Inc.
Los Angeles, CA 90067

Robert A. Major & Associates
San Francisco, CA 94109

Marley Group Ltd.
New York, NY 10003

Meridian Personnel Associates, Inc.
New York, NY 10036

Metro Vantage Associates, Inc.
New York, NY 10168

Alan Metz Legal & Executive Search Consultants
New York, NY 10021

Michaelson Associates
New York, NY 10021

Ruth Miles Associates, Inc.
New York, NY 10017

Susan C. Miller Associates, Inc.
Washington, DC 20006

William Moore Associates, Inc.
New York, NY 10017

National Employment Consultants— Brandywine Inc.
Wilmington, DE 19806

New England Legal Search, Inc.
Boston, MA 02116

New York Legal Search, Inc.
New York, NY 10178

NHS Legal Search Consultants, Inc.
Los Angeles, CA 90017

Nobel, Albach & Associates
Dallas, TX 75218

The NRI Group
Rockville, MD 20850

The NRI Group
Washington, DC 20036

NRI Legal
Washington, DC 20006

O'Crowley & O'Toole Executive Search
Portland, OR 97223

Walter Parnes Management Co.
New York, NY 10019

Personnel Resources Organization
Philadelphia, PA 19107

Phillps Personnel Search
Denver, CO 80202

PM Legal Search Consultants
Dallas, TX 75201

PM Legal Search Consultants
Houston, TX 77057

PPS Consultants
Phoenix, AZ 85004

Prescott Legal Search
Houston, TX 77046

The Psi-Com Group, Ltd.
New York, NY 10019

Pursuant Legal Consultants
Palm Springs, CA 92262

Railey & Associates
Houston, TX 77069

Lloyd Richards Personnel Service
Tulsa, OK 74103

Rivera Legal Search Consultants, Inc.
Santa Monica, CA 90403

The Robert Group
New York, NY 10021

Alan Roberts & Associates, Inc.
New York, NY 10178

Melissa S. Sacks Legal Search Firm
Annandale, VA 22003

Samuelson Associates
Chicago, IL 60602

Seaton/Russo Inc.
Beverly Hills, CA 90212

Robert Sirny & Associates
Minneapolis, MN 55431

Raymond James Smith & Associates
Cary, IL 60013

Alan R. Stone, Esq., Attorney Placement Consultant, Inc.
Boston, MA 02108

Sullivan Associates
Chicago, IL 60606

Thai, Inc.
Libertyville, IL 60048

Waldorf Associates, Inc.
Los Angeles, CA 90049

Walz Associates
New York, NY 10155

Washington Legal Search
Washington, DC 20036

Washington Legal Search, Inc.
Washington, DC 20036

Wells International
Los Angeles, CA 90067

Wells International
Washington, DC 20005

Wells International
Chicago, IL 60601

Wells International
New York, NY 10017

Wells International
Houston, TX 77046

David J. White & Associates Inc.
Chicago, IL 60606

R. M. Whiteside Company
Hilton Head Island, SC 29925

Winship Associates
San Francisco, CA 94104

Xavier Associates, Inc.
Brockton, MA 02401

Ziskind, Greene & Associates
Beverly Hills, CA 90211

Ziskind, Greene, & Associates
San Francisco, CA 94111

MANUFACTURING

Action Personnel Services
Charlotte, NC 28209

The Adams Consulting Group
Columbus, OH 43206

Agri-Associates
Davenport, IA 52803

Aim Executive Recruiting & Search
Cleveland, OH 44132

Alan & Associates Employee Search
Shreveport, LA 71104

William Alder Associates
Leonia, NJ 07605

Thomas R. Aldrich & Associates
Westford, MA 01886

Alexander & Associates, Inc.
Elkhart, IN 46515

Allied Search
Norcross, GA 30092

American Executive Search Services, Inc.
San Jose, CA 95135

American Executive Search Services, Inc.
Santa Clara, CA 95051

Ames & Wyand Associates, Inc.
Brunswick, ME 04011

Ames-O'Neill Associates, Inc.
Hauppauge, NY 11788

Amity Consultants, Inc.
Fairfield, CT 06430

Analytic Recruiting, Inc.
New York, NY 10017

Anderson-Gest & Associates
Bellevue, WA 98004

Anderson, Graham & Stewart
Marietta, GA 30061

The Andre Group, Inc.
King of Prussia, PA 19406

Arancio Associates
Needham, MA 02192

Armstrong & Associates
Los Alamitos, CA 90720

Arthur Personnel
Caldwell, NJ 07006

Ashway Ltd. Agency
New York, NY 10017

Ashworth Consultants
Boston, MA 02109

Associates Business Consultants, Inc.
Los Angeles, CA 90017

Associates Business Consultants, Inc.
Medford, NJ 08055

Atomic Personnel, Inc.
Philadelphia, PA 19102

Aubin International Inc.
Waltham, MA 02154

Austin-Allen Co.
Memphis, TN 38119

Availability Personnel Consultants
Bedford, NH 03102

James Bangert Associates, Inc.
Wayzata, MN 55391

Banner Personnel Service
Chicago, IL 60602

Barclays Recruiting Services, Inc.
Denver, CO 80222

Barger & Sargent, Inc.
Concord, NH 03301

Barone Associates
Woodbridge, NJ 07095

Battalia & Associates, Inc.
New York, NY 10016

Beall Associates—Greensboro
Greensboro, NC 27419

Beall Associates of Greenville
Greenville, SC 29608

Beck, Gerstenfeld & Associates
Woodburn, OR 97071

Becker Associates
North Kingstown, RI 02852

Robert Becker & Co.
Allison Park, PA 15101

Richard Beers & Associates, Ltd.
Glenview, IL 60025

Gary S. Bell Associates, Inc.
Wyckoff, NJ 07481

John Bell & Associates, Inc.
Chicago, IL 60611

Benham & Co., Inc.
Thorndale, PA 19372

Benton, Schneider & Associates, Inc.
Naperville, IL 60540

Leslie Berglass Associates, Inc.
New York, NY 10022

C. Berke & Associates
Doylestown, PA 18901

E. J. Bettinger Co.
Philadelphia, PA 19102

Charles A. Binswanger Associates
Baltimore, MD 21209

Blaine & Associates, Inc.
Encino, CA 91436

J. L. Bohart & Co.
San Mateo, CA 94401

Bonner Gladney Associates
Devon, PA 19333

The Borton-Wallace Company
Asheville, NC 28801

Bossler/Brown & Associates
Topeka, KS 66612

Bowden & Company, Inc.
Cleveland, OH 44131

Breitmayer Associates
Guilford, CT 06437

Brennan & Associates, Inc.
Dallas, TX 75234

K. Robert Brian
Philadelphia, PA 19103

Britt Associates, Inc.
Chicago, IL 60604

BRJ Associates, Inc.
Mountainside, NJ 07092

Brucks Personnel Corp
East Rochester, NY 14445

Bryant Associates, Inc.
Chicago, IL 60611

Burns Personnel Inc.
Rochester, NY 14604

Buzhardt Associates
Jackson, MS 39211

Daniel Cades & Associates
Philadelphia, PA 19107

Douglas Campbell & Associates, Inc.
Santa Ana, CA 92701

Caprio & Associates, Inc.
Oak Brook, IL 60521

Career Dynamics, Inc.
Melrose, MA 02176

Career Specialists, Inc.
Bellevue, WA 98004

Carpenter Consultants, Inc.
Chestnut Hill, MA 02167

CBA Personnel Services
Cincinnati, OH 45202

CBS Personnel Services
Dayton, OH 45402

Chevigny Personnel Agency
Merrillville, IN 46410

Christensen & Montgomery
Morristown, NJ 07960

Christopher, Drew & Associates, Inc.
Cleveland, OH 44122

Citizens Employment Service
Fort Lee, NJ 07024

Richard Clark Associates
West Hartford, CT 06017

Clark Associates, Inc.
Atlanta, GA 30345

Darryl Clausing & Associates
Frankfort, IL 60423

Claveloux, McCaffrey & Associates, Inc.
New York, NY 10018

CMA Technical Search, Inc.
New York, NY 10017

Cochran, Cochran & Yale, Inc.
Rochester, NY 14623

Cole, Warren & Long, Inc.
Philadelphia, PA 19102

Coleman Lew & Associates, Inc.
Charlotte, NC 28202

Colton Bernard Inc.
San Francisco, CA 94118

Concept Corp.
Sausalito, CA 94966

Consultants, Inc.
North Brunswick, NJ 08902

Continental Search Group
New York, NY 10016

Corporate Career Consultants
San Francisco, CA 94111

The Corporate Connection, Ltd.
Richmond, VA 23230

Corporate Environment Ltd.
Crystal Lake, IL 60014

Corporate Recruiters, Inc.
Philadelphia, PA 19126

Corporate Resources, Inc.
Minneapolis, MN 55426

Corporate Service Group, Ltd.
San Francisco, CA 94102

Corporate Staffing Group
Horsham, PA 19044

Cowin Associates
Carle Place, NY 11514

Craighead Associates
Stamford, CT 06901

Cretney & Associates
Cleveland, OH 44143

Crippin, Inc.
Overland Park, KS 66210

Cross Country Consultants, Inc.
Baltimore, MD 21218

Timothy D. Crowe, Jr.
Chelmsford, MA 01824

Daly & Co., Inc.
Boston, MA 02116

N. Dean Davic Associates
Pittsburgh, PA 15235

Robert H. Davidson Associates
Norwood, MA 02062

Davies Associates International, Ltd.
Houston, TX 77218

Gene Davis & Associates
Oklahoma City, OK 73156

The Dean Group
Maplewood, NJ 07040

DEI Executive Services
Cincinnati, OH 45209

Deven Associates, Inc.
Verona, NJ 07044

Ned E. Dickey and Associates
Rockford, IL 61110

Dimmerling & Associates
Atlanta, GA 30339

Donaldson & Wharton Associates
New York, NY 10001

Dorison & Company
Coral Gables, FL 33134

Downer & Starbuck
Rockford, IL 61111

J. H. Dugan & Co.
Chicago, IL 60611

Dumont Kiradjieff & Moriarty
Boston, MA 02109

Dunhill Personnel Service
Philadelphia, PA 19102

Dyna-Search
Chicago, IL 60604

Eastern Executive Associates
Clifton, NJ 07012

E.D.P. World, Inc.
San Francisco, CA 94111

The Elliott Company, Inc.
Woburn, MA 01801

David M. Ellner Associates
New York, NY 10121

Employment Unlimited Agency
Baltimore, MD 21231

ExecuSource International
El Paso, TX 79902

Executive Locators of America
Metairie, LA 70004

Executive Personnel Consultants
Memphis, TN 38117

Executive Placement Corporation
Rochester, NY 14604

Executive Recruiters, Inc.
Milwaukee, WI 53226

Executive Register, Inc.
Danbury, CT 06810

Executive Search Company
Conshohocken, PA 19428

First Recruiting Group
Houston, TX 77024

Fleming Associates
Miami, FL 33166

Fleming Associates
Sarasota, FL 33577

Fleming Associates
Atlanta, GA 30339

Fleming Associates
Columbus, IN 47202

Fleming Associates
Louisville, KY 40220

Fleming Associates
Metairie, LA 70002

Fleming Associates
Dublin, OH 43017

Fleming Associates
Memphis, TN 38111

Fleming Associates
Houston, TX 77024

Flinn Consultants, Inc.
Highland Park, IL 60035

Flowers and Associates
Maumee, OH 43537

Ford and Ford
Dedham, MA 02026

Fortune of Providence
Providence, RI 02903

Foster & Associates, Inc.
San Francisco, CA 94105

Walter Frederick Friedman and Co., Inc.
West Orange, NJ 07052

Futures Personnel Services
Baltimore, MD 21204

General Employment Enterprises
Fremont, CA 94538

General Employment Enterprises
Torrance, CA 90503

General Employment Enterprises
Oak Brook, IL 60521

Genovese & Co. Management Consultants
Los Angeles, CA 90067

Glynn, Brooks & Co.
Fort Lee, NJ 07024

B. Goodwin, Ltd.
Fairfield, CT 06430

Gordon, Cook & Associates
Clayton, MO 63105

Graham & Associates Employee Consultants
Greensboro, NC 27408

Granger & Associates, Inc.
Cincinnati, OH 45242

E. W. Greeen & Associates
Solana Beach, CA 92075

Griffith & Werner, Inc.
Hollywood, FL 33021

Group IV Recruitment Consultants
New York, NY 10036

Grover & Associates
Worthington, OH 43085

The Hamilton/Ryker Company
Martin, TN 38237

Robert Harkins Associates
Ephrata, PA 17522

Haskell & Stern Associates, Inc.
New York, NY 10017

Haskell & Stern Associates, Inc.
Fort Worth, TX 76112

T. J. Hayes Associates
Assonet, MA 02702

Hayman & Company
Dallas, TX 75201

Health Industry Consultants, Inc.
Englewood, CO 80112

F. P. Healy & Company
New York, NY 10169

Heberling Personnel
Harrisburg, PA 17105

E. B. Hendrick Associates
Liverpool, NY 13088

Horizon Associates
Redondo Beach, CA 90277

Horizon Personnel
York, PA 17402

Horizon Personnel
Franklin, TN 37064

Houchins & Associates, Inc.
Atlanta, GA 30308

Robert Howe & Associates
Atlanta, GA 30341

Jack Hurst & Associates, Inc.
Richardson, TX 75080

Huxtable Associates, Inc.
Bridgeton, MO 63044

Indusearch
Newington, CT 06111

Industrial Recruiters Associates, Inc.
West Hartford, CT 06110

Industry Consultants
Atlanta, GA 30338

Interface Group, Ltd.
Washington, DC 20007

International ExecuSearch, Ltd.
Scottsdale, AZ 85254

International Staffing Consultants, Inc.
Newport Beach, CA 92260

Charles Irish Co., Inc.
New York, NY 10170

Charles Irish Co., Inc.
Raleigh, NC 27609

Robert J. Irmen Associates
Hinsdale, IL 60521

Johnson & Genrich, Inc.
Chicago, IL 60630

Johnson Personnel
Canton, OH 44718

J. L. Jordan Associates
Dallas, TX 75240

Karam Associates
Denver, CO 80224

Martin Kartin & Company
New York, NY 10021

KBK Management Associates
Youngstown, OH 44512

Hubert L. Kelly, Personnel Consultants
Chicopee, MA 01020

Kendall and Davis Company
St. Louis, MO 63102

Kenfield Research Associates, Inc.
New York, NY 10016

Joseph Keyes Associates
Hackensack, NJ 07601

Kiley-Owen Associates, Inc.
Philadelphia, PA 19107

Robert Kleven & Co., Inc.
Lexington, MA 02173

KMS Associates
Kingston, NY 12401

Krow Associates, Inc.
West Caldwell, NJ 07006

Kuhnmuench & Cook Associates
Arcadia, CA 91006

Lacrosse Associates, Inc.
Union, NJ 07083

Gilbert Lane Associates
Atlanta, GA 30339

Larsen Personnel
Needham, MA 02192

Paul W. Larson Associates, Inc.
San Juan Capistrano, CA 92675

Michael Latas & Associates, Inc.
St. Louis, MO 63132

Locke & Associates
Charlotte, NC 28280

Arthur J. Loveley Associates
New York, NY 10165

James H. Lowry & Associates
Chicago, IL 60601

George P. Lyon Associates
Doylestown, PA 18901

Lyons/Aspen Consultants Group
Englewood, CO 80110

Ross MacAskills Associates, Inc.
Washington, DC 20036

McInturff & Associates, Inc.
Natick, MA 01760

Maetzold Associates, Inc.
Minnetonka, MN 55343

Main Line Personnel Services, Inc.
Bala Cynwyd, PA 19004

J. C. Malone Associates
Louisville, KY 40218

Management Search & Associates
Westport, CT 06880

Thomas Mangum Co.
Los Angeles, CA 90041

Marshall Group
Los Angeles, CA 92660

Masland Management Services
Philadelphia, PA 19118

Mason Associates
Norwalk, CT 06851

Stephen W. Matson Associates, Ltd.
Birmingham, MI 48011

M. D. Mattes & Associates
Timonium, MD 21093

MBA Associates, Inc.
Boston, MA 02109

MKI Recruiting Associates
White Plains, NY 10601

Morgan & Associates
Springfield, MA 01115

J. R. Morrison & Associates, Inc.
San Francisco, CA 94111

Herbert H. Moss, Inc.
Palm Springs, CA 92262

MRG Search & Placement
New Haven, CT 06510

National Career Centers—USA
Fayetteville, NC 28302

National Career Service
Harrisburg, PA 17105

National Recruiting Service
Dyer, IN 46311

Gary Nelson & Associates, Inc.
Cupertino, CA 95014

Gary Nelson & Associates, Inc.
San Rafael, CA 94913

William H. Nenstiel & Associates, Inc.
Scottsdale, AZ 85251

Perry Newcomb & Associates
Cincinnati, OH 45230

New England Consultants
Warwick, RI 02887

Arthur Newman Associates, Inc.
Houston, TX 77027

Paul Norsell & Associates, Inc.
Anaheim, CA 92807

Paul Norsell & Associates, Inc.
Los Angeles, CA 90045

Northern Consultants, Inc.
Hampden, ME 04444

Oliver Associates, Inc.
Melville, NY 11747

O'Neill Executive Search
Buffalo, NY 14223

C. M. Oppenheim & Associates, Inc.
New York, NY 10036

Harry D. Parkhurst & Associates, Inc.
Minneapolis, MN 55426

Patton/Perry Associates
Charlotte, NC 28284

Robert Pencarski & Company
Dedham, MA 02026

Peeney Associates, Inc.
Fanwood, NJ 07023

People Management Inc.
Simsbury, CT 06070

Personnel, Inc.
Spartanburg, SC 29302

Peterson Personnel Recruiters
Warwick, RI 02886

Peyser Associates, Inc.
Miami, FL 33125

Phillips Resource Group
Greenville, SC 29606

Pinkerton & Associates, Inc.
Chicago, IL 60611

Placement Experts
Huntsville, AL 35801

Power Services
North Charleston, SC 29406

Preferred Positions
Nashua, NH 03060

Probe Technology
King of Prussia, PA 19406

Proctor & Davis
Santa Monica, CA 90403

Professional Career Placements
Arlington, TX 76003

Professional Executive Consultants
Northbrook, IL 60062

Professional Personnel Associates
Charlotte, NC 28212

Professional Personnel Consultants
Southfield, MI 48075

Professional Placement Group
Boston, MA 02109

Professional Recruiters Inc.
Auburn, MA 01501

Professional Specialists
Euclid, OH 44132

Queens Employment Service
Long Island City, NY 11101

Rainess Associates
West Caldwell, NJ 07006

The R & L Group
Arlington Heights, IL 60004

Redmond & Associates, Inc.
Danbury, CT 06810

Renhil Group, Inc.
Perrysburg, OH 43551

Research Technologies
Madison, CT 06443

E. J. Rhodes, Inc.
Framingham, MA 01701

Ridgefield Search International
Ridgefield, CT 06877

R. M. Associates
Portland, OR 97223

Robertson, Spoerlein & Wengert
Chicago, IL 60606

Roche Associates
Stamford, CT 06094

Rogers & Sands Inc.
Burlington, MA 02108

Rollins & Co.
La Jolla, CA 92037

Romano McAvoy Associates, Inc.
Smithtown, NY 11787

Sanford Rose Associates of Hartford
Windsor, CT 06095

Roth Young—Los Angeles
Fox Hills, CA 90230

Roth Young Personnel
St. Louis, MO 63105

Louis Rudzinsky Associates, Inc.
Lexington, MA 02173

Charles Russ Associates, Inc.
Kansas City, MO 64114

Russ Fallstad and Associates
Minneapolis, MN 55426

Sales Executives, Inc.
Troy, MI 48084

Scope Services, Inc.
St. Joseph, MI 49085

Search Source Inc.
Granite City, IL 62040

David Shane & Associates
Galesburg, IL 61404

Siegel & Bishop, Inc.
San Francisco, CA 94112

Siegel Shotland & Associates
Encino, CA 91436

Sinclair & Potts Associates, Inc.
Pittsburgh, PA 15235

James F. Smith & Associates
Atlanta, GA 30342

Sollmar Incorporated
Tustin, CA 92681

David Solol Personnel Consultant
Kutztown, PA 19530

Soltis Management Services
Radnor, PA 19087

S. P. Associates
Charlotte, NC 28231

Stanislaw & Associates, Inc.
Brookfield, WI 53005

John R. Stephens & Associates
Houston, TX 77002

Lawrence A. Stich
Milwaukee, WI 53207

STM Associates
Salt Lake, UT 84111

Stumbaugh Associates, Inc.
Atlanta, GA 30035

Successmove, Inc.
Blue Bell, PA 19422

John J. Sudlow & Co.
Chicago, Il 60611

John J. Sudlow & Co.
Seattle, WA 98101

Technical Support Etc.
Marlboro, MA 01752

Tecmark Associates, Inc.
New York, NY 10123

J. Robert Thompson Co., Inc.
Houston, TX 77027

M. D. Treadway & Company
Olive Branch, MS 38654

K. W. Tunnell Co., Inc.
King of Prussia, PA 19406

Harry F. Twomey Associates
Philadelphia, PA 19102

Uni/Search of New Haven
Woodbridge, CT 06525

United Consultants
York, PA 17403

Varo & Lund Corp.
Los Angeles, CA 90028

Vezan-West & Co.
West Hartford, CT 06107

VIP Personnel of Raleigh
Raleigh, NC 27619

R. J. Waggett & Associates
Houston, TX 77056

Gordon Wahls Company
Villanova, PA 19085

Albert J. Walsh & Associates
Newtown, PA 18940

John H. Warner Associates, Inc.
Hartford, CT 06103

R. H. Warner Consulting
Westerville, OH 43081

Webster Positions, Inc.
Hicksville, NY 11801

Emanuel Weintraub Associates, Inc.
Fort Lee, NJ 07024

Werner Management Consultants, Inc.
New York, NY 10018

Western Reserve Associates
Bath, OH 44210

Whittaker & Associates, Inc.
Atlanta, GA 30339

E. N. Wilkins and Company, Inc.
Chicago, IL 60606

Duane I. Wilson Associates, Inc.
Birmingham, MI 48011

Winguth, Schweichler Associates, Inc.
San Francisco, CA 94111

Winter Wyman & Co.
Bedford, MA 01730

Jim Woodson & Associates
Jackson, MS 39216

John Wylie Associates, Inc.
Tulsa, OK 74136

Zackrison Associates, Inc.
Fairfield, CT 06430

Zackrison Associates, Inc.
Stamford, CT 06905

Zackrison Associates, Inc.
West Hartford, CT 06110

The Zammataro Company
Hudson, OH 44236

MARKETING

Jerome Ackels Associates
Great Neck, NY 11021

Jeffrey C. Adams & Co., Inc.
San Francisco, CA 94104

Agra Placements, Ltd.
Lincoln, IL 62656

Agra Placements, Ltd.
Peru, IN 46970

Agra Placements, Ltd.
West Des Moines, IA 50265

Agri-Associates
Davenport, IA 52803

M. L. Alber Associates
Columbia, SC 29210

Thomas R. Aldrich & Associates
Westford, MA 01886

Alexander-Edward Associates, Inc.
Philadelphia, PA 19107

Don Allan Associates, Inc.
New York, NY 10017

American Executive Search Services, Inc.
San Jose, CA 95135

American Executive Search Services, Inc.
Santa Clara, CA 95051

Analytic Recruiting, Inc.
New York, NY 10017

The Andre Group, Inc.
King of Prussia, PA 19406

Armstrong & Associates
Los Alamitos, CA 90720

Aronow Associates, Inc.
New York, NY 10001

Arthur Personnel
Caldwell, NJ 07006

Artists Counselor & Placement Service
Chicago, IL 60601

Ashworth Consultants
Boston, MA 02109

Associated Personnel Technicians, Inc.
Wichita, KS 67214

Associated Ventures
Dellwood, MO 63136

Auguston & Associates
Portland, OR 97232

Banner Personnel Service
Chicago, IL 60602

Barger & Sargent, Inc.
Concord, NH 03301

Barone Associates
Woodbridge, NJ 07095

Barry & Co.
Los Angeles, CA 90017

Nathan Barry Associates, Inc.
Boston, MA 02109

Bay Search Group
Providence, RI 02903

BCL Corporation
Cleveland, OH 44107

Beck, Gerstenfeld & Associates
Woodburn, OR 97071

Robert Becker & Co.
Allison Park, PA 15101

Richard Beers & Associates, Ltd.
Glenview, IL 60025

Gary S. Bell Associates, Inc.
Wyckoff, NJ 07481

Benham & Co., Inc.
Thorndale, PA 19372

Benton, Schneider & Associates, Inc.
Naperville, IL 60540

Leslie Berglass Associates, Inc.
New York, NY 10022

C. Berke & Associates
Doylestown, PA 18901

E. J. Bettinger Co.
Philadelphia, PA 19102

Bialla & Associates, Inc.
Sausalito, CA 94965

The Bradbeer Co.
Gulph Mills, PA 19406

Breitmayer Associates
Guilford, CT 06437

Brennan & Associates, Inc.
Dallas, TX 75234

Roberta Brenner Associates, Inc.
New York, NY 10022

Britt Associates, Inc.
Chicago, IL 60604

BRJ Associates, Inc.
Mountainside, NJ 07092

Brown-Bernardy, Inc.
Los Angeles, CA 90049

Bryant Associates, Inc.
Chicago, IL 60611

Buzhardt Associates
Jackson, MS 39211

Daniel Cades & Associates
Philadelphia, PA 19107

Caprio & Associates, Inc.
Oak Brook, IL 60521

Career Builders, Inc.
New York, NY 10017

Career Dynamics, Inc.
Melrose, MA 02176

Career Resource Associates, Inc.
Houston, TX 77288

Career Specialists, Inc.
Bellevue, WA 98004

Careers Unlimited
Elkhart, IN 46516

Carpenter Consultants, Inc.
Chestnut Hill, MA 02167

Carroll/Church Associates, Inc.
Bellevue, WA 98004

CDH & Associates
Irvine, CA 92715

Christopher, Drew & Associates, Inc.
Cleveland, OH 44122

Toby Clark Associates, Inc.
New York, NY 10022

Clark, Clark & Clark Associates
College Park, MD 20740

Claveloux, McCaffrey & Associates, Inc.
New York, NY 10018

The Clayton Group, Inc.
Oak Brook Terrace, IL 60181

Cole, Warren & Long, Inc.
Philadelphia, PA 19102

Concept Corp.
Sausalito, CA 94966

Corporate Environment Ltd.
Crystal Lake, IL 60014

Corporate Recruiters, Inc.
Philadelphia, PA 19126

Corporate Service Group, Ltd.
San Francisco, CA 94102

Corporate Staffing Group
Horsham, PA 19044

Craighead Associates
Stamford, CT 06901

Crandall Associates, Inc.
New York, NY 10017

Creative Search Affiliates
New York, NY 10021

Cretney & Associates
Cleveland, OH 44143

Crippin, Inc.
Overland Park, KS 66210

Cris Associates, Inc.
New York, NY 10016

Damon & Associates, Inc.
Dallas, TX 75231

Robert H. Davidson Associates
Norwood, MA 02062

Gene Davis & Associates
Oklahoma City, OK 73156

The Dean Group
Maplewood, NJ 07040

DEI Executive Services
Cincinnati, OH 45209

DeLalla-Fried Associates
New York, NY 10021

DeLoughrey & Co.
Wellesley Hills, MA 02181

W. J. Derden Consultants
Tallahassee, FL 32317

Ned E. Dickey and Associates
Rockford, IL 61110

Dimmerling & Associates
Atlanta, GA 30339

R. M. Donaldson Personnel
Cranford, NJ 07016

Dorison & Company
Coral Gables, FL 33134

J. H. Dugan & Co.
Chicago, IL 60611

Dumont Kiradjieff & Moriarty
Boston, MA 02109

Dunhill of Greater Stamford
Wilton, CT 06897

Dunhill of Cedar Rapids
Cedar Rapids, IA 52401

Dunhill of Paramus
Parmaus, NJ 07652

Dunsmore & Associates, Ltd.
Guilford, CT 06437

The Elliott Company, Inc.
Woburn, MA 01801

David M. Ellner Associates
New York, NY 10121

Employment Unlimited Agency
Baltimore, MD 21231

ERA Placements
Pawtucket, RI 02861

Evans Associates, Inc.
San Francisco, CA 94104

Executive Career Development
Clearwater, FL 33546

Executive Locators of America
Metairie, LA 70004

Executive Personnel Consultants
Memphis, TN 38117

Executive Recruiters, Inc.
Milwaukee, WI 53226

Executive Resources
New Milford, CT 06776

Executive Search Company
Conshohocken, PA 19428

Jerry Fields Associates, Inc.
New York, NY 10019

Finley & Co.
Greenville, SC 29615

First Recruiting Group
Houston, TX 77024

A. G. Fishkin & Associates, Inc.
Rockville, MD 20852

Flinn Consultants, Inc.
Highland Park, IL 60035

Florapersonnel
Deland, FL 32721

Forum Personnel
New York, NY 10017

Foster & Associates, Inc.
San Francisco, CA 94105

The Fry Group
New York, NY 10017

Genovese & Co. Management Consultants
Los Angeles, CA 90067

Glynn, Brooks & Co.
Fort Lee, NJ 07024

Graham & Associates Employee Consultants
Greensboro, NC 27408

Graham & Associates, Inc.
Dallas, TX 75240

Granger & Associates, Inc.
Cincinnati, OH 45242

Paul C. Green & Associates, Ltd.
Green Valley, AZ 85614

Greene Personnel Consultants
Providence, RI 02903

Griffith & Werner, Inc.
Hollywood, FL 33021

Group IV Recruitment Consultants
New York, NY 10036

The Gruen Co.
Oakland, CA 94618

Hahn & Associates, Inc.
Dayton, OH 45402

Hardwick Resources
Clearwater, FL 33575

Harmon Anderson International
Westlake Village, CA 91362

Harreus & Strotz, Inc.
San Francisco, CA 94111

Haskell & Stern Associates, Inc.
Fort Worth, TX 76112

Hayden & Refo, Inc.
Boston, MA 02110

Health Industry Consultants, Inc.
Englewood, CO 80112

F. P. Healy & Company
New York, NY 10169

J. D. Hersey & Associates
Columbus, OH 43221

Higbee Associates, Inc.
Rowayton, CT 06853

Hipp Waters Professional Recruiters
Stamford, CT 06901

HiTech Consulting Group
Los Angeles, CA 90067

Horton Associates, Inc.
Helendale, CA 92342

Houchins & Associates, Inc.
Atlanta, GA 30308

Robert Howe & Associates
Atlanta, GA 30341

H. S. Placements
Green Bay, WI 54302

Huxtable Associates, Inc.
Bridgeton, MO 63044

Industrial Recruiters Associates, Inc.
West Hartford, CT 06110

Robert J. Irmen Associates
Hinsdale, IL 60521

Nancy Jackson, Inc.
Scranton, PA 18503

Janus Consultants, Inc.
Washington, DC 20007

Jean's Personnel
Memphis, TN 38137

JM & Company
Wayne, PA 19087

Johnson, Smith and Knisely
New York, NY 10017

Judd-Falk Inc.
New York, NY 10016

Karam Associates
Denver, CO 80224

Martin Kartin & Company
New York, NY 10021

Kenfield Research Associates, Inc.
New York, NY 10016

Jack Kennedy Associates, Inc.
Chicago, IL 60601

Melvin Kent & Associates
Columbus, OH 43215

Kiley-Owen Associates, Inc.
Philadelphia, PA 19107

Kingsley Quinn, Ltd.
New York, NY 10022

Kinkead Associates
Hartford, CT 06103

Krow Associates, Inc.
West Caldwell, NJ 07006

Kuebler Associates
Portland, ME 04101

Kuhnmuench & Cook Associates
Arcadia, CA 91006

Kunzer Associates, Ltd.
Chicago, IL 60604

Marvin Laba & Associates
Los Angeles, CA 90028

Lacrosse Associates, Inc.
Union, NJ 07083

Lamay Associates, Inc.
Riverside, CT 06878

Gilbert Lane Associates
Atlanta, GA 30339

Paul W. Larson Associates, Inc.
San Juan Capistrano, CA 92675

J. Lee & Associates
Atlanta, GA 30358

Lee Calhoon & Co., Inc.
Birchrunville, PA 19421

Arthur J. Loveley Associates
New York, NY 10165

Lovewell & Associates, Inc.
Atlanta, GA 30361

James H. Lowry & Associates
Chicago, IL 60601

Lyman & Co.
Glendale, CA 91203

Ross MacAskills Associates, Inc.
Washington, DC 20036

MacFarlane & Co., Inc.
Atlanta, GA 30318

Bob Maddox Associates
Atlanta, GA 30326

Maetzold Associates, Inc.
Minnetonka, MN 55343

J. C. Malone Associates
Louisville, KY 40218

Management Resource Associates
Woburn, MA 01801

Management Search & Associates
Westport, CT 06880

Management Search Inc.
Minneapolis, MN 55426

Management South, Inc.
Minneapolis, MN 55426

Thomas Mangum Co.
Los Angeles, CA 90041

Market Search, Inc.
Thiensville, WI 53092

Marshall Consultants, Inc.
Seattle, WA 98111

Marshall Group
Los Angeles, CA 92660

Masland Management Services
Philadelphia, PA 19118

Mason Associates
Norwalk, CT 06851

Medical Recruiters of America
Tampa, FL 33607

James Mercer & Associates, Inc.
Atlanta, GA 30356

Midland Consultants—Pittsburgh
Carnegie, PA 15106

MKI Recruiting Associates
White Plains, NY 10601

Morris Madden & Rice, Inc.
New York, NY 10176

J. R. Morrison & Associates, Inc.
San Francisco, CA 94111

Herbert H. Moss, Inc.
Palm Springs, CA 92262

MRG Search & Placement
New Haven, CT 06510

Multi Technology Inc.
Framingham, MA 01701

National Career Centers—USA
Fayetteville, NC 28302

Nation-Wide Recruiting, Inc.
Encino, CA 91316

William H. Nenstiel & Associates, Inc.
Scottsdale, AZ 85251

Perry Newcomb & Associates
Cincinnati, OH 45230

Paul Norsell & Associates, Inc.
Anaheim, CA 92807

Paul Norsell & Associates, Inc.
Los Angeles, CA 90045

Robert E. Nurse Associates, Inc.
White Plains, NY 10530

O'Grady Associates, Inc.
West Concord, MA 01742

Oliver & Rosner Associates
New York, NY 10022

Oliver Associates, Inc.
Melville, NY 11747

OMNI Executive Search, Inc.
Atlanta, GA 30328

O'Neill Executive Search
Buffalo, NY 14223

C. M. Oppenheim & Associates, Inc.
New York, NY 10036

O'Shea System of Employment
Philadelphia, PA 19107

Carol Palmer Associates, Ltd.
New York, NY 10017

Robert Parella Associates
New York, NY 10103

Peeney Associates, Inc.
Fanwood, NJ 07023

People Management Inc.
Simsbury, CT 06070

Personnel, Inc.
Spartanburg, SC 29302

Personnel Management Associates
Woburn, MA 01801

Peyser Associates, Inc.
Miami, FL 33125

Philadelphia Search Group, Inc.
Philadelphia, PA 19102

Phillips Resource Group
Greenville, SC 29606

Pierce Associates, Inc.
San Francisco, CA 94111

Pinkerton & Associates, Inc.
Chicago, IL 60611

Proctor & Davis
Santa Monica, CA 90403

Professional Executive Consultants
Northbrook, IL 60062

Professional Personnel Consultants
Southfield, MI 48075

The Recruiter
Des Moines, IA 50311

Redmond & Associates, Inc.
Danbury, CT 06810

The Pamela Reeve Agency, Inc.
Los Angeles, CA 90069

Reichelt & Associates, Inc.
Los Angeles, CA 90024

Ridenour & Associates
Chicago, IL 60601

Ridgefield Search International
Ridgefield, CT 06877

RJS Associates
Hartford, CT 06103

R. M. Associates
Portland, OR 97223

Robertson, Spoerlein & Wengert
Chicago, IL 60606

Romano McAvoy Associates, Inc.
Smithtown, NY 11787

Roth Young Personnel of Minneapolis
Edina, MN 55435

Roth Young Personnel
St. Louis, MO 63105

Louis Rudzinsky Associates, Inc.
Lexington, MA 02173

Charles Russ Associates, Inc.
Kansas City, MO 64114

St. Clair International
Menlo Park, CA 94025

Sales & Management Search, Inc.
Chicago, IL 60606

Sales Consultants of Hartford
Hartford, CT 06067

Sales Consultants—New Haven
Rocky Hill, CT 06067

Sales Consultants of Boston
Boston, MA 01803

Sales Consultants of Wellesley
Wellesley, MA 02181

Sales Executives, Inc.
Troy, MI 48084

Sales Recruiters International
Yonkers, NY 10701

Saxon Morse Associates
Pomona, NY 10970

Allan Schoenberger & Associates
Memphis, TN 38138

Scott/Hubbard Associates
Winnetka, IL 60093

Scott, Rogers Associates
New City, NY 10956

Search Source Inc.
Granite City, IL 62040

Search Tech Associates
Calabasas, CA 91302

William A. Sharon & Associates
Essex, CT 06426

Charles Sharp & Associates
Los Angeles, CA 90024

RitaSue Siegel Agency Inc.
New York, NY 10019

Siegel & Bishop, Inc.
San Francisco, CA 94112

Siegel Shotland & Associates
Encino, CA 91436

James F. Smith & Associates
Atlanta, GA 30342

Smith Hanley Associates, Inc.
New York, NY 10165

Carolyn Smith Paschal International
Del Mar, CA 92014

Smith's Fifth Avenue
New York, NY 10017

Sollmar Incorporated
Tustin, CA 92681

Specialized Search Associates
Greenwich, CT 06830

John R. Stephens & Associates
Houston, TX 77002

L. W. Stern Associates, Inc.
New York, NY 10016

Stonehill Management Consultants, Inc.
New York, NY 10175

Successmove, Inc.
Blue Bell, PA 19422

John J. Sudlow & Co.
Chicago, IL 60611

John J. Sudlow & Co.
Seattle, WA 98101

Tanzi Executive Search
San Diego, CA 92101

Tanzi Executive Search
San Francisco, CA 94104

Tecmark Associates, Inc.
New York, NY 10123

Tesar-Reynes, Inc.
Chicago, IL 60601

Richard Theobald & Associates
San Mateo, CA 94404

The Trattner Network
Citrus Heights, CA 95610

Harry F. Twomey Associates
Philadelphia, PA 19102

VanMaldegiam Associates, Inc.
Chicago, IL 60606

Varo & Lund Corp.
Los Angeles, CA 90028

Viking Recruiting Consultants, Inc.
Montvale, NJ 07645

Vine Associates Inc.
North Hollywood, CA 91602

Vlcek & Company
Los Angeles, CA 92660

Wachtel & Associates, Ltd.
New York, NY 10017

Walker Recruitment
Minneapolis, MN 55416

Ward Liebell Associates, Inc.
Greenwich, CT 06830

Wayne Associates, Inc.
Virginia Beach, VA 23452

Emanuel Weintraub Associates, Inc.
Fort Lee, NJ 07024

Werbin Associates Executive Search, Inc.
New York, NY 10175

Werner Management Consultants, Inc.
New York, NY 10018

Western Reserve Associates
Bath, OH 44210

Whittaker & Associates, Inc.
Atlanta, GA 30339

Whittlesey & Associates
West Chester, PA 19380

E. N. Wilkins and Company, Inc.
Chicago, IL 60606

J. W. Willard Associates, Inc.
Syracuse, NY 13201

Duane I. Wilson Associates, Inc.
Birmingham, MI 48011

Winchester Consultants Inc.
New Canaan, CT 06840

Winguth, Schweichler Associates, Inc.
San Francisco, CA 94111

Witt Associates, Inc.
Oak Brook, IL 60521

The Woodward Group
Chicago, IL 60601

Xagas & Associates
Geneva, IL 60134

Yorkshire Consulting Group, Inc.
Newton Upper Falls, MA 02164

Zachary & Sanders, Inc.
New York, NY 10119

Zackrison Associates, Inc.
Fairfield, CT 06430

Zackrison Associates, Inc.
Stamford, CT 06905

Zackrison Associates, Inc.
West Hartford, CT 06110

NONPROFIT

Brakeley, John Price Jones Inc.
Stamford, CT 06905

Garofalo, Curtiss & Company
Glen Falls, NY 12801

Garofalo, Curtiss & Company
Washington, DC 20036

Garofalo, Curtiss & Company
Boston, MA 02110

Garofalo, Curtiss & Company
Ardmore, PA 19003

William Harris Associates
New York, NY 10086

Hilton Research Associates
Woburn, MA 01801

Ketchum, Inc. Executive Recruiting Service
Boston, MA 02109

Ketchum, Inc. Executive Recruiting Service
Chicago, IL 60601

Ketchum, Inc. Executive Recruiting Service
Pittsburgh, PA 15219

Ketchum, Inc. Executive Recruiting Service
Dallas, TX 75250

Kors, Marlar, Savage & Associates
Annapolis, MD 21401

D. A. Kreuter Associates
Philadelphia, PA 19103

Ross MacAskills Associates, Inc.
Washington, DC 20036

Marshall Rice
Weston, CT 06883

The Oram Group, Inc.
New York, NY 10016

Tabor Search Group, Inc.
Washington, DC 20003

Carolyn Smith Paschal International
Del Mar, CA 92104

OFFICE ADMINISTRATION

Jerome Ackels Associates
Great Neck, NY 11021

Alaska Executive Search, Inc.
Anchorage, AK 99501

Alexander-Edward Associates, Inc.
Philadelphia, PA 19107

The Andre Group, Inc.
King of Prussia, PA 19406

E. J. Ashton & Associates, Ltd.
Arlington Heights, IL 60004

Austin-Allen Co.
Memphis, TN 38119

Availability of Hartford
Hartford, CT 06103

Belle Oaks of America
Kansas City, MO 64106

Berman Associates
Atlanta, GA 30309

E. J. Bettinger Co.
Philadelphia, PA 19102

E. A. Butler Associates, Inc.
New York, NY 10020

Cantor & Co., Inc.
Philadelphia, PA 19103

Career Specialists, Inc.
Bellevue, WA 98004

Closman & Asociates, Inc.
New York, NY 10001

Columbia EDP Agency, Inc.
New York, NY 10173

The Computer Resources Group, Inc.
San Francisco, CA 94111

The Computer Resources Group, Inc.
Walnut Creek, CA 94596

Consultant Group—Langlois & Associates,
 Inc.
Needham, MA 02194

Corporate Advisors Inc.
Miami, FL 33137

Crippin, Inc.
Overland Park, KS 66210

Crown, Michaels & Associates, Inc.
Los Angeles, CA 90067

William S. DeFuniak, Inc.
Hinsdale, IL 60521

Drew International Corp.
King of Prussia, PA 19406

Drum/Companies, Inc.
Atlanta, GA 30346

Dumont Kiradjieff & Moriarty
Boston, MA 02109

Dunhill of St. Petersburg
St. Petersburg, FL 33713

Dunhill of Austin
Austin, TX 78723

Dunhill of Greater Jackson
Jacksonville, FL 39206

Dunhill of Fort Collins
Fort Collins, CO 80525

Dunhill of Cedar Rapids
Cedar Rapids, IA 52401

Dunhill of Huntington
Melville, NY 11747

Dunhill of Troy
Troy, MI 48084

Dunhill of Greenville
Greenville, NC 27834

Dunhill of Albuquerque
Albuquerque, NM 87110

Dunhill of Greater Stamford
Wilton, CT 06897

Dunhill Personnel of N.E. Tulsa
Tulsa, OK 74128

Dunhill of Atlanta
Atlanta, GA 30326

Dunhill of Paramus
Paramus, NJ 07652

Dunhill of Hickory, N.C.
Hickory, NC 28601

Dunhill of Greensboro
Greensboro, NC 27408

Dunhill of Montgomery
Montgomery, AL 36117

Dynamic Search Systems, Inc.
Arlington Heights, IL 60004

Dyna-Search
Chicago, IL 60604

Edwards & Sowers, Inc.
Chicago, IL 60611

Evans Associates, Inc.
San Francisco, CA 94104

Executive Careers, Inc.
Conshohocken, PA 19428

Executive Locators of America
Metairie, LA 70004

Executive Recruiting Consultants, Inc.
Des Plaines, IL 60016

Executive Search of New England, Inc.
Portland, ME 04112

Fanning Personnel of Boston
Boston, MA 02116

Fortune of Providence
Providence, RI 02903

Garrett Associates, Inc.
Atlanta, GA 30339

Edward Gaylord & Associates
Mill Valley, CA 94942

General Employment Enterprises, Inc.
Naperville, IL 60540

Graduates Unlimited Personel, Inc.
Union, NJ 07083

Group IV Recruitment Consultants
New York, NY 10036

Robert Half, Inc.
Chicago, IL 60601

Robert Half of Philadelphia
King of Prussia, PA 19406

Robert Half of Boston
Boston, MA 02110

Robert Half of Wilmington
Wilmington, DE 19810

Robert Half of New York, Inc.
New York, NY 10036

Robert Half of Philadelphia, Inc.
Trevose, PA 19047

Robert Half of Philadelphia, Inc.
Philadelphia, PA 19103

Robert Half of Northern California
San Francisco, CA 94111

Robert Half of Orange County
Newport Beach, CA 92660

Robert Half of Dayton
Dayton, OH 45402

Robert Half of Cincinnati
Cincinnati, OH 45202

**Robert Half of Los Angeles Personnel
  Service**
Los Angeles, CA 90010

Hayden & Refo, Inc.
Boston, MA 02110

Hayman & Company
Dallas, TX 75201

Health Industry Consultants, Inc.
Englewood, CO 80112

W. Warner Hinman & Co.
Chicago, IL 60611

HiTech Consulting Group
Los Angeles, CA 90067

Internal Data Sciences
New York, NY 10118

JDG Associates, Ltd.
Rockville, MD 20850

Howard L. Karr & Associates, Inc.
San Mateo, CA 94402

Kenmore Executive Personnel, Inc.
New York, NY 10017

Melvin Kent & Associates
Columbus, OH 43215

Knorps Computer Consultants, Inc.
Winnetka, IL 60093

John Lawrence Agency of Los Angeles
Chatsworth, CA 91311

Lyman & Co.
Glendale, CA 91203

MacFarlane & Co., Inc.
Atlanta, GA 30318

Management Recruiters of Puerto Rico, Inc.
Hato Rey, PR 00918

Management Recruiters of Columbus
Columbus, OH 43229

Management Resources Executive
  Recruiters
Long Beach, CA 90803

Marbrook
New York, NY 10017

Medical Recruiters of America
Tampa, FL 33607

James Mercer & Associates, Inc.
Atlanta, GA 30356

Metricor, Inc.
Oak Brook Terrace, IL 60181

The NRI Group
Rockville, MD 20850

The NRI Group
Vienna, VA 22180

C. M. Oppenheim & Associates, Inc.
New York, NY 10036

O'Shea System of Employment
Philadelphia, PA 19107

Paul-Tittle Associates, Inc.
Silver Spring, MD 20910

Personnel Pool of America
Fort Lauderdale, FL 33335

Probe Technology
King of Prussia, PA 19406

Professional Recruiters of Salt Lake
Salt Lake, UT 84107

Rogers & Seymour Inc.
Portland, ME 04103

Rohn Rogers Associates
New York, NY 10036

Romac & Associates of Columbus
Columbus, OH 43215

Roth Young Personnel of Minneapolis
Edina, MN 55435

Roth Young of Atlanta
Atlanta, GA 30359

Roth Young of Columbus
Columbus, OH 43229

Sales Consultants of Wellesley
Wellesley, MA 02181

Sales Consultants of Boston
Boston, MA 08103

Sales Recruiters of Kansas City
Kansas City, MO 64106

Sales Consultants of Hartford
Hartford, CT 06067

Sanford Rose Associates of Hartford
Windsor, CT 06095

Howard W. Smith Associates
Hartford, CT 06103

John R. Stephens & Associates
Houston, TX 77002

Successmove, Inc.
Blue Bell, PA 19422

F. L. Taylor & Co., Inc.
New York, NY 10016

Technical Placement, Inc.
King of Prussia, PA 19406

Richard Theobald & Associates
San Mateo, CA 94404

K. W. Tunnell Co., Inc.
King of Prussia, PA 19406

Uni/Search of New Haven
Woodbridge, CT 06525

VIP Personnel of Raleigh
Raleigh, NC 27619

Albert J. Walsh & Associates
Newtown, PA 18940

Emanuel Weintraub Associates, Inc.
Fort Lee, NJ 07024

Wells International
Los Angeles, CA 90067

Werbin Associates Executive Search, Inc.
New York, NY 10175

Werner Management Consultants, Inc.
New York, NY 10018

Duane I. Wilson Associates, Inc.
Birmingham, MI 48011

Witt Associates, Inc.
Oak Brook, IL 60521

Dennis Wynn Associates, Inc.
St. Petersburg, FL 33704

PERSONNEL

Abbott Smith Associates, Inc.
Millbrook, NY 12545

Jeffrey C. Adams & Co., Inc.
San Francisco, CA 94104

Alaska Executive Search, Inc.
Anchorage, AK 99501

Thomas R. Aldrich & Associates
Westford, MA 01886

The Andre Group, Inc.
King of Prussia, PA 19406

Arthur Personnel
Caldwell, NJ 07006

Associated Personnel Technicians, Inc.
Wichita, KS 67214

Austin-Allen Co.
Memphis, TN 38119

BCL Corporation
Cleveland, OH 44107

Robert Becker & Co.
Allison Park, PA 15101

Richard Beers & Associates, Ltd.
Glenview, IL 60025

Daniel Benjamin Inc.
New York, NY 10016

E. J. Bettinger Co.
Philadelphia, PA 19102

K. Robert Brian
Philadelphia, PA 19103

Bryant Associates, Inc.
Chicago, IL 60611

Buzhardt Associates
Jackson, MS 39211

Daniel Cades & Associates
Philadelphia, PA 19107

Cantor & Co., Inc.
Philadelphia, PA 19103

Career Resource Associates, Inc.
Houston, TX 77288

Clark Associates, Inc.
Atlanta, GA 30345

Coker, Tyler & Co.
Atlanta, GA 30341

Conaway Personnel Associates, Inc.
Baltimore, MD 21202

John Conway Associates
Milwaukee, WI 53233

Corporate Service Group, Ltd.
San Francisco, CA 94102

Craighead Associates, Inc.
Stamford, CT 06901

Cretney & Associates
Cleveland, OH 44143

Crippin, Inc.
Overland Park, KS 66210

Robert H. Davidson Associates
Norwood, MA 02062

The Dean Group
Maplewood, NJ 07040

Jerry Demaso & Associates
Metairie, LA 70002

Dice Cowger & Associates
St. Louis, MO 63131

R. M. Donaldson Personnel
Cranford, NJ 07016

Dumont Kiradjieff & Moriarty
Boston, MA 02109

Earley Kielty & Associates, Inc.
New York, NY 10121

Edwards & Sowers, Inc.
Chicago, IL 60611

Employment Unlimited Agency
Baltimore, MD 21231

Henry H. Eskay
West Orange, NJ 07052

Estar Execu/Search, Ltd.
Palatine, IL 60067

Executive Search Company
Conshohocken, PA 19428

Flinn Consultants, Inc.
Highland Park, IL 60035

Ford & Ford
Dedham, MA 02026

George W. Fotis & Associates, Inc.
Greenwich, CT 06830

Fox & Fleischer
Richardson, TX 75080

Walter Frederick Friedman and Co., Inc.
West Orange, NJ 07052

Fulton, Longshore & Associates, Inc.
Haverford, PA 19041

Garrett Associates, Inc.
Atlanta, GA 30339

B. Goodwin, Ltd.
Fairfield, CT 06430

Griffith & Werner, Inc.
Hollywood, FL 33021

Hahn & Associates, Inc.
Dayton, OH 45402

Haskell & Stern Associates, Inc.
Fort Worth, TX 76112

Hayden & Refo, Inc.
Boston, MA 02110

Hayman & Company
Dallas, TX 75201

Health Care Executive Search
Lafayette, CA 94549

The Hite Company
Chicago, IL 60603

Hospitality Personnel, Inc.
Valley Forge, PA 19481

Houston Associates, Inc.
Hauppauge, NY 11788

Daniel D. Howard Associates, Inc.
Chicago, IL 60601

Robert Howe & Associates
Atlanta, GA 30341

Huxtable Associates, Inc.
Bridgeton, MO 63044

The Interface Group, Inc.
Washington, DC 20007

Johnson, Smith and Knisely
New York, NY 10017

Karam Associates
Denver, CO 80224

Howard L. Karr & Associates, Inc.
San Mateo, CA 94402

The Keating Division (Division Nordeman Grimm)
New York, NY 10022

Kenfield Research Associates, Inc.
New York, NY 10016

Kenmore Executive Personnel, Inc.
New York, NY 10017

Kiley-Owen Associates, Inc.
Philadelphia, PA 19107

Kingsley Quinn, Ltd.
New York, NY 10022

Robert Kleven & Co., Inc.
Boston, MA 02109

Robert Kleven & Co., Inc.
Lexington, MA 02173

Kunzer Associates, Ltd.
Chicago, IL 60604

Lacrosse Associates, Inc.
Union, NJ 07083

Gilbert Lane Associates
Atlanta, GA 30339

Lee Calhoon & Co., Inc.
Birchrunville, PA 19421

Lineback Associates
Dallas, TX 75240

Lineback Associates
Houston, TX 77042

Ross MacAskills Associates, Inc.
Washington, DC 20036

McCormack & Farrow
Long Beach, CA 90802

MacFarlane & Co., Inc.
Atlanta, GA 30318

Maetzold Associates, Inc.
Minnetonka, MN 55343

Management Resource Associates
Woburn, MA 08101

Management Search & Associates
Westport, CT 06880

Management Search Inc.
Minneapolis, MN 55426

Thomas Mangum Co.
Los Angeles, CA 90041

Marbrook
New York, NY 10017

Marshall Consultants, Inc.
Seattle, WA 98111

Masland Management Services
Philadelphia, PA 19118

MD Resources, Inc.
Miami, FL 33173

Medical Recruiters of America
Tampa, FL 33607

Martin H. Meisel Associates, Inc.
New York, NY 10028

Morris Madden & Rice, Inc.
New York, NY 10176

J. R. Morrison & Associates, Inc.
San Francisco, CA 94111

Richard Mowell Associates, Inc.
Tallahassee, FL 32303

NPF Associates, Ltd.
Coral Springs, FL 33065

Robert E. Nurse Associates, Inc.
White Plains, NY 10530

Oliver & Rosner Associates
New York, NY 10022

O'Neill Executive Search
Buffalo, NY 14223

C. M. Oppenheim & Associates, Inc.
New York, NY 10036

PA Executive Search Group
New York, NY 10017

Peeney Associates, Inc.
Fanwood, NJ 07023

The Personnel Laboratory
Stamford, CT 06901

Phillips Associates
Englewood, NJ 07631

Pinkerton & Associates, Inc.
Chicago, IL 60611

Norman Powers Associates, Inc.
Saxonville, MA 01701

Redmond & Associates, Inc.
Danbury, CT 06810

Ridgefield Search International
Ridgefield, CT 06877

Robertson, Spoerlein & Wengert
Chicago, IL 60606

Romano McAvoy Associates, Inc.
Smithtown, NY 11787

Louis Rudzinsky Associates, Inc.
Lexington, MA 02173

Charles Russ Associates, Inc.
Kansas City, MO 64114

Allan Sarn Associates, Inc.
New York, NY 10017

Search Source Inc.
Granite City, IL 62040

Leo J. Shea Associates, Inc.
Miami, FL 33129

Siegel Shotland & Associates
Encino, CA 91436

Sinclair & Potts Associates, Inc.
Pittsburgh, PA 15235

James F. Smith & Associates
Atlanta, GA 30342

Howard W. Smith Associates
Hartford, CT 06103

Sollmar Incorporated
Tustin, CA 92681

Soltis Management Services
Radnor, PA 19087

Stevens, Thurow & Associates, Inc.
Chicago, IL 60603

Carter Stone & Co., Inc.
New York, NY 10006

Stoneburner Associates, Inc.
Shawnee Mission, KS 66204

Stumbaugh Associates, Inc.
Atlanta, GA 30035

John J. Sudlow & Co.
Chicago, IL 60611

John J. Sudlow & Co.
Seattle, WA 98101

Richard Theobald & Associates
San Mateo, CA 94404

Harry F. Twomey Associates
Philadelphia, PA 19102

VanMaldegiam Associates, Inc.
Chicago, IL 60606

Vantage Careers, Inc.
Stamford, CT 06904

Vantage Careers, Inc.
White Plains, NY 10601

Vezan-West & Co.
West Hartford, CT 06107

Vine Associates, Inc.
North Hollywood, CA 91602

Vinicombe, Nitka & Associates, Inc.
Garden City, NY 11530

Wachtel & Associates, Ltd.
New York, NY 10017

Walker Recruitment
Minneapolis, MN 55416

John H. Warner Associates, Inc.
Hartford, CT 06103

Western Personnel Associates, Inc.
Phoenix, AZ 85012

David J. White & Associates Inc.
Chicago, IL 60606

J. W. Willard Associates, Inc.
Syracuse, NY 13201

Winguth, Schweichler Associates, Inc.
San Francisco, CA 94111

John Wylie Associates, Inc.
Tulsa, OK 74136

Winter, Wyman & Co.
Bedford, MA 01730

Witt Associates, Inc.
Oak Brook, IL 60521

Woltz & Associates, Inc.
Wood Dale, IL 60191

Xavier Associates, Inc.
Brockton, MA 02401

Zackrison Associates, Inc.
Fairfield, CT 06430

Zackrison Associates, Inc.
Stamford, CT 06905

Zackrison Associates, Inc.
West Hartford, CT 06110

The Zivic Group
San Francisco, CA 94111

PHARMACEUTICALS

Agri-Associates
Davenport, IA 52803

Battalia & Associates, Inc.
New York, NY 10016

Blendow, Crowley & Oliver, Inc.
New York, NY 10022

Career Personnel Service
Montgomery, AL 36116

Coker, Tyler & Co.
Atlanta, GA 30341

Cole, Warren & Long, Inc.
Philadelphia, PA 19102

Curry, Telleri, Ziegler, Inc.
Highland Park, NJ 08904

Employment Opportunities
Danbury, CT 06810

Futures Personnel Services
Baltimore, MD 21204

Hardwick Resources
Clearwater, FL 33575

Health Industry Consultants, Inc.
Engelwood, CO 80112

Kingsley Quinn, Ltd.
New York, NY 10022

Samuel F. Leigh Associates, Inc.
Darien, CT 06820

Lynn Associates
Farmington, CT 06032

Marshall Group
Los Angeles, CA 92660

George R. Martin Executive Search
Doylestown, PA 18901

Matthews Professional Employment
  Services, Inc.
Waukegan, IL 60085

Herbert H. Moss, Inc.
Palm Springs, CA 92262

Robert Ottke Associates
Newport Beach, CA 92660

Pascal Associates
Rutherford, NJ 07070

Peeney Associates, Inc.
Fanwood, NJ 07023

Pharmacists Exchange
Des Moines, IA 50309

E. J. Pritz & Associates
Greenvale, NY 11548

Ryan/Smith & Associates, Inc.
Westfield, NJ 07091

S. P. Associates
Charlotte, NC 28231

Sampson, Neill & Wilkins, Inc.
Upper Montclair, NJ 07043

Torretto & Associates, Inc.
Sausalito, CA 94965

PRINTING AND PACKAGING

Thomas R. Aldrich & Associates
Westford, MA 01886

American Executive Search Services, Inc.
Santa Clara, CA 95051

American Research Institute
Long Beach, CA 90804

Ames & Wyand Associates, Inc.
Brunswick, ME 04011

Artists Counselor & Placement Service
Chicago, IL 60601

Banner Personnel Service
Chicago, IL 60602

Leslie Berglass Associates, Inc.
New York, NY 10022

Charles A. Binswanger Associates
Baltimore, MD 21209

Bowden & Company, Inc.
Cleveland, OH 44131

Britt Associates
Chicago, IL 60604

Caprio & Associates, Inc.
Oak Brook, IL 60521

Concept Corp.
Sausalito, CA 94966

Bert Davis
New York, NY 10017

Douglas Campbell & Associates, Inc.
Santa Ana, CA 92701

Dyna-Search
Chicago, IL 60604

Gilmore Personnel Consultants Inc.
Ridgewood, NJ 07450

Graphic Search Associates, Inc.
Newton Square, PA 19073

Industry Consultants
Atlanta, GA 30338

Robert J. Irmen Associates
Hinsdale, IL 60521

Samuel F. Leigh Associates, Inc.
Darien, CT 06820

George R. Martin Executive Search
Doylestown, PA 18901

William H. Nenstiel & Associates, Inc.
Scottsdale, AZ 85251

Phillips Resource Group
Greenville, SC 29606

Pro Select
Montclair, CA 91763

RitaSue Siegel Agency Inc.
New York, NY 10019

S.P. Associates
Charlotte, NC 28231

Spencer Sanders Associates
New York, NY 10175

Stumbaugh Associates, Inc.
Atlanta, GA 30035

Gordon Wahls Company
Villanova, PA 19085

E. T. Wharton Associates
New York, NY 10001

Zachary & Sanders, Inc.
New York, NY 10119

PUBLIC RELATIONS

Berkley and Associates
Atlanta, GA 30339

Brown-Bernardy, Inc.
Los Angeles, CA 90049

The Cantor Group, Inc.
New York, NY 10016

Career Builders, Inc.
New York, NY 10017

Careers/Inc.
Hato Rey, PR 00918

Toby Clark Associates, Inc.
New York, NY 10022

Bert Davis
New York, NY 10017

J. V. DeMoss & Associates
Hato Rey, PR 00918

Gwen Dycus, Inc.
Winter Park, FL 32790

Executive Locators of America
Metairie, LA 70004

Jerry Fields Associates, Inc.
New York, NY 10022

The Fry Group
New York, NY 10017

William Harris Associates
New York, NY 10086

Higbee Associates, Inc.
Rowayton, CT 06853

Ruth Hirsch Career Builders, Inc.
New York, NY 10017

Ketchum, Inc., Executive Recruiting Service
Chicago, IL 60601

Lovewell & Associates, Inc.
Atlanta, GA 30361

Marshall Consultants
Seattle, WA 98111

Marshall Consultants, Inc.
New York, NY 10021

MRG Search & Placement
New Haven, CT 06510

Robert Parrella Associates
New York, NY 10103

Reichelt & Associates, Inc.
Los Angeles, CA 90024

Charles Sharp & Associates
Los Angeles, CA 90024

Leo J. Shea Associates, Inc.
Miami, FL 33129

Carolyn Smith Paschal International
Del Mar, CA 92014

PUBLISHING

Caprio & Associates, Inc.
Oak Brook, IL 60521

Bert Davis
New York, NY 10017

Ryan/Smith & Associates, Inc.
Westfield, NJ 07091

Gordon Wahls Company
Villanova, PA 19085

Zachary & Sanders, Inc.
New York, NY 10119

Professional Career Placements
Arlington, TX 76003

Scott/Hubbard Associates
Winnetka, IL 60093

Winter Wyman & Co.
Bedford, MA 01730

PURCHASING

Barry & Co.
Los Angeles, CA 90017

Clark Associates, Inc.
Atlanta, GA 30345

Florapersonnel
Deland, FL 32721

Heberling Personnel
Harrisburg, PA 17105

Lyons/Aspen Consultants Group
Englewood, CO 80110

McInturff & Associates, Inc.
Natick, MA 01760

Marbrook
New York, NY 10017

Herbert H. Moss, Inc.
Palm Springs, CA 92262

The P & L Group
Jericho, NY 11753

Positions, Inc.
Providence, RI 02904

REAL ESTATE

Accounting Resources International
Laguna Niguel, CA 92677

Analytic Recruiting, Inc.
New York, NY 10017

Anderson, Johnston & Roberts Agency, Inc.
Newport Beach, CA 92660

Anderson, Johnston & Roberts Agency, Inc.
Santa Ana, CA 92705

Charles P. Aquavella & Associates
Dallas, TX 75229

Ashworth Consultants
Boston, MA 02109

Availability Personnel Consultants
Bedford, NH 03102

J. W. Bell & Co.
Newport Beach, CA 92660

Paula Berns, Inc.
New York, NY 10017

Christensen & Montgomery
Morristown, NJ 07960

Deven Associates, Inc.
Verona, NJ 07044

Gwen Dycus, Inc.
Winter Park, FL 32790

Fine Personnel Agency
New York, NY 10017

T. G. Harper & Co., Inc.
Philadelphia, PA 19106

Haskell & Stern Associates, Inc.
Fort Worth, TX 76112

J. D. Hersey & Associates
Columbus, OH 43221

The Hite Company
Chicago, IL 60603

Huntress Real Estate Executive Search, Inc.
Kansas City, MO 64114

Kennedy and Company
Chicago, IL 60606

Kingston and Associates
Tucson, AZ 85710

Lamont-Bruckner, Inc.
Tulsa, OK 74135

Largent Parks & Partners, Inc.
Dallas, TX 75240

George P. Lyon Associates
Doylestown, PA 18901

Main Hurdman
Fort Lauderdale, FL 33394

Main Hurdman
West Palm Beach, FL 33409

MBA Associates, Inc.
Boston, MA 02109

Morgan Research
New York, NY 10175

Richard Mowell Associates, Inc.
Tallahassee, FL 32303

O'Crowley & O'Toole Executive Search
Portland, OR 97223

Patton/Perry Associates
Charlotte, NC 28284

Power & Co.
Boston, MA 02109

Professional Placement Group
Boston, MA 02109

Real Estate Executive Search, Inc.
Napa, CA 94559

Rogers & Sands Inc.
Burlington, MA 02108

Ropes Associates, Inc.
Fort Lauderdale, FL 33394

Mark Rosen
New York, NY 10017

Ryan/Smith & Associates, Inc.
Westfield, NJ 07091

Sockwell & Hendrix
Charlotte, NC 28284

Speciality Consultants, Inc.
Pittsburgh, PA 15222

Stephens & Associates
San Diego, CA 92109

F. L. Taylor & Co., Inc.
New York, NY 10016

J. Robert Thompson Co., Inc.
Houston, TX 77027

RESEARCH
AND
DEVELOPMENT

Abbington Associates
East Northport, NY 11731

American Research Institute
Long Beach, CA 90804

Anderson-Gest & Associates
Bellevue, WA 98004

Ashway Ltd. Agency
New York, NY 10017

Associated Business Consultants, Inc.
Medford, NJ 08055

Aubin International, Inc.
Waltham, MA 02154

Nathan Barry Associates, Inc.
Boston, MA 02109

Gary S. Bell Associates, Inc.
Wyckoff, NJ 07481

Belzano, Deane & Associates
Irvine, CA 92715

Bennett Munson, Inc.
Odessa, TX 79762

Leslie Berglass Associates, Inc.
New York, NY 10022

C. Berke & Associates
Doylestown, PA 18901

BMR Associates
Hollywood, FL 33020

Brennan & Associates, Inc.
Dallas, TX 75234

BRJ Associates, Inc.
Mountainside, NJ 07092

Burns Personnel Inc.
Rochester, NY 14604

Caprio & Associates, Inc.
Oak Brook, IL 60521

Charles A. Binswanger Associates
Baltimore, MD 21209

Christopher, Drew & Associates, Inc.
Cleveland, OH 44122

Claveloux, McCaffrey & Associates, Inc.
New York, NY 10018

Concept Corp.
Sausalito, CA 94966

Consultants, Inc.
North Brunswick, NJ 08902

The Corporate Connection, Ltd.
Richmond, VA 23230

Corporate Search Group, Inc.
Homewood, IL 60430

Corporate Recruiters, Inc.
Philadelphia, PA 19126

Corporate Environment Ltd.
Crystal Lake, IL 60014

Corporate Career Consultants
San Francisco, CA 94111

Corporate Resources, Inc.
Minneapolis, MN 55426

Cross Country Consultants, Inc.
Baltimore, MD 21218

Robert H. Davidson Associates
Norwood, MA 02062

Eastern Executives Associates
Clifton, NJ 07012

Gilmore Personnel Consultants, Inc.
Ridgewood, NJ 07450

The Gruen Co.
Oakland, CA 94618

Health Industry Consultants, Inc.
Engelwood, CO 80112

J. D. Hersey & Associates
Columbus, OH 43221

Horizon Associates
Redondo Beach, CA 90277

Industrial Recruiters Associates, Inc.
West Hartford, CT 06110

Industry Consultants
Atlanta, GA 30338

Nancy Jackson, Inc.
Scranton, PA 18503

J. M. & Company
Wayne, PA 19087

Johnson & Genrich, Inc.
Chicago, IL 60630

Martin Kartin & Company
New York, NY 10021

Robert Kleven & Co., Inc.
Lexington, MA 02173

Robert Kleven & Co., Inc.
Boston, MA 02109

Kors, Marlar, Savage & Associates
Annapolis, MD 21401

Kunzer Associates, Ltd.
Chicago, IL 60604

Lacrosse Associates, Inc.
Union, NJ 07083

Gilbert Lane Associates
Atlanta, GA 30339

Paul W. Larson Associates, Inc.
San Juan Capistrano, CA 92675

Thomas Mangum Co.
Los Angeles, CA 90041

Mason Associates
Norwalk, CT 06851

James Mercer & Associates, Inc.
Atlanta, GA 30356

MPI Associates
Boulder, CO 80302

Paul Norsell & Associates, Inc.
Los Angeles, CA 90045

Paul Norsell & Associates, Inc.
Anaheim, CA 92807

Oliver & Rosner Associates
New York, NY 10022

OMNI Executive Search, Inc.
Atlanta, GA 30328

O'Neill Executive Search
Buffalo, NY 14223

Harry D. Parkhurst & Associates, Inc.
Minneapolis, MN 55426

People Management Inc.
Simsbury, CT 06070

Phillips Resource Group
Greenville, SC 29606

Norman Powers Associates, Inc.
Saxonville, MA 01701

Probe Technology
King of Prussia, PA 19406

The R & L Group
Arlington Heights, IL 60004

Rambert & Co., Inc.
Lake Bluff, IL 60044

Ridgefield Search International
Ridgefield, CT 06877

Lowell N. Ross & Associates
Corte Madera, CA 94925

R. V. M. Associates, Inc.
White Plains, NY 10604

RitaSue Siegel Agency, Inc.
New York, NY 10019

Siegel & Bishop, Inc.
San Francisco, CA 94112

Sollmar Incorporated
Tustin, CA 92681

John R. Stephens & Associates
Houston, TX 77002

Successmove, Inc.
Blue Bell, PA 19422

Tecmark Associates, Inc.
New York, NY 10123

J. Robert Thompson Co., Inc.
Houston, TX 77027

Harry F. Twomey Associates
Philadelphia, PA 19102

Varo & Lund Corp.
Los Angeles, CA 90028

Vezan-West & Co.
West Hartford, CT 06107

Albert J. Walsh & Associates
Newtonown, PA 18940

Webster Positions, Inc.
Hicksville, NY 11801

Western Reserve Associates
Bath, OH 44210

Western Personnel Associates, Inc.
Phoenix, AZ 85012

E. N. Wilkins and Company, Inc.
Chicago, IL 60606

Winchester Consultants, Inc.
New Canaan, CT 06840

John Wylie Associates, Inc.
Tulsa, OK 74136

RETAIL

Albany Personnel Service
Albany, GA 31701

Ashworth Consultants
Boston, MA 02109

James Bangert Associates, Inc.
Wayzata, MN 55391

J. L. Bohart & Co.
San Mateo, CA 94401

Bowden & Company, Inc.
Cleveland, OH 44131

Career Management
New York, NY 10001

CBS Personnel Services
Cincinnati, OH 45202

CBS Personnel Services
Dayton, OH 45402

Chevigny Personnel Agency
Merrillville, IN 46410

William J. Christopher Associates, Inc.
West Chester, PA 19380

Coleman Lew & Associates, Inc.
Charlotte, NC 28209

Continental Search Group
New York, NY 10016

John Davidson & Associates
Dallas, TX 75229

Deven Associates, Inc.
Verona, NJ 07044

Dunhill of Atlanta
Atlanta, GA 30326

Gwen Dycus, Inc.
Winter Park, FL 32790

Eggers Personnel & Consulting
Omaha, NB 68144

Executive Locators of America
Metairie, LA 70004

Executive Recruiters
Bethesda, MD 20814

Ford and Ford
Dedham, MA 02026

Futures Personnel Services
Baltimore, MD 21204

Gendason Cooper Associates
Englewood Cliffs, NJ 07632

Greene Personnel Consultants
Providence, RI 02903

D. Jackson and Associates
Hershey, PA 17033

Kenzer Corp.
New York, NY 10017

Key Employment Services
West Des Moines, IA 50265

Marvin Laba & Associates
Los Angeles, CA 90028

Michael Latas & Associates, Inc.
St. Louis, MO 63132

Alan Lerner Associates
Chestnut Hill, MA 02167

Alan Lerner Associates
Boca Raton, FL 33432

George P. Lyon Associates
Doylestown, PA 18901

Management Recruiters Midwest
Thousand Oaks, CA 91360

MBC Systems, Ltd.
Towson, MD 21204

Perry Newton Associates
Rockville, MD 20850

Nicholson & Associates, Inc.
New York, NY 10169

Al Perkell
New York, NY 10017

The Placers, Inc.
Wilmington, DE 19806

E. J. Pritz & Associates
Greenvale, NY 11548

Retail Personnel Associates
Glastonbury, CT 06033

Retail Recruiters
Rocky Hill, CT 06067

Retail Recruiters
Providence, RI 02906

**Retail Recruiters, Spectra Professional
Search**
Fort Lauderdale, FL 33311

Retail Recruiters/Spectra Search
Rockville, MD 20852

E. J. Rhodes Personnel Consultants
New York, NY 10036

Lloyd Richards Personnel Service
Tulsa, OK 74103

Roth Young—Los Angeles
Fox Hills, CA 90230

Roth Young of Atlanta
Atlanta, GA 30359

Roth Young Personnel of Minneapolis
Edina, MN 55435

Roth Young Personnel
St. Louis, MO 63105

Roth Young Associates
New York, NY 10036

Roth Young of Columbus
Columbus, OH 43229

Roth Young
Houston, TX 77008

A. William Smyth, Inc.
Ross, CA 94957

Spectra Professional Search
Atlanta, GA 30346

F. L. Taylor & Co., Inc.
New York, NY 10016

Torretto & Associates, Inc.
Sausalito, CA 94965

Viro Executive Search, Inc.
New York, NY 10018

Walker Recruitment
Minneapolis, MN 55416

Whittaker & Associates, Inc.
Atlanta, GA 30339

Joel H. Wilensky Associates, Inc.
Sudbury, MA 01776

Sales

ACI
Orlando, FL 32803

Ackerman Johnson Career Consultants, Inc.
Houston, TX 77008

The Adams Consulting Group
Columbus, OH 43206

Advancement Concepts
Norcross, GA 30093

Advantage Personnel Agency
Miami, FL 33155

Agra Placements, Ltd.
Lincoln, IL 62656

Agra Placements, Ltd.
Peru, IN 46970

Agra Placements, Ltd.
West Des Moines, IA 50265

Agri-Associates
Davenport, IA 52803

Agri-Business Services
St. Paul, MN 55113

Alan & Associates Employee Search
Shreveport, LA 71104

Albany Personnel Service
Albany, GA 31701

Thomas R. Aldrich & Associates
Westford, MA 01886

Alexander-Edward Associates, Inc.
Philadelphia, PA 19107

Don Allan Associates, Inc.
New York, NY 10017

Allied Careers, Inc.
Denver, CO 80237

Amity Consultants
Fairfield, CT 06430

Anderson, Graham & Stewart
Marietta, GA 30061

Arista Corporation
Atlanta, GA 30338

Associated Business Consultants, Inc.
Medford, NJ 08055

Associated Ventures
Dellwood, MO 63136

Auguston & Associates
Portland, OR 97232

Babich & Associates
Dallas, TX 75206

Babich & Associates
Fort Worth, TX 76102

Bales Sales Recruiters
Jacksonville, FL 32207

Barclays/Recruiting Services, Inc.
Denver, CO 80222

Nathan Barry Associates, Inc.
Boston, MA 02109

Belle Oaks of America
Kansas City, MO 64106

**Benson & Associates Personnel &
  Management Consultants**
Fort Lauderale, FL 33309

Berkley and Associates
Atlanta, GA 30339

Career Consultants
Indianapolis, IN 46204

Career Consultants
Towson, MD 21204

Career Personnel Service
Montgomery, AL 36116

Career Specialists
Los Altos, CA 94022

Careers, Ltd.
Denver, CO 80203

CDH & Associates
Irvine, CA 92715

Chevigny Personnel Agency
Merrillville, IN 46410

Clark, Clark & Clark Associates
College Park, MD 20740

The Clayton Group, Inc.
Oakbrook Terrace, IL 60181

Cole International
Berkeley, CA 94709

The Concord Group, Ltd.
Barrington, IL 60010

Cretney & Associates
Cleveland, OH 44143

Frank Cuomo & Associates
Tuckahoe, NY 10707

Damon & Associates, Inc.
Dallas, TX 75231

Davies Associates International, Ltd.
Houston, TX 77218

William S. DeFuniak, Inc.
Hinsdale, IL 60521

DeLoughrey & Co.
Wellesley Hills, MA 02181

Ned E. Dickey and Associates
Rockford, IL 61110

Dotson Benefield & Associates, Inc.
Atlanta, GA 30345

J. H. Dugan & Co.
Chicago, IL 60611

Dunhill of Greater Stamford
Wilton, CT 06897

Dunhill of Atlanta
Atlanta, GA 30326

Dunhill of Cedar Rapids
Cedar Rapids, IA 52401

Eggers Personnel & Consulting
Omaha, NB 68144

Ells Personnel Systems
Minneapolis, MN 55402

Employment Opportunities
Danbury, CT 06810

Employment Unlimited Agency
Baltimore, MD 21231

Executive Career Development
Clearwater, FL 33546

Executive Finders
Pittsburgh, PA 15219

Executive Locators of America
Metairie, LA 70004

Executive Personnel Consultants
Memphis, TN 38117

Executive Placement Corporation
Rochester, NY 14604

The Executive Suite
Seattle, WA 98101

Far Western Placement Services
Phoenix, AZ 85012

Finley & Co.
Greenville, SC 29615

First Recruiting Group
Houston, TX 77024

A. G. Fishkin & Associates, Inc.
Rockville, MD 20852

Florapersonnel
Deland, FL 32721

Fox Morris
Baltimore, MD 21204

Futures Personnel Services
Baltimore, MD 21204

Gather, Inc.
Chartley, MA 02712

Robert Gee & Associates
Pittsburgh, PA 15235

General Employment Enterprises
Oak Brook, IL 60521

S. Gorlick & Associates
Irvine, CA 92714

Granger & Associates, Inc.
Cincinnati, OH 45242

Hardwick Resources
Clearwater, FL 33575

Hipp Waters Professional Recruiters
Stamford, CT 06901

HiTech Consulting Group
Los Angeles, CA 90067

Horton Associates, Inc.
Helendale, CA 92342

H. S. Placements
Green Bay, WI 54307

D. Jackson and Associates
Hershey, PA 17033

JAMAR Personnel Service
Rock Island, IL 61201

Job Finders/Jobs Temporary
Des Moines, IA 50312

Johnson & Genrich, Inc.
Chicago, IL 60630

JPM Associates, DBA
San Clemente, CA 92672

E. A. Keepy—National Recruiters
Davenport, IA 52805

Keshlear Associates
Aiken, SC 29210

Key Employment Services
West Des Moines, IA 50265

Kingston & Associates
Tucson, AZ 85710

J. Lee & Associates
Atlanta, GA 30358

Longs Personnel Service
Mobile, AL 36616

McMahon & Associates
Stone Mountain, GA 30086

Bob Maddox Associates
Atlanta, GA 30326

Mahony Associates
Atlanta, GA 30328

Management Recruiters Midwest
Thousand Oaks, CA 91360

Management South
Charlotte, NC 28246

Margolin
New York, NY 10016

George S. May International Company
Park Ridge, IL 60068

MBC Systems Ltd.
Towson, MD 21204

Morris Madden & Rice, Inc.
New York, NY 10176

Multi Technology, Inc.
Framingham, MA 01701

Murphy Employment Service
Tampa, FL 33609

National Career Centers—USA
Fayetteville, NC 28302

National Hospitality Associates, Inc.
Tempe, AZ 85282

National Recruiters Corporation
Woodland Hills, CA 91364

National Recruiting Service
Fairfield, OH 45014

Nation-Wide Recruiting, Inc.
Encino, CA 91316

Perry Newcomb & Associates
Cincinnati, OH 45230

O'Grady Associates, Inc.
West Concord, MA 01742

Personnel Center
Gainesville, FL 32602

Personnel, Inc.
Spartanburg, SC 29302

Personnel Search
Omaha, NB 68124

Philadelphia Search Group, Inc.
Philadelphia, PA 19102

Phillips Personnel Search
Denver, CO 80202

Pierce Associates, Inc.
San Francisco, CA 94111

Professional Executive Consultants
Northbrook, IL 60062

Professional Specialists
Euclid, OH 44132

Purcell Group Management Consultants
Houston, TX 77057

Lloyd Richards Personnel Service
Tulsa, OK 74103

Ridgefield Search International
Ridgefield, CT 06877

R.M. Associates
Portland, OR 97223

Roche Associates
Stamford, CT 06094

Romac & Associates
Bala Cynwyd, PA 19004

Roth Young—Los Angeles
Fox Hills, CA 90230

Roth Young Personnel of Minneapolis
Edina, MN 55435

Royal Recruiters
Fort Lauderdale, FL 33334

Sales & Management Search, Inc.
Chicago, IL 60606

Sales Consultants—Birmingham
Birmingham, AL 35223

Sales Consultants Encino
Encino, CA 91436

Sales Consultants of Hartford
Hartford, CT 06067

Sales Consultants—New Haven
Rocky Hill, CT 06067

Sales Consultants of Boston
Boston, MA 01803

Sales Consultants of Wellesley
Wellesley, MA 02181

Sales Consultants International
Cleveland, OH 44115

Sales Executives, Inc.
Troy, MI 48084

Sales Recruiters International
Yonkers, NY 10701

Sales Recruiters of Kansas City
Kansas City, MO 64106

Salesworld Inc.
Towson, MD 21204

Savannah Personnel Consultants
Savannah, GA 31406

Schneider, Hill & Spangler, Inc.
Philadelphia, PA 19107

Allan Schoenberger & Associates
Memphis, TN 38138

Search Tech Associates
Calabasas, CA 91302

Security Jobs Corporation
Honolulu, HI 96813

SHS International—Charlotte
Charlotte, NC 28202

RitaSue Siegel Agency, Inc.
New York, NY 10019

S. J. Associates
St. Louis, MO 63109

Snelling & Snelling
Lexington, SC 29072

Southwestern Placement
Memphis, TN 37202

Specialized Search Associates
Greenwich, CT 06830

Stanislaw & Associates, Inc.
Brookfield, WI 53005

Status, Inc.
Atlanta, GA 30326

Stevens, Thurow & Associates, Inc.
Chicago, IL 60603

Sun Valley Personnel Agency
Walnut Creek, CA 94596

Systems Network Assistance
Glenview, IL 60048

The Trattner Network
Citrus Heights, CA 95610

C. J. Vincent Associates, Inc.
Columbia, MD 21044

Gordon Wahls Company
Villanova, PA 19085

Don Waldron & Associates
New York, NY 10123

Hank Ward Associates, Ltd.
Latham, NY 12110

Wayne Executive Search
Portland, OR 97266

Western Personnel Associates, Inc.
Phoenix, AZ 85012

Whittlesey & Associates
West Chester, PA 19380

Woltz & Associates, Inc.
Wood Dale, IL 60191

SCIENCE AND TECHNOLOGY

The Adams Consulting Group
Columbus, OH 43206

Alexander & Associates, Inc.
Elkhart, IN 46515

Alexander & Zier Associates
Trumbull, CT 06611

American Research Institute
Long Beach, CA 90804

Ames-O'Neill Associates, Inc.
Hauppauge, NY 11788

Amity Consultants, Inc.
Fairfield, CT 06430

ASC & Co.
Houston, TX 77056

Ashway Ltd. Agency
New York, NY 10017

Atomic Personnel, Inc.
Philadelphia, PA 19102

Aubin International, Inc.
Waltham, MA 02154

Beck, Gerstenfeld & Associates
Woodburn, OR 97071

Gary S. Bell Associates, Inc.
Wyckoff, NJ 07481

Berman Associates
Atlanta, GA 30309

Blendow, Crowley & Oliver, Inc.
New York, NY 10022

The Borton-Wallace Co.
Asheville, NC 28801

Bowden & Company, Inc.
Cleveland, OH 44131

Dr. Will G. Bowman, Inc.
Weston, MA 02193

Brault & Associates, Ltd.
Reston, VA 22090

The Caldwell Partners International
Houston, TX 77010

Career Personnel Service
Montgomery, AL 36116

Andrew B. Carr & Associates
San Angelo, TX 76902

Center for Health Care Personnel
Wethersfield, CT 06109

CHASE, Inc.
Rosemont, PA 19010

Chemical Scientific Services
Columbus, OH 43227

Robert Clifton Associates, Inc.
Pittsburgh, PA 15220

Corporate Environment Ltd.
Crystal Lake, IL 60014

Corporate Resources, Inc.
Minneapolis, MN 55426

Cowin Associates
Carle Place, NY 11514

R. J. Evans & Associates, Inc.
Beachwood, OH 44122

ExecuSource International
El Paso, TX 79902

Executive Finders
Pittsburgh, PA 15219

Executive Personnel Consultants
Memphis, TN 38117

Executive Resources
New Milford, CT 06776

Friends & Co.
Huntington, NY 11743

Gilmore Personnel Consultants, Inc.
Ridgewood, NJ 07450

Gold Card Recruiters
Camden, AR 71701

Graham & Associates, Inc.
Dallas, TX 75240

Great Southwestern Personnel Co.
Phoenix, AZ 85016

Harris & U'Ren, Inc.
Phoenix, AZ 85003

Haskell & Stern Associates, Inc.
New York, NY 10017

F. P. Healy & Co., Inc.
New York, NY 10169

Heberling Personnel
Harrisburg, PA 17105

A. R. Hutton Agency
Yuma, AZ 85364

Charles Irish Company, Inc.
Raleigh, NC 27609

JPM Associates, DBA
San Clemente, CA 92672

Martin Kartin & Company
New York, NY 10021

Richard Kaye Personnel Agency, Inc.
New York, NY 10017

Robert Kleven & Co., Inc.
Boston, MA 02109

Knudsen & Co.
Oak Brook, IL 60521

Paul W. Larson Associates, Inc.
San Juan Capistrano, CA 92675

Charles R. Lister International, Inc.
Carmel-by-the-Sea, CA 93921

Ross MacAskills Associates, Inc.
Washington, DC 20036

McCormack & Farrow
Long Beach, CA 90802

Management Recruiters-Hamden
Hamden, CT 06518

Management South
Charlotte, NC 28246

F. L. Mannix & Co., Inc.
Boston, MA 02109

Midgette Consultants, Inc.
Waterbury CT 06702

Multi Processing, Inc.
Lexington, MA 02173

Murphy Symonds and Stowell
Portland, OR 97204

National Recruiting Service
Fairfield, OH 45014

Gary Nelson & Associates, Inc.
Cupertino, CA 95104

Arthur Newman Associates, Inc.
Houston, TX 77027

Richard E. Nosky & Associates
Scottsdale, AZ 85251

Oliver & Rosner Associates
New York, NY 10022

Robert Ottke Associates
Newport Beach, CA 92660

Harry D. Parkhurst & Associates, Inc.
Minneapolis, MN 55426

People Management Inc.
Simsbury, CT 06070

Perry-White & Associates, Inc.
San Francisco, CA 94104

Perry-White & Associates, Inc.
Waltham, MA 02154

Perry-White & Associates, Inc.
Dallas, TX 75240

Perry-White & Associates, Inc.
Houston, TX 77074

Pinsker and Shattuck, Inc.
San Francisco, CA 94104

Pinsker and Shattuck, Inc.
Saratoga, CA 95070

Polytechnical Consultants, Inc.
Chicago, IL 60659

Pro, Inc.
La Jolla, CA 92037

Purcell Employment Systems
Los Angeles, CA 90010

Purcell Group Management Consultants
Houston, TX 77057

Quantum
New York, NY 10016

Lloyd Richards Personnel Service
Tulsa, OK 74103

Lowell N. Ross & Associates
Corte Madera, CA 94925

Louis Rudzinsky Associates, Inc.
Lexington, MA 02173

Schattle Personnel Consultants, Inc.
Warwick, RI 02886

Scientific Placement, Inc.
Houston, TX 77224

Search Northwest & Affiliates
Portland, OR 97204

Search Tech Associates
Calabasas, CA 91302

Slovin Personnel Associates
Worcester, Ma 01609

Thomas E. Sowell
Jenks, OK 74037

S. K. Stewart & Associates
Cincinnati, OH 45240

STM Associates
Salt Lake City, UT 84111

Torretto & Associates, Inc.
Sausalito, CA 94965

The Trattner Network
Citrus Heights, CA 95610

Vision
New York, NY 10018

Vlcek & Company
Los Angeles, CA 92660

Gordon Wahls Company
Villanova, PA 19085

Wallach Associates, Inc.
Rockville, MD 20852

Wargo & Co., Inc.
Waukesha, WI 53186

Webster Positions, Inc.
Hicksville, NY 11801

Whitman Stone Associates
Orange, CA 92668

Wilkinson & Ives, Inc.
Orinda, CA 94563

William H. Willis, Inc.
New York, NY 10022

Woodson Associates
Ashland, MA 01721

Yelverton & Company
San Francisco, CA 94111

SECURITIES AND INVESTMENTS

Allen Personnel Agency
New York, NY 10038

Benson & Associates Personnel & Management Consultants
Fort Lauderdale, FL 33309

Brandon Associates
Fort Lee, NJ 07024

Clayton Personnel
New York, NY 10038

W. Hoyt Colton Associates, Inc.
New York, NY 10005

JAMAR Personnel Service
Rock Island, IL 61201

JPM Associates, DBA
San Clemente, CA 92672

Kanon
New York, NY 10018

Kennedy and Company
Chicago, IL 60606

Lancaster
New York, NY 10038

McWilliams Personnel, Inc.
New York, NY 10038

Morgan Research
New York, NY 10175

Nicholson & Associates, Inc.
New York, NY 10169

The Placers, Inc.
Wilmington, DE 19806

Professional Placement Group
Boston, MA 02109

Ken Richardson
Bethesda, MD 20817

Riley Recruiting Enterprises
Denver, CO 80218

Romac & Associates, Inc.
Portland, ME 04112

Wehinger Service, Inc. Agency
New York, NY 10038

Wellesley, Ltd.
Providence, RI 02903

TELECOMMUNICATIONS

Abbington Associates
East Northport, NY 11731

Albany Personnel Service
Albany, GA 31701

Don Allan Associates, Inc.
New York, NY 10017

Allied Search
San Francisco, CA 94123

AMCR
Akron, OH 44313

AMD Associates
Silver Spring, MD 20906

American Research Institute
Long Beach, CA 90804

Amity Consultants
Fairfield, CT 06430

Analytic Recruiting, Inc.
New York, NY 10017

Aronow Associates, Inc.
New York, NY 10001

Atomic Personnel, Inc.
Philadelphia, PA 19102

Baker Scott & Company
Parsippany, NJ 07054

Banner Personnel Service
Chicago, IL 60602

Battalia & Associates, Inc.
New York, NY 10016

Bay Search Group
Providence, RI 02903

Berman Associates
Atlanta, GA 30309

Marc-Paul Bloome Ltd.
New York, NY 10107

Bonner Gladney Associates
Devon, PA 19333

Botal Associates
New York, NY 10007

Bradstreet Management, Inc.
New York, NY 10165

Broadcast Personnel Inc.
New York, NY 10020

Daniel Cades & Associates
Philadelphia, PA 19107

Career Builders, Inc.
New York, NY 10017

Career Enterprises Agency
Long Beach, CA 90807

Career Specialists
Los Altos, CA 94022

CBS Personnel Services
Dayton, OH 45402

CDH & Associates
Irvine, CA 92715

Clark, Clark & Clark Associates
College Park, MD 20740

CMA Technical Search, Inc.
New York, NY 10017

Commonwealth Personnel
Rockville, MD 20852

The Comnet Group
Garden City, NY 11530

Com-tek Agency
New York, NY 10017

Consultants, Inc.
North Brunswick, NJ 08902

COR Management Services Ltd.
New York, NY 10170

Corporate Search Group, Inc.
Homewood, IL 60430

Corporate Staffing Group
Horsham, PA 19044

Corporate Staffing Group
Largo, FL 33541

Data Management Resources
Stamford, CT 06901

Gene Davis & Associates
Oklahoma City, OK 73156

Dunhill of Huntington
Melville, NY 11747

Dynamic Search Systems, Inc.
Arlington Heights, IL 60004

Eastern Executive Associates
Clifton, NJ 07012

Phil Ellis Associates
Raleigh, NC 27658

Executive Resources
New Milford, CT 06776

Richard Farber Associates, Inc.
Great Neck, NY 11021

A. G. Fishkin & Associates
Rockville, MD 20852

Fortune Personnel Consultants
Nashua, NH 03062

Forum Personnel
New York, NY 10017

General Employment Enterprises
Oak Brook, IL 60521

Glynn, Brooks & Co.
Fort Lee, NJ 07024

Graham & Associates, Inc.
Dallas, TX 75240

E. W. Green & Associates
Solana Beach, CA 92075

The Gruen Co.
Oakland, CA 94618

Hazel Associates
New York, NY 10017

HDB Inc.
St. Louis, MO 63011

W. Warner Hinman & Co.
Chicago, IL 60611

Information Resources Group
Westlake Village, CA 91361

Input Search Agency
Lake Forest, CA 92630

Input Search Agency
Los Angeles, CA 90036

Internal Data Sciences
New York, NY 10018

International Staffing Consultants, Inc.
Newport Beach, CA 92260

Janus Consultants, Inc.
Washington, DC 20007

JDG Associates, Ltd.
Rockville, MD 20850

Johnston & Associates
Naperville, IL 60565

King Computer Search
Dallas, TX 75238

Knorps Computer Consultants, Inc.
Winnetka, IL 60093

Knudson & Co.
Oak Brook, IL 60521

Lane Employment Service
Worcester, MA 01608

Linker Personnel Systems Ltd.
New York, NY 10017

Littman Associates
Troy, MI 48084

London Scott Associates
Clifton Park, NY 12065

McCulloch and Company
Greenville, SC 29603

McSherry & Associates
Chicago, IL 60601

Management Recruiters Midwest
Thousand Oaks, CA 91360

Management Scientists, Inc.
New York, NY 10016

Marbrook
New York, NY 10017

Mogul Consultants, Inc.
Jericho, NY 11753

National Career Centers—USA
Fayetteville, NC 28302

N.E. Power and Electronics Personnel
Ballston Spa, NY 12020

The NRI Group
Rockville, MD 20852

Omni
New York, NY 10016

Paul-Tittle Associates, Inc.
Silver Spring, MD 20910

Perry-White & Associates, Inc.
Santa Clara, CA 95050

Pierce Associates, Inc.
San Francisco, CA 94111

PPS Consultants
Phoenix, AZ 85004

Renhil Group, Inc.
Perrysburg, OH 43551

Research Technologies
Madison, CT 06443

Lloyd Richards Personnel Service
Tulsa, OK 74103

Roche Associates
Stamford, CT 06094

Richard R. Rosche
St. Louis, MO 63163

Lowell N. Ross & Associates
Corte Madera, CA 94925

Schuyler Associates, Ltd.
Atlanta, GA 30339

Search Division
Los Angeles, CA 90048

Siegel & Bishop, Inc.
San Francisco, CA 94112

William Snyder Associates
Tucson, AZ 85710

Soltis Management Services
Radnor, PA 19087

W. J. Stuart & Co.
Los Angeles, CA 90068

Sumrall Personnel Consultants
Dallas, TX 75234

Synergistics Associates Ltd.
Chicago, IL 60601

Systems Personnel
Media, PA 19063

Systems Search II
Millburn, NJ 07041

Technical Search Associates
Danbury, CT 06810

P. T. Unger Associates
Washington, DC 20036

Varone Personnel
Pawtucket, RI 02860

Webster Positions, Inc.
Hicksville, NY 11801

Went MacKenzie
Atlanta, GA 30360

William H. Willis, Inc.
New York, NY 10022

Dennis Wynn Associates, Inc.
St. Petersburg, FL 33704

XXCAL
Los Angeles, CA 90025

Yelverton & Company
San Francisco, CA 94111

TRANSPORTATION

Alexander & Associates, Inc.
Elkhart, IN 46515

Analytic Recruiting, Inc.
New York, NY 10017

Arancio Associates
Needham, MA 02192

Aviation Personnel International
New Orleans, LA 70174

Bowker, Brown & Co.
Miami, FL 33129

Dotson Benefield & Associates, Inc.
Atlanta, GA 30345

Kearney: Executive Search Group
Englewood, CO 80111

Patton/Perry Associates
Charlotte, NC 28202

Robert Sage & Associates
Denton, TX 76201

Search Division
Los Angeles, CA 90048

Torretto & Associates, Inc.
Sausalito, CA 94965

TR Recruiters
New York, NY 10038

Wilkinson & Ives, Inc.
Orinda, CA 94563

GLOSSARY

Applicant   The job hunter who is seeking a position.

Candidate   In executive search, an individual who may be well suited to a specific opening at a client company.

Career counselor   A trained professional providing vocational guidance to individuals, for a fee. He or she is not involved in placement.

Client   The employer (a corporation, partnership, or sole proprietor) who authorizes an outside agent (executive recruiter, personnel agency, or other search consultant) to find a suitable candidate for a job. The client pays the fee for this service.

Contingency   A payment arrangement in which the search professional will be paid a fee only after finding a suitable candidate for a particular opening. The fee is paid by the client once a candidate has been hired. If the employment professional does not find an acceptable candidate for the specific job, no fee is paid.

Employment agency (or **licensed personnel agency**)   These firms serve as matchmakers between employers and applicants, by interviewing job seekers and evaluating their qualifications, experience, and appropriateness for the particular opening. Employers contact agencies when they have openings; the agency recommends or tries to locate suitable candidates for the job, so that interviews can be arranged between employer and applicant. Fees may be paid by either applicant or employer, but no fee is ever paid until an individual accepts a position with an employer to which an employment agency referred him or her. Many states license personnel agencies.

Executive marketing   A specialty in which individuals pay a fee for assistance in planning their job-hunting strategies. Executive marketing firms assist in résumé preparation, recommend ways to compile a mailing list of possible employers, or send out mass mailings introducing a job seeker to prospective employers. Fees are paid by the user of the service, whether or not a position is secured.

Executive search   A specialty in which consultants work for an employer seeking a high-level worker to fill a particular position. The individual executive never pays a fee. Executive search consultants are paid by the employer for their efforts to locate a well-suited candidate. Search consultants are reimbursed for expenses (such as travel, telephone, or advertising).

Head hunter   A slang term for recruiters, or executive search consultants. The unflattering allusion is to the fact that their assignments require locating and presenting new opportunities to well-qualified executives who are currently employed in respectable positions. The hope is to entice an outstanding professional into pursuing a good job with a new employer.

Job register   A fee-based service maintaining a clearinghouse through which résumés can be channeled to interested employers. Executives submit résumés, which the job register classifies; when an employer reports a specific opening, the job register forwards appropriate résumés to the employer. A set fee is paid by each individual wishing to be registered in the data bank, whether or not a position is ever obtained.

Off limits   This is an ethic in executive search, which specifies that once an executive search firm has placed a candidate with a client company, no other executives at that employer can be solicited for openings elsewhere, generally for a period of two years. Many firms will not even accept résumés from employees of an off-limits company. (Some questions are raised in the field about how rigorously this ethic is enforced.)

Retainer   A method of payment in which a search consultant is paid a fee for taking on an assignment to fill a particular opening. Regardless of how long the search process takes, the consultant is paid for making a diligent effort to find a suitable candidate. Sometimes the best candidate is already working for the client company, and the search consultant will recommend that the staff member be appointed to the vacancy. The client company pays the retainer, whether or not the position is ever filled.

Rusing   A set of ploys used by recruiters to gain information about, or access to, employed professionals who may not be actively job-hunting. Ruses are as varied as the people who use them. To collect data about possible candidates for an opening, recruiters may claim they're gathering biographical facts for Who's Who, performing a survey, putting together a testimonial dinner, or doing anything their imaginations can create. Rusing is thoroughly frowned upon by professionals in the executive search field.

BIBLIOGRAPHY

Boll, Carl. Executive Jobs Unlimited. New York: The Macmillan Publishing Company, 1980.

Cohen, William. The Executive Guide to Finding a Superior Job. rev. ed. New York: AMACOM, 1983.

Fleming, Charles. Executive Pursuit. New York: Mentor, 1984.

Gerraughty, William B. How to Seek a New and Better Job. Consultant News, 1984.

Half, Robert. The Robert Half Way to Get Hired in Today's Job Market. New York: Bantam Books, 1983.

Irish, Richard K. Go Hire Yourself an Employer. Garden City, N.Y.: Doubleday/Anchor Books, 1978.

Lewis, William. Resumes for College Graduates. New York: Monarch Press, 1982.

Payne, Richard. How to Get a Better Job Quicker. New York: Mentor Book, New American Library, 1979.

Perry, Robert H. How to Answer a Head Hunter's Call: A Complete Guide to Executive Search. New York: AMACOM, 1984.

Traxel, Robert G. Manager's Guide to Successful Job Hunting. New York: McGraw-Hill Book Company, 1978.

Wilkinson, William. Executive Musical Chairs. San Mateo: Warrinton & Company, 1983.

NOTE: Several of the books listed above are available from:

> The Consultants Bookstore
> Templeton Road
> Fitzwilliam, NH 03447
> 603-585-2200

Some directories and publications that can be helpful are:

Access: the membership directory of the National Association of Personnel Consultants. Available from: NAPC, 1432 Duke Street, Alexandria, CA 22314. $12.50 (1985).

The Executive Employment Guide: capsule descriptions of 150 search firms, compiled by the American Management Association, 135 West 50th Street, New York, NY 10020. $3.00 (1985).

Executive Recruiters News: a monthly newsletter for the executive search industry, published by Kennedy & Kennedy, Inc. Their Directory of Executive Recruiters lists over 2,500 recruiting firms and costs $21.00 (1985) prepaid. Both publications are available from the Consultants Bookstore.

INDEX